The Constitution of European Democracy

The Constitution of European Democracy

Dieter Grimm

Professor of Law, Humboldt University of Berlin, Former Justice of the Federal Constitutional Court of Germany, Former Director of the Wissenschaftskolleg zu Berlin Institute for Advanced Study

Translations by Justin Collings, Professor of Law, Brigham Young University

OXFORD
UNIVERSITY PRESS

OXFORD
UNIVERSITY PRESS

Great Clarendon Street, Oxford, OX2 6DP,
United Kingdom

Oxford University Press is a department of the University of Oxford.
It furthers the University's objective of excellence in research, scholarship,
and education by publishing worldwide. Oxford is a registered trade mark of
Oxford University Press in the UK and in certain other countries

The translation of this work was funded by Geisteswissenschaften International–Translation Funding for Humanities and Social Sciences from Germany, a joint initiative of the Fritz Thyssen Foundation, the German Federal Foreign Office, the collecting society VG WORT and the Börsenverein des Deutschen Buchhandels (German Publishers & Booksellers Association)

Europa ja – aber welches?

First Edition published in 2017

Impression: 2

Published in the United States of America by Oxford University Press
198 Madison Avenue, New York, NY 10016, United States of America

British Library Cataloguing in Publication Data
Data available

Library of Congress Control Number: 2017944689

ISBN 978–0–19–880512–0

Printed and bound by
CPI Group (UK) Ltd, Croydon, CR0 4YY

Preface to the English Edition

When this book was published in German in March 2016 Brexit still appeared as a distant and unlikely eventuality. Meanwhile it has become a reality. It was a shock for the European Union. For the first time a Member State had decided to leave the Union. Until then European countries had been longing for membership. Some are still on the waiting list. But in a number of Member States political forces that advocate an exit find growing popular support. In spite of these movements, European integration is an achievement if one looks back to the devastating wars among European states and if one looks forward to the growing global activity of powerful private actors, which nation-states are unable to control. These are good reasons to preserve and even expand the European Union (EU). However, preserving the Union requires reforming it so that the legitimacy gap from which it suffers at present can be bridged. This book draws attention to the least noticed source of the crisis in acceptance of the EU, namely its over-constitutionalization, and rejects the most favoured reform option, namely a full parliamentarization of the EU. The book instead offers some other solutions that might bring the EU closer to its citizens, without whose support the ambitious project is bound to fail.

I am extremely grateful to Professor Justin Collings for an outstanding translation of the book and to "Geisteswissenschaften International" for a generous grant that made the translation possible.

Berlin
January 2017

Dieter Grimm

Preface

As the title of this book makes clear, a dichotomy lies at the heart of these essays. On the one hand, they are animated by a deep conviction that European integration is a necessity. On the other hand, they are inspired by an equally deep concern that European integration is on the wrong path. The European Union (EU) is paying for this with the alienation of its citizens. Without citizen acceptance, however, the project of integration is doomed to failure. A critique of the current status of the Union stands, therefore, in the foreground of this book. My purpose, however, is not to plead for less Europe, but to plead for a better Europe. Avenues towards such a better Europe will be highlighted along the way.

All of the essays share a few fundamental observations. Among these is that the EU has morphed from an economic to a political community, without however reflecting that transition in its decisional structure. Decisions of high political moment are taken in a non-political way. This has been made possible because the executive and judicial institutions of the EU have largely divorced themselves from the democratic processes of both the Member States and of the EU itself. The opportunity for this has been provided by the 'constitutionalization' of the European treaties—the most widely overlooked source of Europe's legitimacy deficit. Democratic legitimacy may be regained only through a re-politicization of the European decision-making process.

A further fundamental observation is that the EU does not possess sufficient legitimacy resources to hold up on its own. It draws, rather, as it always has, on the legitimation that emanates from the Member States, which for their part are democratic. For this reason, the most frequent proposal for the resolution of Europe's democracy problem—namely, the transformation of the EU into a parliamentary system of government—misses the mark. Parliamentarization on the state model would sever the flow of legitimacy from the Member States without being able to fill the gap with an adequate legitimation of Europe's own. The distance between the EU and its citizens would increase rather than diminish. The EU, therefore, does itself no favours when through a subtle erosion of competences it steadily weakens the democracy of the Member States.

These observations run through the various contributions in this volume. Some overlap, therefore, is inevitable. Because each of the articles was published independently, knowledge of the premises could not be taken for granted. Each article, however, appeared in a different context and deals with a different aspect of the integration process. Only the first two essays strongly resemble one another. The first gives the book its title. I have decided nevertheless to include the second, because it provided the opportunity to satisfy the wish for a more precise elucidation of my general approach. I do not mean to suggest, however, that the causes for the legitimation weaknesses of the EU enumerated here are the only ones. Nor do I mean to suggest that the only possible remedies are the ones I propose.

My discipline is law, and law plays a predominant role in this book, both with respect to the diagnosis and with respect to the cure. What is economically sound must be decided by others on the basis of their expertise. But because the EU came into being as a legal community and can only persist as such (for it is unable to draw upon the pre-legal sources for unity available to states), economic decisions are also dependent on legal form. A great deal depends on wise legal organization, especially in the EU.

Dieter Grimm

Contents

1 Europe, Yes—But Which Europe? 1

2 In Search of Acceptance 21

3 Sovereignty in Europe 39

4 On the Status of the EU's Democratic Legitimacy after Lisbon 57

5 The Democratic Costs of Constitutionalization—The European Case 81

6 The Cause of the European Democracy Deficit is Sought in the Wrong Place 105

7 The Necessity of Europeanized Elections and Parties 117

8 The Significance of National Constitutions in a United Europe 131

9 The Role of National Parliaments in the European Union 167

10 The Role of National Constitutional Courts in European Democracy 181

11 The Basic Law as a Barrier against a Transformation of the EU into a State 207

12 Europe Needs Principles, Not Pragmatism 233

References 243

Index 245

1

Europe, Yes—But Which Europe?

European integration is a product of the Second World War, which in its turn was a product of the First, and which prompted greater efforts to prevent war, both globally and especially in Europe, than had been undertaken with the League of Nations after the First World War. It is the great achievement of European integration that a renewed war among the states who have banded together in the European Union (EU) has become improbable. If one were to pose the question, 'Why Europe?', this achievement is, for the generations that remember the Second World War, the first thing that comes to mind. Within the EU there is no risk of war. A sorrowful chapter of European history appears to be closed.

But when it comes to contemporary acceptance of the process of European unification, this achievement no longer plays an essential role. It is not linked to the EU in any meaningful symbolic way. The distance between the EU's founding and the Second World War's end is too great for that, and the EU's beginnings as a customs union too prosaic. The experience of contemporary generations is that of a peaceful Europe. Even if one were to imagine a Europe without the EU, there is no threat of war among the European states. War has yielded to other dangers—terrorism, for instance. Peace, on the other hand, which was once an achievement, is now a given. It no longer rouses enthusiasm for the European cause. As the English political scientist, Richard Rose, has recently written, the call for more Europe on the basis of an achievement now more than half a century old holds no greater attraction than a black and white television.

War, of course, has not disappeared. But it happens elsewhere. Those exposed to war envy Europe; many make their way towards Europe. Bordering states crowd into the EU. Within the EU itself, scepticism predominates and spreads quickly even in the newly acceded countries whose greatest wish, just a short time before, was EU membership. One might quarrel with one's own state and execrate its current rulers, but the state's purpose and right to exist remain undisputed. Things are different, however, with the EU. One thinks one could do without it. European politicians cannot win over a majority of EU citizens for the project. Even the European Parliament, the representative of those citizens, brings them no closer to the EU. The more powers the Parliament acquires, the fewer EU citizens go to the polls.

It was not always thus. There was in the past a genuine enthusiasm for Europe. Even after that abated, there was broad and enduring approval. What motivated such attitudes? Why have they been lost? After 1945, weariness with war and its consequences were so great, among both victors and vanquished, that all hopes centred in European unification. For Germany even more was at stake. After the National-Socialist bid for European domination, the only path back into the circle of civilized nations ran through European integration. The path was smoothed by an escalating East–West confrontation and by the Korean War. The dismantling of West German industry was halted. A West German state was established and rearmed.

France found all of this unsettling. European integration was France's answer to a development that it was not strong enough to prevent. The European Coal and Steel Community (ECSC) was set up to remove war-related industries from German control; the European Defence Community (EDC) was created to place the German military under European control; and the European Political Community (EPC) was initiated to hold German sovereignty at bay. Adenauer, on the other hand, saw Europeanization as a gateway to equal status. As it happened, only the founding of the ECSC succeeded; it became a forerunner of the European Economic Community (EEC).

The EEC became a substitute for the EDC and the EPC, which no longer commanded majority support after a change of government in France. France now turned its attention to economic integration, without however losing sight of political integration. Sooner or later, economic integration would drag political integration inexorably in its wake.

One must remember this initial position if one is to compare the initial Europe-euphoria with today's Europe-lethargy. The situation-dependent justifications for Europe faded with the gradual return of normality. Economic integration, which was all that remained of the great post-war plans, did not inspire enthusiasm—but neither did it elicit protest. Economic integration provided Europe with a broad-based approval because it progressed inconspicuously, presented itself as apolitical, and brought increased prosperity. This was entirely consistent with the aims of the founders. A common market was not dependent on democratic legitimacy. It legitimated itself through its usefulness. Politics remained a matter for the Member States. What happened at the European level was of a technical nature. Or so, at least, it might have seemed.

This was also reflected in the construction of the EEC. Its legal foundation was an international treaty among sovereign states; its guiding institution and legislature the Council, in which the Member-State governments sat. Decisions of the Council required unanimity. No dissenting state could be outvoted. The Commission was constructed by the Member States, but was independent of them in its operations—beholden only to the programme of integration, which it was to pursue consistent with guidelines established by the states. There was no provision for popular participation. There was only a parliamentary assembly, without decision-making power, composed of members of the national parliaments. Democratic legitimation in the EU came only from the democratic Member States.

That much more was going on behind this institutional façade remained hidden for a long time. Integration was driven primarily by what, based on its functions, was the least likely European institution: the European Court of Justice (ECJ). The Court was supposed to mediate disputes of a European nature—particularly those between the community and the Member States—and to provide binding clarifications of norms of community law. And yet when France, under De Gaulle, pursued a 'Europe of fatherlands'—i.e. an intergovernmental rather than an integrated Europe—it was the Court that fuelled the integration process judicially when it stagnated politically.

How did this come about? From the very beginning, the ECJ understood its mandate to be achieving economic integration even against the frequently obstinate resistance of the Member States. The Court interpreted the treaties with this objective in mind. A methodological pre-determination provided the basis for such interpretations. According to the traditional practice of interpreting international treaties, the intentions of the signatory states were decisive. Provisions restricting sovereignty were to be construed narrowly. The ECJ broke with this principle and construed the treaties as if they were the constitution of a nation-state, focusing on an objective purpose rather than on the intentions of the founders. The Court saw itself neither as the guardian of the rights of the signatory states, nor as a neutral arbiter between the states and the Community, but rather as the driving force of integration. It was a court with an agenda.

In two revolutionary judgments, the Court ruled first, in 1963, that community law was directly applicable within the Member States. The result was that economic actors could challenge the compatibility of national laws with European law before national courts, which could then refer the question of compatibility to the ECJ. This stood in stark contrast to the original conception, which was that community law addressed itself to the Member States, requiring the latter to bring national law into conformity with community law. A year later, the ECJ declared that community law was not only directly applicable within the Member States, but was to take precedence over national law—even over the constitutions of the Member States. National courts were forbidden to apply national law that was incompatible with community law, and they need not refer the question beforehand to their national constitutional courts. Article 100 of the German Basic Law, which required just such a referral to the German Federal

Constitutional Court, is still technically part of the German constitution, but holds no longer true when the applicability of EU law is at stake.

The judgments were revolutionary because the principles they announced were not agreed upon in the treaties and almost certainly would not have been agreed upon had the issues been raised. The process has been described, with good reason, as a 'constitutionalization' of the treaties. The legal foundation of the EU remained, technically, an international treaty. The Member States retained their position as 'Masters of the Treaties'. Only they determine the EU's legal foundation. But, based on the ECJ's jurisprudence, the treaties functioned as a constitution. Alongside political integration by treaty and the promulgation of secondary European law, there was now an alternative, judicial path towards integration. That path consisted in overcoming national legal diversity by means of treaty interpretation. This is how the EEC (later the EC and the EU) became what it is today: a singular, supranational entity somewhere between an international organization and a federal state.

Everything depended, in these circumstances, on how the ECJ understood the treaties. The Court's approach privileged the four basic economic freedoms (the free movement of goods, services, persons, and capital) and their more detailed implementation in the treaties. The four freedoms were originally conceived of as guidelines for the legislature in establishing a common market. National law that favoured domestic firms at the expense of foreign competitors was to be invalidated. The jurisprudence of the ECJ, however, turned the four freedoms into fundamental rights of economic actors. This allowed the judiciary to take integration into its own hands. The legislature was no longer necessary for the realization of the common market.

Instead, the ECJ worked all the more resolutely towards the goal of a common market. Thus, the Court expanded bans on discrimination into bans on regulation. Any good that was legally produced in one Member State could be marketed in every other Member State without regard to the relevant national laws. What's more, every provision of national law that proved a hindrance to cross-border trade became a potential victim of the Court's interdiction. The precept of European law that forbade only 'quantitative restrictions' on imports and 'measures having equivalent effect' thereby lost its limiting force. Measures now fell under suspicion of European illegality that had no discriminatory motive, or even an economic motive, but which served other legal values such as the protection of health, the environment, workers, etc.

In this way, national legislatures lost the power to establish the standards of protection they thought politically necessary. This raised the risk that the minimal standard of protection would prevail throughout Europe. This risk could be met only by European legislation. Broad interpretation of the four freedoms thus expanded automatically the EU's lawmaking powers. It was easier, of course, to quash national law than to create European law. A decision of the Commission or a judgment of the Court sufficed to invalidate a national law. Making a European law required a unanimous resolution of the Council. Sometimes that happened, but often it did not. The result was the well-known asymmetry between negative (norm-abolishing) and positive (norm-establishing) integration, and its economically liberal impact.

The treaties' ban on market-distorting state subsidies to corporations experienced a similar expansion. The ECJ applied this provision not only to private corporations, but to public service institutions as well. So long as there were private competitors, whether domestic or foreign, for the relevant services, state financing of public institutions became a subsidy and potentially market-distorting. The upshot was that the Member States could no longer freely decide which areas to leave to the market and which to govern themselves. Although many states had removed certain services from the market for reasons of general welfare, those considerations played no role in this development, which has partially driven the wave of privatization in recent years.

Alongside, then, the explicit transfer of powers from the Member States to the EU, there has also been a clandestine loss of powers through the ECJ's expansive interpretation of the treaties. A transfer of powers presupposes a conscious decision of the Member States—one that must be compatible with their national constitutions. But a loss of powers via interpretation is something that the Member States must simply endure. What national constitutions say about the matter is, for the ECJ, irrelevant. All of this undermines a fundamental principle of the treaties—the principle of conferral. An action for annulment before the Court with an agenda had little hope of success. If a Member State refused to surrender its right or to abolish a public service agency, and if the Commission chose to chasten that state in a treaty violation proceeding, the Commission could count on a victory before the ECJ. A Member State, on the other hand, that filed a complaint against the Commission for overstepping its powers faced almost inevitable defeat.

In response to this development, Roman Herzog, Germany's former federal president, called some time ago for the ECJ to be 'stopped'. But it is not so easy to stop a court. For functional reasons, courts operate under the protective shield of judicial independence. They do not depend either on political direction, on votes, or on the recourse (provided by voting) to the views of the society for which they interpret the law. From a democratic point of view, this is acceptable because courts are subject to another obligation—namely an obligation to the law, which is itself the product of a democratic process and which the courts are supposed simply to apply.

And yet nothing highlights better than the ECJ's jurisprudence the limitations of the binding force of legal norms. Such norms are necessarily framed in general and abstract terms, but they must be applied to specific cases. This gap must be bridged through interpretation. Interpretation is a process guided by method, but it would be a mistake to think of interpretive method as a neutral tool for ascertaining meaning already lodged definitively in the text of the norm. In the process of applying law, choices are always made between alternative interpretations—and meaning is always generated. In this respect the ECJ, both through its chosen interpretive method—the canons of constitutional law, rather than of international law—and through its use of that method, has proven extraordinarily creative.

Political scientists are quick to explain judicial activism in terms of institutional self-interest. They see in judicial activism a form of self-empowerment in the service of the court's own position of power. But this assessment pays too little attention to the internal logic of the jurist. One must distinguish, instead, between effect and intention. As a general rule, courts have the intention of aiding the law they are entrusted to enforce towards the greatest possible realization. This is especially true of a court, like the European Court of Justice, with an agenda. The effect, of course, is an increase in the Court's powers at the expense of other institutions. However, the implementation of law is not a pretext; it is a motivation.

Yet, this does not explain why the Member States have not put a stop to the development. For even if the prospects of a successful legal complaint were slim, the governments of the Member States constituted, through the Council, the legislature of the European Union—originally the sole legislature, but still the principal one. There are, however, several reasons why the Member States have not tried to check the ECJ legislatively. To begin with, the full reach of the Court's decisions was often unclear. Courts decide individual controversies on the basis of a pre-existing body of law, and they explain their decisions in such a manner that they seem to be derived ineluctably from that pre-existent body of law. The decisions are written, moreover, in a technical language that is often opaque and provides few potential targets for extrajudicial criticism. The impact of a decision beyond the individual case often becomes visible only when it has been consolidated into 'settled case law'.

But even if the Member States took note of what was happening, they were limited in their possibilities of reaction. Politicians guide courts, if at all, through legislation. When politicians no longer recognize their own intentions in the courts' interpretation of laws, or when they deem the consequences of those interpretations to be noxious, or when they simply wish to change course (after an election, for instance), they can reformulate the law for the future. But they cannot eliminate the need for interpretation, and they cannot dictate to the courts the method that will inform that interpretation. This does not mean, of course, that changing course by amending the laws would be entirely hopeless. Why, then, is this path so seldom taken?

One reason is that the Council is not an adequate counterweight to the ECJ. The Council, it is true, represents the interests of the Member States; but the Member States have no unified interest. As a result, the Council's decision-making follows the pattern of bargaining. The form of decision in the Council is not, as in national parliaments, deliberation, but rather, as in international conventions, negotiation. Unanimity, which was for many years the norm in the Council, but also qualified majorities, which suffice today, are difficult to achieve for the purpose of correcting the ECJ's jurisprudence—to say nothing of the fact that the Council depends on the initiative of the Commission to promulgate secondary law. And the Commission, as a general rule, is uninterested in correcting the ECJ's jurisprudence.

There is, however, another reason for all of this, which has heretofore barely been noted. It has to do with the peculiarity of the European treaties. Although technically international treaties, they have, through the ECJ's jurisprudence, been constitutionalized. They function like a constitution but are not framed as a constitution. Constitutions govern the process of political decision-making both formally and materially, but they leave the political decisions themselves to the political process, thereby ensuring the significance of elections. The victorious party in an election implements its programme through legislation (within the framework of the constitution, of course). The stronger the substantive content of the constitution, the narrower the leeway for politics. Whatever is governed in the constitution is removed from the realm of political decision-making. It is no longer an object, but a premise of politics. It cannot be influenced even by the outcome of an election.

This difference between the conditions for political decisions and the decisions themselves is, for constitutionalism, constitutive. In the EU, however, the two planes get muddled. The treaties are full of provisions that, in a Member State, would be governed by so-called ordinary law. When the Commission and the ECJ construe and apply those provisions, they are implementing the constitution. As a result, not only are the Council and the parliaments not needed to establish the common market, they cannot even amend decisions of the executive and judicial bodies through legislation. The ever-present possibility within a nation-state of redirecting courts through legislation is largely absent in the EU. The ECJ has more freedom than any national court. Its jurisprudence can be repealed only by amending the treaties—which, as everyone knows, is all but out of the question.

It is significant, in terms of the acceptance of European integration by EU citizens, that the important advances in integration were undertaken in an un-political manner and excited correspondingly little public attention. National politicians hardly noticed. The media did not realize what was happening. Even legal scholars missed the mark. Representatives of national law ignored European law. European law was studied primarily by experts who overwhelmingly identified with their subject and who viewed their discipline as part of the European project. In this way, the development of European constitutionalization had no critical bystanders in the relevant scholarly discipline. There prevailed an unspoken ban on criticism, so as not to endanger the European project.

The long phase of European sclerosis finally came to an end with the passage of the Single European Act (SEA) of 1987, which abolished the unanimity requirement in the Council of Europe. The reform won universal applause because the unanimity requirement was seen, not as a guarantee of democratic legitimacy, but as a source of stagnation. Meanwhile, however, the simultaneous development set in motion by the ECJ remained unnoticed. As a result, it was not immediately apparent that the end of unanimity marked the beginning of Europe's democracy problem. As long as political decisions could be taken only unanimously in the Council, the democratic legitimacy that flowed to the EU from the governments of the Member States—which, for their part, were democratically legitimated and controlled—was sufficient.

This remained true for European primary law—the treaties. But as far as secondary law and its application were concerned, the continuous chain of legitimation that ran from the peoples of the Member

States through their parliaments and governments to the Council and the other European institutions was now broken. It was now possible for laws to apply within a Member State that the state had not approved through its political process or had even, in some cases, explicitly rejected. Thus, a legitimation gap opened that could not be closed at the national level. Europe has been in need of reform ever since.

The 1992 Treaty of Maastricht was supposed to meet this need by conferring upon the European Parliament—whose members had been directly elected since 1979—rights of participation in European decision-making. The Union was supposed to move thus from monistic to dualistic legitimation. At the same time, the Treaty was designed to elevate Europe to 'a new stage in the process of creating an ever closer union among the peoples of Europe'. The European Community became the European Union, and a common currency was agreed upon. As became clear, however, the peoples of Europe were not prepared for this. The approval upon which political leaders thought they could still rely had been approval for an economic community that had long since been overstepped. The long phase of steadily advancing integration through hidden, unpolitical channels had been a precondition of progress. As the Treaty of Maastricht pulled back the veil, approval ratings sank. The Treaty of Maastricht, which brought institutional progress, marked a step backward in terms of popular acceptance.

The response to this crisis, and to a further need for reform through expanding the EU, was the constitutional treaty. The institutional reforms themselves were not dependent on the constitutional format. All that was thought necessary in the reforms could have been achieved by amending the treaties. That it was nonetheless to be a Constitution can be explained only by the expectation that this would somehow solve the problem of acceptance: Integration through Constitution. Within nation-states this sometimes, if rarely, succeeds. For the most part it is gratifying enough when constitutions perform their legal function—namely, to guide politics within certain channels and to constrain politicians within certain limits. If, beyond this, a constitution is to exert an integrative influence as well, certain supplementary conditions must prevail. Those conditions were absent in Europe.

The problem, which became obvious with the Maastricht Treaty, was that broad segments of the population believed that integration had gone too far. The proposed constitution, by contrast, envisioned not less Europe, but more. This was one reason for its rejection by referendum in France and the Netherlands. In response, the Treaty of Lisbon—which now forms the legal foundation of the EU—disavowed all the trappings of a constitution. The Lisbon Treaty significantly expanded the powers of the European Parliament, which was now to be the representative body, not of the peoples of the Member States, but of EU citizens. The Treaty also introduced the so-called European Citizens' Initiative. None of this, however, resolved the acceptance problem. And the financial crisis intensified it.

Under the current Treaty, decisions of extraordinary political importance continue to be made through a non-political mechanism. In many political decisions, the Commission and the Court continue to go it alone. Upgrading the European Parliament did nothing to alter the fact that the Commission, in decisions designed to advance integration, remains unaffected by the outcome of parliamentary elections. The real democracy problem of the EU lies in the autonomy of its executive and judicial institutions vis-à-vis its political institutions and the will of the Member States.

The problem is aggravated by a yawning gap between decision-making power and accountability. This stems from the fact that, because the EU lacks an administrative infrastructure of its own, it is unable, acting alone, to implement its decisions. It relies instead on the governments of the Member States. While the Commission, which actually makes the decisions, cannot be held democratically accountable anywhere, the national governments, who have not decided anything, can be held accountable in domestic elections. National governments can be punished by voters, while the Commission, immunized against citizen protest, risks only a diffuse sense of displeasure. The ECJ, as a court, evades the question of democratic accountability entirely.

Integration through the non-political mechanism of treaty interpretation is often recounted as a success story. And indeed it is a success story. Without the contribution of the ECJ, the EU would in all likelihood remain just one international organization among many—with more powers, to be sure, and a thicker organizational structure than others, but not the singular novelty that it is today. But the success story masks several important factors. For one thing, many citizens cannot identify with the outcome. The judge-driven development was not supported by the political will of those affected by it. Their opinion was not asked, and they have responded by withdrawing legitimation. The question, 'Why Europe?', is a plea for plausible explanations of integration.

Is there, then, a grand narrative of Europe that convinces the reason and captures the heart, and in which the mass of EU citizens can find themselves? The first condition is easier to satisfy than the second. There is a highly plausible justification for Europe—namely, that the benefits promised by Europeanization are to be had in no other way. This is so because of a growing number of cross-border problems, for which a political solution is expected, but for which a solution is no longer possible in the narrow confines of the European nation-states. Between the sphere of action of powerful, globally influential private actors and the sphere of action of national politics there is a gap that can be closed only through the internationalization of public authority.

Nation-states have been pursuing this path since 1945, sometimes globally, as with the UN, the WTO, and international courts, and sometimes regionally. Nowhere, however, has the effort to increase the problem-solving capacity of public authority through internationalization been undertaken as it has been in Europe. One can ask whether communalization has gone too far or not far enough. But there is little sense in questioning communalization as such. The alternative would require an agreement among states for every problem in need of supranational regulation. This would foster neither efficiency nor coherence.

This is a pragmatic justification of integration—admittedly, a powerful one. But it appeals to the reason, not to the heart. Hence the second question is all the more important: how must the European Union be arranged so as to find greater acceptance? As we have seen, efficiency could carry the EU only as long as it was regarded as an economic community without political implications. A return to that condition, however, could come only at the cost of the EU's capacity to solve problems. The question, with respect to communalization, is how to subject the power of transnational actors to rules that serve the general interest. And that is a political question. Transforming the EU back into a common market would thus be inconsistent with the basis of its legitimacy.

On the other hand, the pattern that has heretofore characterized European politics—the pattern of making political decisions through non-political channels—cannot continue. Political decisions require a political mechanism, which in Europe can only mean a democratic mechanism. The democratic capacity of the EU is therefore of pivotal importance. Since the EU will always remain a federal structure, and since EU citizens will, for the foreseeable future, feel a stronger bond to their Member States than to the EU itself, there must be an appropriate balance between the functions undertaken by the community and those reserved to the Member States with their respective preferences. There must be constraints, that is, on the EU's insatiable jurisdictional appetite.

Efforts undertaken previously have either failed or been insufficient. The attempt to secure greater acceptance for the EU by transforming international treaties into a constitution has failed. The attempt to constrain the incessant growth of the EU's powers through the principle of subsidiarity can also be deemed a failure. The subsidiarity principle has been in force since 1992, but because it has never succeeded in acquiring any justiciable content, it has had no impact. It serves well enough as a legal-political maxim for the establishment of a federal order, but not as a standard for adjudicating concrete jurisdictional disputes. The right of complaint granted to national parliaments under the Treaty of Lisbon cannot compensate for this vagueness of content.

Current discussions focus on enhancing the representation of EU citizens—that is, on the European Parliament. It is proposed that the Parliament be endowed with the same plethora of powers typically wielded by national parliaments, such that the EU becomes a parliamentary system. This could not happen, of course, without repercussions for the other EU institutions. The Commission would be upgraded to the status of a European government. The great losers would be the European Council, which would be limited to revising the treaties, and would lose the power to set the guidelines of European politics; and the Council of Ministers, which would no longer be the central legislative body, but would be degraded into a second chamber of the European Parliament.

This is clearly the pattern of a federal state, and in fact such an institutional reform of the EU would closely resemble a federal state. Whether the German Federal Republic could pursue this goal is, in light of the Federal Constitutional Court's jurisprudence on the limits of European integration, highly questionable. But apart from this obstacle, one must ask whether this proposed solution can remedy the EU's legitimacy deficit. If the solution to the problem is to upgrade the Parliament, then it must be presumed that the EU's weak legitimacy stems from the fact that the central legitimating institution is not the Parliament, which is directly elected by the EU's citizens, but the Council, which is filled by the national governments of the Member States. Only then would reordering external and internal legitimation be the appropriate response.

Parliament's legitimating function is not secured, however, merely by the fact that it is elected every five years by EU citizens. That would reflect a purely formal conception of democracy. The Parliament's legitimating power depends rather on how the elections are structured and, even more, on its being embedded, between elections, in an unbroken societal process in which opinions are formed and interests articulated—a process that culminates in, but is not exhausted by, elections. There must be a continual, mutual interaction between the electorate and the political institutions, such that the views and needs of the public find expression in the Parliament and influence political decision-making within the other institutions.

Neither happens currently. European elections do not fulfil their legitimating potential. Elections are governed by national election law. In each Member State, the national parties compete with one another and campaign on the basis of national themes. But there is no correlation between the parties that stand for election and those that sit in the Parliament. Instead, the Parliament is dominated by European factions composed of numerous national parties. These factions have other questions to decide than those raised during the election campaign, and in response to those questions they must agree upon a programme that is no longer that of the national parties. Consequently, the voter who can vote only for national parties has no prospect of seeing those parties' platforms realized in the European Parliament.

Things are even worse with respect to the Parliament's being embedded in an ongoing societal process of shaping opinions and articulating interests. This leaves much to be desired even in the Member States, where parliamentarism is undermined by broad tendencies that make politics increasingly expert-based and international. An upgraded European Parliament would not be immune to these tendencies either. In Europe, however, these tendencies are especially acute because the underlying basis of a living democracy is underdeveloped. Insofar as European parties even exist, they make no appearance in society, leaving the field instead to the national parties. Interests are articulated and citizens engaged essentially only within a national framework. But above all else, there are no European media that can sustain a genuinely European public discourse, and not merely twenty-eight national discourses on European issues. While the deficiencies of European elections could be at least partially rectified by introducing a European electoral system with European parties, a European public sphere that even remotely resembles the national public spheres is unlikely to emerge any time soon.

The European Parliament, therefore, is further removed from a societal basis than the national parliaments, and it faces difficulties in generating a Europe-wide public opinion that could be channelled into the decision-making processes of other institutions. But one must not end the diagnosis with the European Parliament. One must also take into account the other institutions, which would incur the costs of full parliamentarization. These are the institutions that confer upon the EU a democratic legitimacy derived from the Member States—the European Council and the Council of Ministers. As a result, the EU's increasing independence from the Member States would not increase its internal legitimacy. One must conclude, then, that the EU would emerge from full parliamentarization democratically weakened rather than strengthened.

On the other hand, one should not conclude from these observations that the powers of the European Parliament must be further reduced. On the contrary: the Parliament is indispensable as a counterweight to the national egotisms of the Council and the technocratic tendencies of the Commission. But the Parliament cannot carry the burden of legitimacy alone. The EU's legitimacy continues to rest upon two pillars—one grounded in the democratically elected and accountable governments of the Member States, and one grounded in a European Parliament elected by EU citizens. The two pillars, however, are not equally sturdy. The flow of legitimacy from the Member States is considerably stronger, in part because the Council wields more significant powers, in part because the conditions for a living (not merely a formal) democracy are much more promising in the Member States than in the EU.

Current deliberations about reform focus on the EU's internal legitimation. If, in pursuit of this objective, the EU were to become a parliamentary system, the flow of legitimacy from the Member States would be blocked, or at least impeded, without increasing the EU's internal legitimacy. External and internal legitimacy do not interact like communicating vessels. They are not rivals in a zero-sum game. Weakening the national flow of legitimacy does not strengthen the European flow—to say nothing of the fact that parliamentarization would not address at all the problem of the non-political mechanism of decision that results from overloading the constitutionalized treaties with ordinary law.

What needs to happen, then, to increase acceptance of the EU? If the EU's legitimacy problem stems from the fact that its executive and judicial institutions have separated themselves from the will of the legitimating Member States, and that they make decisions of great political importance through non-political means, then measures must be taken to limit this separation and ensure that political decisions are made in a political manner. And if it is true that the EU will long remain dependent on the Member States for its democratic legitimacy, then one must ensure that this flow of legitimacy is not hindered by reconfiguring the EU according to a nation-state model.

Since the treaties have by now been constitutionalized, it would be appropriate to re-classify all provisions of a non-constitutional nature as ordinary law—basically the entire Treaty on the Functioning of the European Union (TFEU). Undesirable interpretations could then be corrected by legislation, as happens in every democratic state. But in Europe this possibility is not even mentioned. The expansion of powers through interpretation has been possible (among other reasons) because the EU knows no division of legislative subject matters—with the exception of areas of exclusive jurisdiction, such as customs—but follows instead the general principle that the EU may govern anything that helps to establish and maintain the common market. In response, there must be a catalogue, based on subject matter, in which certain areas are reserved to the states—even if under certain conditions those areas affect the common market.

Even if these proposals were embraced, one would expect additional transfers of powers to the EU. This is because the number of cross-border problems is constantly increasing, and every transnational crisis brings pressure for further Europeanization—as the financial crisis has recently demonstrated anew. The tendency to treat every gain of ground as incomplete but also irreversible will surely persist. It is all the more important, then, to establish criteria that are not dictated by the crisis but that will govern choices during the crisis.

But this means nothing more than that there needs to be a discussion of ultimate goals.

The EU has long since outgrown the original economic community. But what it should become in the end remains unsettled. Is the goal a European State—a United States of Europe—or a community of interest for matters that the Member States can better solve together than apart? What should be the relationship between unity and diversity, exclusion and inclusion, social justice and the market? The solution to Europe's problems will differ depending on one's answers to these questions. Politicians, however, shun discussions of ultimate questions and respond to demands for clarification of first principles with reassurances: the questions will be addressed when the time for decision arrives.

But this gesture towards the future does not stop politicians from making decisions today that, while suppressing the question of ultimate goals, will have weighty consequences tomorrow and that will prejudice the answer to the question of ultimate goals. When the consequences come, it is too late to discuss goals. The monetary union has taught this lesson anew. In the end, the Maastricht experience will repeat itself, though on a grander scale. We are gradually approaching a state of affairs that was never subject to debate and about which EU citizens never had the chance to form an opinion. As a result, they experience this state of affairs as something dictated from above, not as something they have chosen. And if they then dispute the state of affairs, they are told simply that they are too late—that there is now no alternative. That is not a formula for increasing legitimacy.

2

In Search of Acceptance

On the Legitimacy Deficit and the Legitimacy Resources of the European Union

No one disputes that the European Union suffers from a shortage of acceptance on the part of its citizens. Nor does anyone dispute that this shortage of acceptance endangers the project of integration. Less clear is the source of this weakness and how—if one accepts that there are good reasons for integration—it is to be overcome. In the early phases of European integration, there was no doubt that there were good reasons for it. Approval was high. The question arises, then, why this was so, and why that high approval has been lost.

To answer the first part of the question one must look back to the Second World War. After the sufferings of that global conflict, which affected both victors and vanquished, there was a great willingness to confront the danger of war more effectively than had been done after the First World War. For those generations with a living memory of the 1939–45 war, the greatest achievement of European integration has been the prevention of renewed war among the European states.

But this achievement seems to have paled in the course of time. Peace is not symbolically associated with the European Union. The distance between the end of the Second World War and the founding of the European Economic Community is too great for that, and the Union's beginnings as a customs union are too prosaic. The experience of contemporary generations is of a peaceful Europe, and even if one imagines life without the EU, there is no risk of war among the Member States. Peace, once an achievement, is now a given.

For Germany there was yet another reason to embrace integration. After the deep fall through the National Socialist tyranny, the route back to the circle of civilized nations ran only through European integration. At the same time, European integration provided France with the means to bring a newly strengthening Germany under control—economically through the communalization of war-related coal and steel industries in the European Coal and Steel Community (ECSC); militarily through the European Defence Community (EDC); and politically through the European Political Community (EPC). Of the three, only the economic association materialized. The military and political plans fell by the wayside because they no longer enjoyed majority support in France.

These early motivations have also faded over time. The founding motives for Germany as well as for its wartime antagonists have been exhausted. Germany is once more a respected member of the community of states and is closely integrated within that community. It is no longer regarded as a threat to peace. The EU has expanded. Since the founding, twenty-two European states have joined for entirely different reasons.

One must keep this in mind when comparing the original Europe-euphoria with the current Europe-lethargy. The early enthusiasm was largely situation-dependent, but the situation is no longer the same. Of the original grand plans, only the common market survived, an inadequate object for enthusiasm, but also—because it appeared apolitical and enhanced prosperity—not a source of rejection. The common market legitimated itself through its usefulness.

This is one side of the process of alienation between the European Community and its citizens. It first gained significance, however, through another side introduced by the European Community itself. Under the cloak of economic integration, changes took place that went beyond establishing and maintaining the common market. These changes were not perceived by the public, much less made the subject of a political debate.

It was the 1992 Treaty of Maastricht that removed the cloak from this development and confronted the citizens of the Member States with a level of integration concerning which their opinion had never been asked. The Europe that the Maastricht Treaty was to secure and advance was not the Europe on which the acceptance of its citizens had been based. European integration and European consciousness had fallen out of step.

With respect to integration, the Maastricht Treaty was a momentous step forward; with respect to acceptance, a step backward. It marks a turning point in public attitudes towards the European project—the beginning of the EU's weak acceptance. In the long run it fostered the spread of anti-European parties, which have since won seats in the European Parliament and are held at bay only by grand coalitions of pro-European factions.

Responses to these developments are of long-standing. The EU spends a great deal of money trying to foster a European identity from above, but without perceptible success. The creation of a European constitution was another attempt to bring the EU closer to its citizens. The constitutional proposal can only be explained in these terms. All the reforms that seemed necessary in light of the increased number of Member States and Europe's altered role in a post-1989 world could have been achieved by amending the treaties.

The choice of a constitution rather than an improved treaty can be explained by reference to the EU's legitimacy deficit. It was hoped that a constitution would provide a stronger bond between the Union's citizens and the EU. But this too misfired. The constitution envisioned more Europe when many thought there was already too much Europe. Not coincidentally, the constitutional treaty failed precisely in those countries where it depended on popular referenda.

The constitutional idea will not be revived in the near future. Today's preferred institutional reforms focus on strengthening citizen representation. Towards this end, it is proposed that the European Parliament be endowed with the powers typically possessed by national parliaments. This proposal is made in the hope that a full parliamentarization of the EU will solve the legitimacy problem by placing the elected representatives of the people, rather than the governments of nation-states, at the centre of the EU.

These hopes, of course, will be fulfilled only if the EU's legitimacy deficit stems from the European Parliament's lack of powers. It is far from obvious, however, that this is the case. All appearances suggest the contrary. The more powers the European Parliament has acquired, the lower voter participation has sunk. Voter participation is particularly low in new Member States—states whose greatest desire, just a short time ago, was EU membership.

This too has multiple causes. A particularly weighty one is the weak representativeness of the European Parliament. This, in turn, is related to the voting system. European voting is not Europeanized. Elections are conducted in accordance with national election laws and for national allotments that do not correspond with the varying populations of the Member States. Campaigns are conducted by national parties on the basis of national themes. The results are overwhelmingly assessed from national perspectives.

Consequently, the legitimacy to be gained through elections is relatively slight because the connection between election results and European politics is slight. For one thing, the EU's central institution—the Council—is unaffected by European elections. For another, the voting system actually blocks, to some degree, the flow of legitimacy. EU citizens can vote only for national parties. But those parties do not appear as such in the European Parliament. Instead, they operate within European factions that have no roots in society.

For this reason, parties cannot even credibly promise that the goals they championed during the campaign will later exert any influence in the European Parliament. The parties that one can elect do not set the parliamentary agenda. The parties that do set the parliamentary agenda, one cannot elect. The Europeanization of the national programmes comes only after the election. Furnishing the European Parliament with a broader array of powers would do nothing to change this.

But suppose that European elections were to be Europeanized and the EU transformed into a parliamentary system. Would this solve the legitimacy problem? There are reasons to doubt that it would. Despite their full array of powers and their role as an intermediary between society and the political system, parliaments everywhere are under pressure. Politics are increasingly expert-based and internationalized, which plays into the hands of governments, while parliaments decline in public favour. It is improbable that, of all parliaments, the European Parliament will be spared this fate.

But there is another, more Europe-specific reason for this. It lies in the growing autonomy of the EU's executive and judicial organs from the democratic processes both of the EU itself and of the Member States. The causes of this have gone largely unexplored. Accordingly, this argument needs to be elaborated in somewhat greater detail. That can be done by comparing the original structure of the European Community with the current structure resulting from changes accrued over time.

Originally, the European Community derived its democratic legitimacy exclusively from the Member States, which for their part are democratic. The Member States agreed upon the legal foundation of the Community in the European treaties. They were also, by way of the Council, the European legislature. The Council was composed of representatives of Member State governments and could make decisions only unanimously.

Under this arrangement, no Member State was ever subject to a law that it had not previously approved. This was true both of the signing of treaties and of the creation of European secondary law—i.e. the directives and regulations promulgated by the Council, for which one could hold the national government accountable at the next election. The European Commission and the European Court of Justice (ECJ) were authorized only to implement law enacted by the Member States, and were thus bound by the states' political will. There was a parliament of sorts known as the Common Assembly, but it was not elected and its role was merely advisory.

Changes set in over time, two of which seem particularly important—one of them obvious, the other less noted. The obvious change was the enactment of the Single European Act, adopted by the Member States in 1987, whose most important innovation was the partial abolition of the unanimity requirement for decisions of the Council.

This innovation was broadly hailed for putting an end to what was perceived as the obstructionist posture of individual Member States. It had consequences, however, for Europe's legitimacy. It was now possible for states to be subjected to laws that they had not approved, and which they may even have rejected explicitly through the national democratic process. The result was a legitimacy gap. For the outvoted state, at least, the flow of legitimacy from citizens of the states through their national parliaments and governments to the institutions of the EU was cut off.

This gap could not be closed at the national level—only at the European. At that level, one could look only to the European Parliament, which had been directly elected since 1979. In this way, external legitimation through the Member States—which was no longer adequate—was replaced by limited internal legitimation through the European Parliament. Since then, the European Parliament's powers have expanded with each amendment of the treaty. These expansions have not, however, made the Parliament the equal of the Council.

The less noted change had come much sooner, but with a soft step—not by amending the treaties, but by interpreting them. These were the ECJ's revolutionary judgments of 1963 and 1964. In the first judgment, community law was declared to be directly applicable in the Member States. The judgment's significance did not lie in the fact that, departing from the usual rules of international law, no further transformation into national law was required. This followed already from the text of the treaties. Rather, under this judgment, community law not only bound the Member States, it also conferred rights on their citizens.

Citizens could now raise obligations of community law against their own states before national courts. This benefited primarily the four economic freedoms (the free movement of goods, services, capital, and labour) and their concretization in the treaties. Originally, these freedoms were objective legal duties of the states to adapt their legal orders to the provisions of community law. The judgment transformed them into subjective rights of economic actors.

After the first judgment, the question of what would happen in the case of a collision between community law and national law remained open. The second judgment answered this question, holding that community law took precedence over national law—including the supreme national law, the constitution. Whether or not there *was* a collision would be decided by the ECJ, to which national courts must refer the question of compatibility and by whose judgments they would then be bound. From then on, the ECJ could take integration into its own hands.

This was not, one must stress, an inevitable conclusion drawn from the text of the treaties. Like all law, European law must be interpreted before it can be applied to concrete cases. At the same time, interpretation entails discretion—not in the sense that the outcome is arbitrary, but in the sense that the outcome is not fully determined by the norm's text. One can construe norms broadly or narrowly.

The ECJ itself had opened the gate to its understanding of the treaties through its choice of method: it would construe the treaties, not as international law was typically construed (i.e., focusing on the will of the treaty's signatories and, in cases involving limitations on sovereignty, narrowly), but as national constitutions were construed (i.e., focusing on an objective purpose and with little regard to the historic intent of the authors).

The question here is not whether these judgments were right or wrong. What the ECJ decided fifty years ago still stands. The only disputed questions are whether there are outer limits to the supremacy of EU law—above all, as many national constitutional courts maintain, in the form of the core identity of national constitutions—and whether only the ECJ may determine that EU institutions have exceeded their powers, or whether national constitutional courts may so determine as well.

The point here is rather to raise awareness of the consequences of this jurisprudence for the EU's legitimacy. To that end, it is important to recognize how these judgments—rightly described as revolutionary—have altered the character of the treaties. Put baldly, the treaties have been constitutionalized. It was American observers who first noticed this consequence of the judgments.

When in the context of national law one speaks of constitutionalization, one usually refers to the transformation and permeation of statutory law by constitutional law. In Europe, constitutionalization means that the treaties are elevated to the stature of a constitution, and that the relevant consequences appear in assessing the validity of sub-constitutional law—secondary European law, but also national law, including national constitutional law. National law that contradicts European law may no longer be applied.

The two judgments provided the point of departure for an enormous thrust towards integration—and this precisely at a time when integration had stagnated politically. From then on, there were two paths towards integration: a political path that only the Member States could take by amending the treaties, and a legal path that the ECJ could take by interpreting the treaties. In the first case, the Member States transferred powers to the EU; in the second, they had powers stripped from them by the EU.

The ECJ pursued the second path with missionary zeal. With this in mind, Rainer Wahl has described the ECJ as a court with an agenda. The Court's path, however, ran largely outside the attention threshold of politicians and the public. Answers to legal questions referred to the ECJ by national courts do not generate great interest, either in the media or among the public at large. Their consequences are often felt only after individual judgments have consolidated into settled jurisprudence.

In retrospect, the history of the ECJ's jurisprudence, as initiated by the two judgments of 1963 and 1964, is often recounted as a success story. And indeed it is a success story, if one looks only at economic integration. But that is a cramped perspective. The economic success story has a legitimacy downside that has never been fully acknowledged.

In its effects, the jurisprudence reaches far beyond the proximate goal of establishing a single market. Instead, the ECJ used its bootstrapped powers to steadily contract the realm of national regulation and to penetrate, through expansive interpretation of the treaties, spheres of competence that the Member States had reserved to themselves. Anna Katharina Mangold has described this process in her book *Gemeinschaftsrecht und deutsches Recht* of 2011 in great detail.

Thus, the ECJ has not only banned national protectionism—which the treaties explicitly required the Member States to do—but has, through expansive interpretation, broadened the ban on protection into a ban on regulation. Since then, the Member States have been unable to establish their own standards of protection—for health, labour, consumers, etc.—regardless of whether the relevant national laws pursue protectionist goals.

Member States cannot even freely decide which services to leave to the market and which to take under state control. This is so because the ECJ applies the ban on state subsidies not only to for-profit businesses, but also to public service institutions. This has led in many cases to the privatization of public institutions and social welfare agencies, often without regard to whether the market can provide comparable services.

This would not be worth emphasizing if satisfactory European regulations and institutions took the place of the national institutions and regulations. Here, however, lies the significance of the asymmetry—highlighted by Fritz Scharpf—between positive and negative integration. Negative integration happens when national law may no longer be applied; positive integration happens when European law fills the resultant regulatory vacuum.

Thanks to the constitutionalization of the treaties, negative integration can take place through the stroke of a pen from the EU's executive and judicial organs; positive integration, by contrast, requires a political act—European legislation—which demanded unanimity until 1987 and must clear high hurdles even today. Sometimes, as in the case of environmental law, the gaps ripped open by negative integration have been closed. Sometimes, however, they have not been.

The asymmetry based on the constitutionalization of the treaties is also responsible for the essentially liberalizing character of European jurisprudence—not in the sense that the ECJ is actively pursuing a policy of liberalization, but rather in the sense that liberalization is a consequence of its jurisprudence. Indirectly, this also undermines the constitutional obligations of the Member States to secure social justice. In a liberalized environment, those obligations come under pressure, since a robust system of social welfare risks becoming a competitive disadvantage for the domestic economy. In the EU, economic policy and social policy have parted paths.

The most recent example of the expansive interpretation of the treaties is the rolling back of national fundamental rights in favour of the European Charter of Fundamental Rights. For the protection of national fundamental rights, the European Charter of Fundamental Rights provides that the European fundamental rights apply to the institutions of the EU, whereas they apply to the Member States 'only' when the Member States are implementing European law. But if the implementation of national law has any connection, however remote, to European law, the ECJ regards that too as the implementation of European law.

This, too, would not be worth emphasizing if there were an essential overlap between European and national fundamental rights. At the textual level there is. While the Charter contains more rights than most national constitutions, it avoids contradictions with them. Considerable differences, however, emerge at the level of interpretation. The ECJ tends to give precedence to economic rights over personal, communicative, and social rights. In the Member States, the reverse is true.

Why have the Member States not resisted? In the European Council, they ultimately determine the contours, the extent, and the pace of integration; in the Council of Ministers, they constitute the EU's principal legislature. They should be able, then, to correct jurisprudence in which they no longer recognize the intentions that led them to sign the treaties, or from which they fear adverse consequences.

It is the constitutionalization of the treaties that prevents their doing so. Constitutions remove certain questions from the realm of political decision-making. What the constitution enshrines is no longer an object, but a premise of politics. That which is regulated in the constitution is independent of the outcome of elections or of particular majorities. Where there are constitutional courts, constitutional provisions can be implemented against the will of the current majority.

This is precisely the point of a constitution. It should channel and constrain political power. It should not, however, make politics superfluous. This requires that the constitution remain limited to a few regulations of fundamental importance. The more a constitution is filled with objects of ordinary legislation, the less democracy is possible. Accordingly, the distinction between a constitution and a statute is, for constitutionalism, fundamental.

In other words, constitutions regulate the production of political decisions, but they do not themselves make political decisions. Rather, they leave such decisions to political institutions, who make them on the basis of preferences expressed by majorities in elections. Only through the distinction of levels between constitutional law and statutory law does an election retain its significance as the foundational democratic act.

There would be little to say against the constitutionalization of the European treaties if the treaties contained only such provisions as constitutions usually contain—e.g. decisions determining the goals of communalization, the polity's institutions with their powers and procedures, and fundamental rights that place substantive limits on public authority.

But this is not the case with the European treaties. They are filled with regulations that in a nation-state would be enacted as ordinary law. Many see this only as the source of the treaties' length. But that is superficial. The real problem appears only when one takes into account the consequences of constitutionalization for the relationship between law and politics.

Because the treaties have been constitutionalized, their application by the ECJ becomes a form of constitutional implementation. As a result, not only are the EU's political institutions (the Council, in which the democratically legitimated governments of the Member States are represented, and the European Parliament) excluded from all participation; they cannot even influence the ECJ's interpretation and application of the treaties through amendatory legislation.

In this way, decisions of great political importance and deep encroachments into the long-standing structures of the Member States come about in Europe through administrative and judicial channels—through a non-political mechanism, that is, and hence outside the democratic process. Insofar as the ECJ's interpretation extends the reach of the treaties, citizens lose the possibility to change anything through elections. This is true of both national and of European elections.

The only means of correction is to amend the treaties. But it is well known how high a hurdle that is. All twenty-eight Member States must agree to the changes and have them ratified in their parliaments or through popular referenda. For the purpose of redirecting jurisprudence, this is as good as unattainable. Thanks to constitutionalization, the Commission and the ECJ have been immunized, within the coverage of the treaties, against politics. The EU is over-constitutionalized. Its Court of Justice is freer than any national court.

It is easy to see how parliamentarization of the EU—widely regarded as a cure for Europe's legitimacy deficit—passes over this problem entirely. As a matter of course, the European Parliament stands below, not above the constitution. Expanding the Parliament's powers would not alter the consequences of over-constitutionalization in the slightest.

In another respect, however, upgrading the Parliament would clearly have consequences. One cannot expand the powers of Parliament without narrowing the powers of other institutions. In reality, the push for parliamentarization of the EU is only part of a more comprehensive project of reform, by which Parliament is to take its place in the centre of European politics, the Commission is to be elevated into a parliamentary government, and the Council is to be degraded into a second chamber of the European Parliament.

What would this mean for the EU's legitimacy? The flow of legitimacy from the Member States through the Council would be throttled. The European Union would be forced to rely on its internal legitimation. The question arises, then, whether it has sufficient resources for such internal legitimation. Given the state of European elections and the shortage of European parties described earlier, the answer is uncertain at best.

The prospects for internal legitimation are reduced further by the weakly developed preconditions for a European public sphere. After all, the democratic substance of a political system is not finally shaped by its institutions. It is determined much more by the societal sphere that precedes those institutions. It is important that there be a constant link between voters and those they elect, even during the period between elections. This requires intermediary institutions—above all, media of mass communication.

The preconditions for this in the Member States, while not uniformly good, are considerably better than they are for the EU as a whole. A European public sphere exists only in its rudiments. European mass media capable of generating a Europe-wide political discourse are missing entirely. There is no prospect of a rapid change in these circumstances. It is improbable, then, that the European Parliament could carry the burden of legitimation alone, or even predominantly.

This must not be understood, however, as a call to narrow the powers of Parliament. On the contrary: the European Parliament is a necessary counterweight to the dominance of national interests in the Council and of technocratic tendencies in the Commission. The point is simply that the EU cannot do without the supply of legitimacy that emanates from the Member States. It is in the EU's self-interest to nurture living democracies in the Member States, rather than erode them through the clandestine transfer of powers.

What, then, is to be done? The answer to this question turns on one's perception of integration's ultimate goal: forward towards a

European state, backward to a common market, or stand fast as a federal polity but not a state? Deciding on a destination would require, beyond addressing the problems of the moment, a discussion of first principles. Such a discussion should take place independent of crises, so that principles are already available when solutions are sought during a crisis. Such discussion is desperately needed. But politicians avoid it.

As a result, reform measures and crisis management are undertaken without a clear conception of the destination of European integration. Such measures, however, prejudice the question of ultimate goals. The financial crisis confirmed this. Warnings that a monetary union would not work without a common economic policy or the transition to a 'union of solidarity', in which stronger states assume liability for the debts of weaker states, were already on the table when the Maastricht Treaty was signed. They were suppressed because it was clear that discussing them would have thwarted plans for a monetary union. What was once an option is now a fait accompli.

In my view, of the three possibilities mentioned only the middle way makes sense. A European state would imperil the richness of European pluralism. But above all it would be overwhelmed by legitimacy challenges. EU citizens would likely feel even greater distance from a European state than they do from the current structure. On the other hand, a purely economic community would ignore the fact that economic decisions have political implications and that many tasks traditionally undertaken by nation-states can no longer be discharged satisfactorily at the state level.

Indeed, as a consequence of globalization, the gap between the operating range of global economic actors and that of national politicians is growing. This gap can only be narrowed by internationalizing public authority. The European Union is a regionally limited, but effective and promising step in that direction. This is a strong reason to preserve integration—one that has persuasive power beyond the founding motives. The task, then, can consist only of taking the EU as it is and making it better. Three recommendations, derived from the foregoing, are submitted to that end.

(1) Because Europe's indispensable internal legitimation runs through the European Parliament, the Parliament must be brought closer to the public. This can happen through a Europeanization of European elections and political parties. Europeanized parties can do what national parties cannot—namely, engage with European society and, even before the election, balance national interests and consolidate them into a European election platform. In this way, voters will have the opportunity to influence European, and not only national, politics.

(2) Because the current structure provides inadequate protection against a creeping erosion of Member-State powers, and because the principle of subsidiarity has proven ineffective and non-justiciable (even upon complaint of the Member States), there must be clearer limits on communalization. Currently, the treaties' goal of establishing and preserving a common market provides a tool for undermining the powers of the Member States. This is so because it is possible to discern in every imaginable Member-State norm a potential impediment to the market.

Hence, the proper way to restrain European expansionism is to replace the final criterion of impact on the market with a division of powers based on subject matter—something that has hitherto existed only for the EU's few exclusive legislative powers. A division of powers based on subject matter—common to every federal state—would reserve specified areas of policy to the responsibility of the Member States, even if the exercise of these powers had repercussions for the common market.

(3) Because the EU's legitimacy deficit has been caused in large measure by the de-politicization of political decisions, and by the autonomy of the EU's administrative and judicial bodies from the democratic processes in both the Member States and in the EU itself, decisions with significant political implications must be re-politicized. This can be achieved by reducing the treaties to the scope necessary for their constitutional function.

To be clear: the point is not to abandon constitutionalization, but to draw proper conclusions from the constitutionalization that has already taken place. If the treaties have been constitutionalized already, they should now be re-structured in the form of a constitution. They should be limited to provisions regarding goals, institutions, powers, procedures, and fundamental rights. Provisions regarding policy should be relegated to the level of secondary European law.

This would not deprive the ECJ of the power to implement European law. The Court would simply lose the unassailable position it has procured through constitutionalization. The EU's political institutions (the Council and the Parliament) would acquire the capacity, should they conclude that the ECJ's interpretation departs from the intentions of the founders or has harmful consequences, to redirect the Court's future jurisprudence by amending laws.

None need fear that any of this will halt or reverse integration. On the contrary: there will be a further transfer of powers to the EU. This is so, on the one hand, because necessary attention to the impact of national policies on other Member States cannot be ensured successfully at the national level. The externalities of national politics for other Member States can be dealt with only at the superior, European level.

Further transfer of powers to the EU will be necessary, on the other hand, because the number of problems that can no longer be resolved effectively at the national level is growing rather than diminishing. This entails, of course, an increasing need for legitimacy. The EU's efforts to meet that need by redirecting towards itself the ties that citizens feel towards their Member States have little hope of success. Rather, the increased need for legitimacy can be met only through concurrent self-limitation.

What are the prospects of success for these recommendations? From a legal perspective, they face no great obstacles. Easiest of all is the Europeanization of elections, which can occur without amending the treaties. It would require only the promulgation of a European election law, which the Lisbon Treaty already envisions. Implementing recommendations 2 and 3, on the other hand, would require treaty amendments. The necessary amendment for recommendation 3, however, would be extremely simple—unlike recommendation 2, it would require no substantive changes. It would simply require a single provision converting the contents of the Treaty on the Functioning of the European Union (TFEU) into secondary EU law.

From a political perspective, the obstacles arising from potential conflict and high requirements of consensus are greater. At the very least, this remains true of the transition to a European election law. While the Member States have already, in principle, agreed to such a law by treaty, uniting upon an election system will be anything but conflict-free. Moreover, because recommendation 2 would selectively limit integration, it might well face political opposition. Yet the need to limit the transfer of powers has also, in principle, been recognized by all Member States through their commitment to subsidiarity.

Although recommendation 3 necessitates no changes in the treaties' content, it might face the greatest political obstacles. In the European Convention, it was not even mentioned. Neither politicians nor the public at large are aware of the legitimacy costs of the treaties' constitutionalization. But slender prospects of success are no reason to ignore the fact that there are paths out of the legitimacy crisis, if one could only summon the will to travel them.

3

Sovereignty in Europe

A. The Relevance of the Question

The question of who is sovereign in political entities composed by states—the members or the whole—is older than the European Union (EU). It has been discussed ever since sovereignty became a key notion of political and legal theory in the era of state formation in the sixteenth century. The question was posed with regard to the Holy Roman Empire of the Germanic Nation, later for the United States where it needed a civil war to settle it, then for the German Confederation of the nineteenth century, the Swiss Federation, and with particular intensity for the German Empire of 1871.[1]

Yet, the current discussion differs from the historical debates on a fundamental point. It is not limited to the question of who is the holder and what is the content of sovereignty. Rather the very existence of sovereignty is at stake. For many observers of the present situation it is not of interest who is sovereign in a novel institution like the EU, but whether it makes sense to analyse this institution in terms of sovereignty in the first place. A number of authors are of the opinion that the notion of sovereignty is outdated and out of touch with reality and consequently not capable of explaining the political world of

[1] Dieter Grimm, *Sovereignty* (New York: Columbia University Press, 2015), p. 23 ss., 51. Dieter Grimm, 'Was the German Empire a Sovereign State?', in S.O. Müller and C. Torp (eds), *Imperial Germany Revisited* (New York: Berghahn, 2011), p. 51.

the twenty-first century.[2] If this were true, a political entity that claims sovereignty would only be holding an empty shell.

Therefore two levels must be distinguished when sovereignty is discussed, the conceptual level and the object level. The two are neither congruent nor unrelated. They may develop asynchronously sometimes with the concept and sometimes with the reality being ahead. Bodin's notion of sovereignty was an anticipation of the real development and, for a certain time, greatly influenced this development. Today the question is more whether the reality has passed over the concept. But even if this were the case the incongruence would not be without impact on the reality; because it makes a difference whether the reality is conceived and interpreted in terms of sovereignty or not.

This is why the search for the location of sovereignty still makes sense. Even if we assume, with the sovereignty sceptics, that an object which deserves the name of sovereignty no longer exists, this would not change the fact that we constantly come across the notion of sovereignty. In the academic world we face a boom of sovereignty literature. Outside academia the term appears in numerous political and legal documents. According to the UN Charter, the UN is based on the equal sovereignty of the Member States whereas the Charter does not claim sovereignty for the UN. The Treaties of the EU avoid the term, but most constitutions of the Member States contain provisions about sovereignty. Court opinions take the existence of sovereignty for granted and draw conclusions from it, most recently the *Lisbon* judgment of the German Constitutional Court.[3]

What follows from this? Notwithstanding scholarly doubts about the existence of sovereignty, and regardless of the dispute about its content, states behave in their international relations as if they were sovereign. They use sovereignty as an argument in order to claim or defend rights and powers. International organizations treat them as sovereign. The concept of sovereignty continues to influence political

[2] Neil MacCormick, *Questioning Sovereignty* (Oxford: Oxford University Press, 1999).

[3] BVerfGE 123, 267 (2009).

and legal thinking and action. This means that, if the object of sovereignty had disappeared, sovereignty is at least present as a social fact, also in the EU. Therefore, it would not be wise to ignore the question of who is sovereign in the EU. The future course of European integration depends on the answer. Hence, the question of the concept of sovereignty is asked more often than the question of its existence: that is, which concept of sovereignty is best suited to understand and explain the EU?[4]

B. Sovereignty in the EU

1. *The development of the concept*

If this is accepted, the meaning of sovereignty cannot be left open. For Bodin, the father of the idea of sovereignty in the modern sense, 'sovereignty' designated the accumulation of all prerogatives, up to then dispersed among many independent holders, into one hand, preferably that of the monarch, and their concentration into one single public power. It included the power to make laws without being bound by law and was indivisible. Hobbes added to this notion the absolute character of public authority. The sovereign was legally omnipotent, but he grounded this authority in the consent of the people, expressed in the social contract.

The idea of sovereignty became immediately attractive, not only in the academic, but also in the political world. The monarchs of many territories tried to shape their rule according to the new model. If they were successful a new form of political entity emerged: the modern territorial state. Sovereignty was the characteristic element that distinguished the state from older forms of political associations. The sovereign state did not share its power with anyone else. Internally it enjoyed self-determination; externally it was independent of any

[4] Cf. for instance Neil Walker (ed), *Sovereignty in Transition* (Oxford: Hart Publishing, 2003).

foreign power. Above the state neither a lawmaker nor an organization for law enforcement existed. Obligations among states could only flow from self-limitation, typically freely concluded treaties.

The strong notion of sovereignty becomes understandable if one takes into account that Bodin and Hobbes wrote under the influence of the religious civil wars which followed Luther's Reformation. Both saw the emergence of a sovereign power as the only way to restore peace. Thus, in the countries rifted by civil wars, sovereignty seemed a dictate of reason, its risks had to be accepted as the inevitable price for peace and security of life, limb, and property. However, the better the modern state fulfilled its historic mission to pacify society, the less plausible seemed its absolute rule. The idea of the social contract, which in the beginning had justified absolutism, now suggested the limitation of public power.

When, in the great revolutions of the late eighteenth century, public power was transferred from the monarch to the people and its exercise was constitutionally limited, sovereignty remained unaffected—only the traditional holder of sovereignty was replaced by another. Constitutions were regarded as a product of sovereign decision-making, not as a negation of sovereignty. The separation of powers and their limitation through constitutional law happened below the level of sovereignty. In their external relations nothing changed. The states, whether constitutionalized or not, were as sovereign as before. International law continued to rely on cooperation, not subordination.

This state of affairs lasted for 300 years. It came to an end after the Second World War. The turning point was the foundation of the UN. It is true that the UN is based on the sovereignty of the Member States. But at the same time the UN gave a blow to state sovereignty. None of the older alliances had the power to create and enforce international obligations. The UN, on the contrary, has such a power. In order to enforce the renunciation of violence declared by the Member States, it may interfere with the right to self-determination of the state, if necessary by applying military means.

It is true that the powers of the UN do not at all equal those of the state. They are but isolated powers, while the vast majority of powers are retained by the states. The states are universally competent; the UN needs a special authorization. Its power is not original, but derived from the states. States have a say in the use of the power, particularly the permanent members of the Security Council. However, the power of the UN can be used against states, and if this happens it is legally superior to that of the states—insofar there is now a power above them against which they cannot rely on their sovereignty.

Over time, the supranational power increased.[5] The seminal changes of 1989–90 accelerated the change. New supranational institutions were created like the WTO and international courts. Within international law a *ius cogens* developed that binds states regardless of their consent. Public international law is no longer limited to regulating the relations of states, but penetrates the borders of states and extends to the individuals within it. Humanitarian intervention is accepted in principle and a responsibility to protect endangered groups is evolving. All this relativizes the prohibition of interference with the internal affairs of states. A similar development can be observed on the regional level.

Concerning the meaning of sovereignty, we can draw a first conclusion. Everyone who, in spite of the changes mentioned, adheres to the existence of sovereignty must give up the understanding according to which the states are the exclusive bearers of public power on their territory with no other power above themselves and that sovereignty means an unlimited right to self-determination. Such a notion is refuted by the facts. Vice versa, everyone who still identifies sovereignty with Bodin's or Hobbes' definition must conclude that sovereignty has disappeared. Sovereignty is either no longer absolute or no longer existent. There is no apparent third way.

It should be added, however, that the original understanding of sovereignty was never uncontested. The great attraction of the concept resulted in many attempts to describe even political entities, which lacked the characteristics of a state, in terms of sovereignty,

[5] See, e.g., Jan Klabbers, Anne Peters, and Geir Ulfstein, *The Constitutionalization of International Law* (Oxford: Oxford University Press, 2009).

which was impossible without adapting the notion to their specific conditions. In particular, Bodin's and Hobbes' assumption that sovereignty is indivisible was never generally accepted. Many authors held that it was sufficient for sovereignty to exist that a political entity or a ruler was the highest authority within his area of powers. It was not necessary that he held the monopoly of public power or was omnipotent in a given territory.

Only when the nation-state predominated in the nineteenth century did the idea of indivisibility of sovereignty dominate once again. A division of sovereignty would have meant a negation of national unity. Many argued that it was logically impossible. Two sovereignties on one and the same territory cancelled each other out. 'There is no half, divided, diminished, dependent, relative sovereignty. There is only sovereignty or no sovereignty', wrote Paul Laband, the leading mind among German constitutionalists during the Empire,[6] and this view was not limited to Germany.

2. *Sovereignty and public powers*

However, exactly the qualifications that Laband declared incompatible with sovereignty re-emerge today when the question for sovereignty in the EU is asked.[7] The EU is certainly in the forefront of the post-national development. Although, unlike the UN, it is not disposed of coercive means vis-à-vis the Member States, the EU constantly exercises public power—legislative, administrative, and judicial—with direct effect within the Member States and superiority over national law. National law is, to a large extent, superseded or modified by EU law. As far as the number of powers and the density of the organizational structure are concerned, the EU does not differ fundamentally

[6] Paul Laband, *Das Staatsrecht des Deutschen Reiches*, vol. 1 (Tübingen: J.C.B. Mohr, 4th edn, 1901), p. 68.

[7] For a discussion see, e.g., Neil Walker, 'Late Sovereignty in the European Union', in: Neil Walker (ed), *Sovereignty in Transition* (Oxford: Hart, 2003), p. 10, and Grainne de Burca, 'Sovereignty and the Supremacy Doctrine of the European Court of Justice', ibid., p. 449.

from the central state in a federal system. Nevertheless, it is not a state, but an entity somewhere between a supranational organization and a federal state, for which a convincing notion is still missing.

As unclear as the legal nature of the EU is, equally unclear is the question of sovereignty in Europe. Five constellations seem possible: (1) Sovereignty lies with the Union. (2) Sovereignty lies with the Member States. (3) Sovereignty is in some way or other divided among the EU and the Member States. (4) The Member States of the EU have pooled their national sovereignty and exercise it through the EU. (5) Sovereignty has dissolved in the EU. Whatever alternative is adopted, the relationship between sovereignty and the various public powers has to be determined since the fact that the latter have been divided is undeniable. The end of the identity between public power and state power is the basic point of departure for all sovereignty discourses after 1945.

Since public powers form the substance of sovereignty and since this substance is divided among the EU and the Member States, the idea suggests itself that sovereignty is divided as well. Many authors are of that opinion. As the history of the notion of sovereignty shows this is by no means a contradiction to sovereignty. It is incompatible with an absolute notion of sovereignty. But this notion can no longer be upheld under present conditions. If there is something like sovereignty in the EU, wherever it may be located, it is undeniably not sovereignty in the sense of Bodin and Hobbes. Authors who reject the existence of sovereignty often do this on the basis of the absolute notion. Authors who find that sovereignty continues to be a useful concept, also in Europe, start from a relative notion.

The assumption of the proponents of a divided sovereignty is that a division of public powers results in a division of sovereignty. However, the situation that public powers are divided is no novelty of the EU. Every federal state must divide the totality of public powers in some way or other. This is a necessary element of federalism. Laband could not ignore this when he formulated his theory of indivisibility of sovereignty. Given the federal character of the German Empire, indivisibility of sovereignty could not mean indivisibility of public powers.

This presupposed that sovereignty meant more than just a bundle of prerogatives that could be untied. Sovereignty and public powers had to be distinguished.

This position is also taken by the German Constitutional Court in its *Lisbon* judgment and in all previous judgments on matters European. The Court insists that the Basic Law authorizes Germany to transfer only public powers to the EU, not sovereignty.[8] Even as Member States of the EU, the states retain their sovereignty altogether and the EU has to respect it. Moreover, according to the *Lisbon* judgment, national sovereignty is the borderline which the Federal Republic may not transgress in the process of European integration. Not even a constitutional amendment could change this. According to the Court, the transfer of sovereignty is prohibited by the eternity clause of the Basic Law.[9]

The question then is: What is the difference between sovereignty and public powers? On what does it depend that, within a federal system, one bearer of public powers is sovereign, the other not? This question was extensively debated in Germany towards the end of the nineteenth century with regard to the *Kaiserreich*. The dispute was finally settled by the answer that Georg Jellinek gave: Sovereign is the entity which decides about the division of powers between the centre and the members. What makes the difference is the *Kompetenz-Kompetenz*. In a federal system sovereignty retreats into the *Kompetenz-Kompetenz*, the power to divide the powers between the two levels. Sovereign is the entity that holds this power.[10]

Again, this is also the answer that the Federal Constitutional Court gives with regard to the EU. Sovereignty in the EU lies with the Member States since they are the 'Masters of the Treaties' and hold the *Kompetenz-Kompetenz*.[11] This is indeed the difference between a federal state and other types of federations. The EU does not have

[8] BVerfGE 123, 267 (p. 347). See Dieter Grimm, ch. 11 of this volume.

[9] Ibid., (p. 343).

[10] Georg Jellinek, *Allgemeine Staatslehre* (Berlin: O. Häring, 1914), 7th edn, 1960, p. 495.

[11] BVerfGE 123, 267 (p. 349).

the right to self-determination about its existence, its legal basis, and its competencies. The decision about these matters is in the hands of the Member States. They decide by way of concluding a treaty under international law, and that means: unanimously. Yet, once public powers have been transferred their exercise is a matter of the EU. Even if the Member States retain a share in exercising these powers, they do so as members of an organ of the EU, the Council. Here the self-determination of the states ends and that of the EU begins.

Is this degree of self-determination as to secondary law-making and law enforcement sufficient to call the EU sovereign? It is true that there is no sovereignty without self-determination. The reverse is, however, not true. Not every right to self-determination makes its bearer sovereign. The type of self-determination, which is an expression of sovereignty, refers exactly to the existence and form of a political entity, i.e. to the constitutional level, in European terms to the primary law. Sovereign is an entity that has this power, whereas it seems difficult to call a political entity sovereign that cannot independently determine its existence, its purpose, its form, and its competencies. This is the case with the EU. It lacks the constituent power. With regard to its legal foundation it is hetero-determined and consequently not sovereign.

3. *Habermas' theory of dual sovereignty*

Yet, in a recent book Habermas denies just this.[12] So, we stay our final judgment until Habermas has been heard. He concedes that the constituent power regarding the EU lies with the Member States, but he adds, no longer alone. With the Lisbon Treaty the constituent power in his view is divided between the Member States and the EU citizens. According to him they participate in the process of amending the Treaties. It is, however, clear from the text of the Lisbon Treaty that the European citizens as such have no say in the

[12] Jürgen Habermas, *Zur Verfassung Europas* (Berlin: Suhrkamp, 2011), pp. 48–82.

amendment process. But Habermas finds that their elected representatives in the European Parliament have a share in the constituent power. The constituent power is therefore divided between the Member States and the European citizens as represented by the European Parliament.

Habermas goes still one step further when he asks whether, on the side of the Member States, it is truly the states which exercise that power. His answer is the following. Since all Member States are representative democracies the treaty-making or treaty-amending power of the Member States belongs ultimately to their peoples, i.e. to their individual citizens. Thus the citizens are the ultimate subject of European public power. What seems to be a subject composed by the Member States and the EU at first glance is in fact one identical subject like in the nation-state. It consists of the individual citizens with the particularity that they exercise it in a double capacity and a double procedure, as citizens of the various Member States and as European citizens.[13]

This is what Habermas understands by divided sovereignty. The division does not exist between two different subjects, but between two capacities or roles of one and the same subject. This means at the same time that the division happens at the source of the entity to be constituted, not at the source of the powers of the already constituted entity. This distinction is important for Habermas because it allows him to reject the argument that sovereign is whoever has the *Kompetenz-Kompetenz*. The existence of one original democratic sovereign excludes the existence of a *Kompetenz-Kompetenz*. Jellinek's solution does not apply in the EU.

[13] Ibid., 66–70. Habermas relies here on Armin von Bogdandy, 'Grundprinzipien' in A. von Bogdandy and J. Bast (eds), *Europäisches Verfassungsrecht* (Berlin: Springer, 2009), p. 64; Christian Callies, *Die neue Europäische Union nach dem Vertrag von Lissabon* (Tübingen: Mohr Siebeck, 2010), p. 71; Claudio Franzius, *Europäisches Verfassungsrechtsdenken* (Tübingen: Mohr Siebeck, 2010), p. 57. See also Alexandra Kemmerer, 'Legitimationssubjekte: Staatsbürger und Unionsbürger' in C. Franzius et al (eds), *Strukturfragen der Europäischen Union* (Baden-Baden: Nomos, 2010), p. 204; Anne Peters, *Elemente einer Theorie der Verfassung Europas* (Berlin: Duncker & Humblot, 2001), p. 390 ss., p. 556 ss.

To be sure, Habermas is not primarily interested in the question discussed here, to wit: who is sovereign in the relationship between the EU and its Member States. He is rather interested in the possibility of transnational democracy.[14] For this possibility, Europe serves as an important test case. Habermas takes the EU as a model for a cosmopolitan entity. Ever since the great revolutions of the late eighteenth century popular sovereignty is the answer to the question of who the holder of sovereignty is within the state. The existence of sovereignty was presupposed. Popular sovereignty as a new paradigm finds its expression in the constituent power. If it can be shown that such a power of the people exists in Europe, then the foundations for a genuine European democracy are laid and the objection that the EU is not sovereign, because it lacks the constituent power, becomes obsolete.

4. *The amendment power according to the Lisbon Treaty*

This is certainly an ambitious construct, the question being, however, whether it is in fact that of the Lisbon Treaty. The answer to this question requires an assessment of the rules governing the amendment process. This process is now regulated in Article 48 of the Treaty on European Union (TEU). The article provides for three modes of amending the treaties instead of one under the previous regime. For each mode a different procedure exists with different levels: a preparatory level, and a decision-making level, and different actors on each level. The Lisbon Treaty itself was still concluded according to the classical international law pattern. The heads of state and government of the Member States negotiated the text. The Member States ratified the text according to the provisions of their constitutions, mostly by a vote of parliament.

The national parliaments when ratifying a treaty decide as representatives of their peoples. The result is attributed to the peoples. Hence, the Lisbon Treaty can be regarded as an expression of the

[14] Habermas, *Zur Verfassung Europas* (n. 12), pp. 39, 48.

will of the peoples of the Member States. Organs of the EU were not involved and likewise the individuals in their capacity as EU citizens were not involved, neither directly nor indirectly. In the future there will be differences. There is a regular amendment procedure and, in addition, there are two simplified procedures. For the sake of simplification, only the decision-making stage will be discussed here, not the preparatory stage, which is not binding for the decision-makers.

The regular procedure, which covers the TEU totally and most of the Treaty on the Functioning of the European Union (TFEU), differs from the previous rule only in the preparatory stage, not in the decision-making stage. The heads of state and government of the Member States negotiate the text of the amendment and adopt it in the form of a treaty under international law. The Member States ratify it according to the provisions of their constitutions, either by a parliamentary vote or by a referendum. This means that at the same time the Member States remain the 'Masters of the Treaty'. It is not the EU that decides about its legal foundation, but the Member States in their capacity as subjects of international law.

This is different for the two simplified procedures. Both have a narrower field of application. None of them applies to the TEU. The first of the two simplified procedures applies to the TFEU, albeit not in its entirety, but only to part three, and does not allow a transfer of competencies. Hence, the *Kompetenz–Kompetenz* remains untouched by this procedure. The decision is taken by the European Council, i.e. an organ of the EU, yet, the organ which is composed by the heads of state and government of the Member States. The decision requires unanimity of the twenty-eight Member States. The European Parliament and the European Commission are heard before the decision. It takes legal force only after ratification by every Member State.

The second simplified procedure applies to two questions regulated in the TFEU. The first one concerns the decision-making mode in the Council, namely the transition from the unanimity rule to majority vote. The second one concerns the role of the European Parliament, namely a transfer of legislative acts from the special procedure to the regular procedure, i.e. from suspending parliamentary veto to full co-decision. These decisions are taken by the European Council unanimously. They require the consent of the European Parliament. Each national parliament has a veto right.

What does that mean with regard to the legitimation subject in Habermas' understanding, i.e. the participation of the individuals in their double capacity as national and EU citizens? In their capacity as *national* citizens they are involved in the first two procedures via the requirement of ratification, directly in the case of a national referendum, indirectly in the case of a parliamentary vote. In the third procedure they are involved via the national parliaments' veto power. In their capacity as *European* citizens they are not at all involved in the first two procedures since neither a European referendum is prescribed nor does the European Parliament play a role here. In the last procedure they are involved through the veto power of the European Parliament.

The result is that the constituent power of the EU remains in the hands of the Member States, albeit in various degrees. In the regular procedure, the constituent power lies exclusively with the Member States. They retain the *Kompetenz–Kompetenz*. In the first simplified procedure the constituent power is given to an organ of the EU, but to that organ which is composed by the heads of state and government of the Member States and which can only decide unanimously. In this sense, the states remain, here as well, the 'Masters of the Treaties'. In the third procedure the EU citizens have an indirect share in a limited number of matters of minor importance.

Regarding sovereignty, it remains true that the EU cannot decide about its own legal foundation, the Treaties, and everything that is regulated in these Treaties. The portion of constituent power that the Member States share with the EU is extremely small and certainly not sufficient to call the EU sovereign. Habermas' construction remains interesting, but not as a description of the legal situation after the Lisbon Treaty, but as a theoretical model of construing sovereignty in a political entity composed of democratic states.

5. *Divided, pooled, or absent sovereignty?*

If it is true that the EU (and with it the individuals in their capacity as EU citizens) does not share the constituent power with the Member States, then it follows that the language of divided sovereignty is incorrect. The EU does not have a portion of the sovereignty. The EU has but a portion of the public powers. Is it, then, at least correct to say that the Member States have pooled their national sovereignty and exercise it jointly through the organs of the EU? Perhaps that could be said, as long as decisions of the Council required unanimity. But this is over. It is now possible that a Member State is subject to a European decision that it explicitly rejected in its national democratic process.

If this happens then the state is not subject to the will of other states, but to the will of the EU. This is even more so if the decision is not taken by the Council, which is composed of members of the national governments, but by the Commission or the ECJ. These EU organs are independent from the Member States in their will formation and do not necessarily represent the joint will of the Member States. It can happen, and often does, that a European act stands in opposition to the will of the Member States. On the level of the exercise of transferred powers, the EU has emancipated itself to a large extent from the Member States. This makes it also incorrect to speak of a pooled sovereignty.

On the other hand, the fact that the EU has not become sovereign does not automatically mean that the Member States have remained sovereign. It is not impossible that in a federal entity no part is sovereign. Carl Schmitt even described it as a characteristic of what he calls a 'Bund', as opposed to a federal state ('Bundesstaat') and a confederation ('Staatenbund'), that the question of sovereignty is left open. Homogeneity among the parts makes this possible. If, on the other hand, the question of sovereignty is raised and answered, this means for him the end of the 'Bund'. Either it turns into a federal state where the central unit is sovereign or it disintegrates into a federation where the members are sovereign.[15]

[15] Carl Schmitt, *Verfassungslehre* (Berlin: Duncker & Humblot, 1928), p. 361 ss.

The Member States of the EU could have given up or lost their sovereignty in a number of ways. One of them is a loss of autonomy with regard to their legal foundation. As a matter of fact, the Member States of the EU are no longer completely free to determine the national constitution. EU law claims primacy even over domestic constitutional law. However, not all constitutional courts of the Member States accept this. They make reservations regarding EU law that touches upon the very identity of the national constitution. But even these reservations leave a considerable part of the domestic constitution that depends on compatibility with EU law. To that extent, the Member States no longer possess unlimited self-determination about their constitutions. It could be regained only by leaving the EU.

Still, the EU and the Member States are not in the same situation with regard to their legal foundations. The EU has no constituent power. It owes its existence and legal foundation to the Member States. They possess the constituent power for the European Union. The Member States, on the contrary, constitute themselves. They possess the constituent power on their territory. In exercising this power they are limited in some respects. The limits flow from the European Treaties that they freely concluded. Insofar, they are self-imposed limitations. National constitutional law that is incompatible with EU law does not become invalid but only inapplicable. The EU cannot enforce the superiority of the Treaties. It can only apply the sanctions provided in the Treaties. These differences seem big enough to still concede a right of self-determination to the Member States.

A loss of national sovereignty could also happen if the number of powers in the hands of the Member States shrink so much that one would hesitate to call the states sovereign. This could be the result of an excessive transfer of powers to the EU. The Federal Constitutional Court of Germany tries to prevent this by defining the limits of a power transfer to the EU.[16] However, the Court has difficulties to draw a clear borderline. If, as the Court admits, there are no subject matters that may by no means be transferred, the limitation becomes a matter

[16] BVerfGE 123, 267 (p. 357 ss.).

of degree. Since power transfers used to happen step by step, it seems difficult for a court to determine the critical moment. A good cause for interference may never arrive.

A loss of sovereignty could, however, also be the result of an arrogation of powers by the EU. In this case, it is not the Member States that transfer too many powers to the EU. Rather, the EU uses the formally transferred powers to informally enlarge them by interpreting the Treaties in a way that amounts to an amendment. Such an interpretation would, of course, be a violation of the Treaties. But if the violation is sanctioned or even committed by the guardian of Treaties itself, the ECJ, the Member States lack a remedy to cure the transgression. If it can easily be circumvented, the *Kompetenz–Kompetenz*, as the place to which national sovereignty retreats, loses its function as a protection of Member State sovereignty.

This is not only a theoretical possibility but a real threat to national sovereignty. It comes as a consequence of the so-called constitutionalization of the European Treaties through the ECJ. They are higher law, not only compared to secondary European law but also to all national law, which automatically loses its applicability in case of conflict. The interpretation and application of the European Treaties is, therefore, enforcement of quasi-constitutional law. This means that the Member States, if they regard the interpretation as legally flawed or politically detrimental, have no chance to correct it by legislation. The only remedy would be an amendment of the Treaties, which requires the consent of all Member States and is usually unavailable.

The potential of eroding national sovereignty by way of interpretation of the European Treaties explains the claim of several constitutional courts of the Member States to be able to review European Union acts, including ECJ decisions, as possible violations of the principle of conferral. The ECJ agrees that *ultra vires* acts of EU organs are invalid. But it claims the exclusive jurisdiction over questions of compatibility of EU acts with the Treaties. Instances where the ECJ found an EU act *ultra vires* are extremely rare, whereas the Court has frequently declared acts of Member States incompatible with the Treaties. The perceived role of the ECJ is still that of a promoter of integration rather than that of a neutral umpire between the EU and its Member States.

Hence the role of the guardian of Member States rights, in particular the principle of conferral, lies in effect with the national constitutional courts. However, in a recent decision the German Constitutional Court raised the threshold, declaring an EU act inapplicable in Germany in a way that makes it rather unlikely that it will ever find a violation.[17] According to this decision, a clear violation of the Treaties is not sufficient to declare an EU act inapplicable in Germany. The act must, in addition, lead to a structural power shift from the Member States to the EU. However, such a power shift will rarely be the work of one decision. Rather, it will be the result of a cumulation of many minor steps, each of which will seem too small to risk open conflict between the courts. The cumulation, in turn, will never be the subject of judicial review which is bound to individual cases.

C. Sovereignty Still Adequate?

The question of who is sovereign in the EU is thereby answered. In spite of some blurring effects, the Member States may still be called sovereign, whereas the EU is not sovereign. However, since it is not necessary that there be sovereignty in an entity like the EU and since it has become more difficult to determine sovereignty clearly, I want to return to the initial problem whether one should maintain the concept of sovereignty or recognize that the era of post-sovereignty has begun, as many authors suggest.

One thing seems clear, however. The traditional holders of full sovereignty, the states, continue to exist and remain the basic units of the emerging post-Westphalian international order. The borders of the states are porous, but have not disappeared. The states share public powers with international organizations, but still hold the far bigger

[17] BVerfGE 126, 286 (2010).

portion of public powers. In particular, they have not given up the monopoly of legitimate use of physical force. When it comes to applying physical force all international organizations, insofar as they have the right to use coercive means, have to borrow them from the states.

In addition, one should not forget that the EU is a very special case of a supranational public power holder. Not all states are as deeply integrated into supranational entities as the Member States of the EU. Less than 15% of all existing states are members of the EU. Sovereignty is still much more evident outside than inside the EU. It would therefore be a mistake to discuss the sovereignty problem only from a European perspective. But even within the EU the changes concern mostly the vertical dimension, the relations between states and the EU; whereas, in the horizontal dimension, the relationship among the states, the traditional pattern still prevails within the EU.

Moreover, the preconditions for democratic government, the degree of identification and solidarity which is indispensable for politics, is far better developed within states than within supranational organizations. This is even true for the EU. The degree of democratic self-legitimation of the EU, as mediated by European elections, is still small, the societal preconditions of a lively democracy still being underdeveloped. This is why the EU depends largely on the legitimation that comes from the Member States. The EU is not in a position to replace it. This should prevent the EU from constantly lowering the political substance of the Member States and the impact of their democratic structures and processes.

Habermas, by the way, is ready to accept this. He refers to this situation in order to show that the Member States must retain a share of European sovereignty. For him, they are the primary guarantors of individual freedom, democracy, and the rule of law. Sovereignty is, in times of increasing internationalization and globalization, a means to secure democratic self-determination to units where democracy has a real chance.[18] It is no longer, as some authors who reject the concept fear, a safe haven for repressive regimes.

[18] Habermas, *Zur Verfassung Europas* (n. 12), p. 20.

4

On the Status of the EU's Democratic Legitimacy after Lisbon

A. Strengthening European Democracy as Goal of the Lisbon Treaty

'Lisbon' lends its name to two legal documents: the treaty, which since 1 December 2009 has formed the legal foundation of the European Union, and the judgment of the German Federal Constitutional Court, dated 30 June 2009, which declared that the German law ratifying the treaty was compatible with the Basic Law, Germany's constitution. The EU's democratic legitimacy plays a major role in both documents. One of the treaty's declared goals is to strengthen European democracy.[1] According to Article 1 § 2 of the Treaty on the European Union (TEU), the treaty 'marks a new stage in the process of creating an ever closer union among the peoples of Europe'. Article 9 and those that follow specify the EU's 'democratic principles'. According to Article 10 § 1 TEU, the Union's operation is founded on representative democracy. The provisions that follow distinguish between two forms of representation. Under Section 2, citizens are directly represented at the EU level in the European Parliament. Under Section 3, the Member States are represented in the European Council by their

[1] Preamble, 7. Recital.

heads of state or government, and in the Council by their governments, which for their part are democratically accountable directly to their national parliaments or their states' citizens. Further provisions promise transparency and introduce a citizens' initiative. The European Parliament receives greater powers.

One must not infer from the German Constitutional Court's approval of the treaty's content that the Court is satisfied with the current state of European democracy. The Court is by no means without misgivings about the treaty, and precisely with regard to democracy its observations are highly critical. 'The Treaty of Lisbon', the judgment states, 'does not lead to a new phase in the development of democracy.'[2] And further: 'Even in the new wording of Article 14 § 2 of the Lisbon Treaty, and contrary to the claim that seems to be made by the text of Article 10 § 1, the European Parliament is not the representative body of a sovereign European people.'[3] Nor, the justices added, could the European public authority's existing democratic deficit (measured by the democratic standards of nation-states) be offset by citizen rights aimed at participation and transparency.[4] On the contrary, the structure of the EU imposes a 'considerable impediment to the personal or substantive implementation of the will of a representative parliamentary majority'.[5] Only with great difficulty, then, does the Court arrive at the conclusion that the treaty is compatible 'as yet' (*noch*) with the German Basic Law.[6]

If, against the backdrop of these diverging views, one wishes to explore the current state of democratic legitimacy for both the EU and the authority it exercises, one must begin with the legal organization and configuration of the flow of democratic legitimacy. In this respect, one must distinguish between the levels of *creating* and *organizing* European public authority—in constitutional terms, the *pouvoir constituant*, and the exercise of European public authority—in constitutional terms the *pouvoir constitué*. Legal institutions, of course, do

[2] BVerfGE123, 267 (379). [3] Ibid., 372. [4] Ibid., 377 ss.
[5] Ibid., 376. [6] Ibid., 370.

not constitute the whole of democracy. They provide only the foundation and the framework of a democratic process that culminates, but does not exhaust itself in constitutional institutions and procedures. The democratic process has its roots in society. It involves citizens, with their associations and spontaneous forms of collective action, as well as intermediary institutions—e.g. the media of a democratic public sphere. The real preconditions and possibilities of development for a polity's democratic substance are determined at this pre-legal level. The community's democratic condition can be determined only by considering both levels.

B. The Levels of European Democracy

1. *The constituting level*

The first principle of every national democracy is that state authority derives from the people. 'The people' means the people of the state. This is the subject of legitimation. It possesses original authority. It cannot, however, constantly exercise this authority on its own. For that, it needs institutions. These derive their authority from the people. The legitimating principle of democratic states is popular sovereignty. Popular sovereignty is expressed through an act of constitution-making. That act determines the form and content of the polity. This usually happens in one of two ways: either the people appoint a constituent assembly that enacts a constitution, or a draft constitution is adopted by the people. Neither of these is essential. It seems sufficient that public power be attributed to the people as the source of all public authority, and that the state be so organized that the exercise of state authority is influenced by the popular will. This requires that state institutions exercise their authority on behalf of the people, and that they be responsible to the people for that exercise. The most important means of forging a link between legitimacy and accountability is the election, the medium for which is the competition among parties for votes.

The European treaties—currently the Treaty of Lisbon, the most recent in a series of founding and amending treaties—form the EU's legal foundation. They give it existence, form, and content. The Lisbon Treaty is the equivalent of a state constitution. It differs from a constitution, however, in the manner of its origin. It came into being in the same manner as all previous European treaties. The heads of state and government of the Member States signed an international treaty, which was then ratified in accordance with the procedures specified in the Member States' national constitutions. The Union's citizens—the treaties do not speak of a 'people' of the Union—played no role in this. The legitimating principle of the treaties is not popular sovereignty, but rather state sovereignty.

This does not mean, however, that the EU lacks democratic legitimacy. The Lisbon Treaty, like its predecessors, gives it democratic legitimacy insofar as the Member States, for their part, approved it in a democratic process. The peoples of the Member States participated in that process—directly where a referendum took place, indirectly where a parliamentary resolution sufficed. But they participated as the peoples of the states (approving the treaty concluded by their national governments), not as the people of the Union. As a result, the treaties' democratic legitimacy stems exclusively from the Member States. The EU was the object, not the subject, of the conclusion of the treaty. As far as its existence, its objectives, and its organization are concerned, it possesses no internal legitimacy. It is legitimated only externally.

This could change, of course. The EU is not committed once and for all to external legitimation. In the course of crafting the treaty, the Member States could, for the future, have shifted the constituent, or constitution-making power to the EU, and thus transformed the international treaties into a constitution. That did not happen, however, and it was not envisioned even in the failed constitutional treaty. In the future, too, changes to the treaty will come about essentially according to the model of international law. But the procedure for amending the treaties, now regulated in Article 48 TEU, has become more differentiated and more complex: more differentiated, because Article 48 distinguishes three types of procedure; more complex, because rules are laid down, not only for the decision itself, but also for its preparation. The rules differ for each type of procedure. This complexity cannot be set forth here in all its details. In summary, one can say that the Union's citizens never come into the picture directly as legitimating subjects. Indirectly, they play a role through the European Parliament.[7] Their participation, however, remains essentially limited to the preliminary phase. The European Parliament is called upon to participate only in one case of a subordinate nature.

In the ordinary amendment procedure, nothing in the decision-making mechanism has changed with respect to the earlier situation. Amendments to the treaty must be adopted unanimously by a conference of the Member State governments (Art. 48(4)(1) TEU), and they enter into force when ratified by all the Member States in accordance with the Member States' constitutions (Art. 48(4)(2) TEU). In simplified amendment proceedings, which apply only to the third part of the Treaty on the Functioning of the European Union (TFEU) and may not lead to an expansion of EU powers (Art. 48(6)(2) TEU), the decision is made by the European Council. The decision in the Council must be unanimous, and it enters into force after being approved by all the Member States (Art. 48(6)(2) TEU). This procedure was first employed in the effort to combat the financial crisis and led to a supplement of Article 136 TFEU. The European Court of Justice (ECJ) has confirmed the validity of this amendment.[8]

Finally, the so-called '*passerelle* clauses' (*passarelle* being French for a small bridge) allow a legislative procedure to be altered without formally amending the treaties. Under these clauses, within the jurisdiction of the TFEU or of Title V of the TEU ('General Provisions on the Union's External Action and Specific Provisions on the Common Foreign and Security Policy'), the unanimity requirement in the Council can be replaced by a qualified majority requirement, and the special legislative procedure can be replaced by the ordinary legislative

[7] The Federal Constitutional Court, however, doubts this. Cf. BVerfGE 123, 267.

[8] *Pringle v. Ireland*, Case C-370/12, Decision 2011/199 (27 November 2012).

procedure in which the Parliament takes part in the decision. The decision to alter the procedure must be made unanimously in the Council and approved by the European Parliament. Each national parliament has a right of veto (Art. 48(6)(7) TEU). Ratification in the Member States is not required.

While the decision in ordinary proceedings is reserved to the Member States—and is thus made independent of the EU—in simplified proceedings and in general *passerelle* proceedings, the decision is made by an EU institution, the Council. As a consequence, the EU in this case is not the object, but the subject of the decision. Even so, the institution involved is one composed of the Member States' heads of state or government, and these must decide unanimously. In the general *passerelle* proceedings, by contrast, there is an element of internal European legitimation, inasmuch as the European Parliament takes part—albeit in a purely negative way—in the decision. The Parliament can only reject decisions of the Council; it cannot initiate them or determine their content.

In its *Lisbon* judgment, the Federal Constitutional Court grappled with the procedures for amending the treaty and for approving amendments, maintaining that, 'in accordance with the powers to pursue European integration granted under Article 23(1) of the Basic Law—in conjunction with the Preamble, Article 20, Article 79(3) and Article 146—there can be no independent legitimating subject for the European Union's public authority that could, on its own initiative and without reference to some external will, constitute itself on a higher level'.[9] Accordingly, in the Court's view, the Member States must remain 'Masters of the Treaties'. In other words, the *pouvoir constituant* may not be transferred to the EU, and the *Kompetenz-Kompetenz*—the power, in jurisdictional questions, to decide who decides—must remain with the Member States. The upshot is a limitation on Germany's readiness to pursue integration and, with it, a limit to Europe's internal democratic legitimacy. The EU must not do away with external legitimation through the Member States.

[9] BVerfGE 123, 267 (349).

This limit is democratically justified in its own right, and at the Basic Law's highest level, Article 79(3), which protects the constitution-making, or constituent, power of the German people. From it, the institutions of the German state receive their mandate. According to Article 79(1)-(2), the mandate even embraces constitutional amendments. A legislature cannot free itself from the mandate by amending the constitution to abolish the existing basis of its powers. The self-determination of the German people—expressed internally through the constituent power, externally through sovereignty—is not at the legislature's disposal. Not only are the institutions of the Federal Republic forbidden to abolish this right or transfer it to the EU, they cannot even amend the constitution in a way that would make such a transfer possible. Such a power could be granted only by the German people. However, because of the Basic Law's restraints on amendment in this regard, such an authorization could be granted only by enacting a new constitution, one in which Germany's membership in a European state is expressly provided or permitted.[10]

As far as the ordinary amendment procedure is concerned, there can be no doubt that the constituent power has not been transferred to the EU. In the simplified procedure—specifically in the general *passerelle* procedure—this is less obvious. The deciding institution in both cases is the European Council, which, unlike the Conference of heads of state and government, is an EU institution. Formally, then, it is no longer a matter of external-determination but of self-determination. Substantively, however, the difference dwindles, for the personnel of the Conference is identical to that of the European Council, and the decisions of both bodies must be unanimous. Thus, no Member State is subjected to an external will. In this respect, one can say that even in the simplified procedure the Member States remain 'Masters of the Treaties'. In the *passerelle* procedure, no treaty amendment that the Member States reject can be forced upon them. But, on the other hand, they cannot implement every amendment

[10] The FCC repeatedly stressed this in the *Lisbon* judgment. Cf. BVerfGE 123, 267 (347–349, 363–369).

that they desire. To this extent, the *passerelle* procedure diminishes full possession of constituent power, but only in a narrow realm of relatively slender importance.

In any event, none of this gives rise to a European legitimating subject for the EU's fundamental legal order. There is no basis in the Lisbon Treaty for the ambitious attempt of Jürgen Habermas to prove the existence of a constituent power of European citizens, which the citizens will exercise in a dual capacity as citizens of the EU and as citizens of the Member States.[11] Where democracy culminates in a nation-state—at the level of the *pouvoir constituant*—there is no European democracy. If there were European democracy at this level, it would mean that the EU—with regard to its existence, its legal foundation, its purposes, and its powers—would have become a self-sufficient entity, independent of its Member States. Decisions about the distribution of powers would take place on the higher rather than the lower plane. In other words: willingly or not, the EU would have become a state.

Because the Basic Law forbids the surrender of sovereign German statehood, the Federal Republic could not join in this endeavour. For Germany, EU statehood is not a goal to be pursued but a danger to be repelled. Admittedly, the risk does not seem acute. The Constitutional Court's concern is directed instead at the more proximate threat presented by revisions to the procedures for amending the treaties. Every expansion of EU powers alters the Basic Law. This is so because every European legal act based on such expansions claims validity in Germany without regard to its conformity with the Basic Law. Accordingly, the Federal Constitutional Court requires that Germany's approval of such expansions comply with the Basic Law's provisions governing constitutional amendments, even where this is not explicitly required by European law or by Article 23(1) GG.

This means that treaty amendments must honour Article 79(2)-(3) GG. The Bundestag bears the 'responsibility for integration'.[12]

[11] Jürgen Habermas, *Zur Verfassung Europas: Ein Essay* (Berlin: Suhrkamp, 2011), pp. 62–74. See also my engagement with Habermas's theses in ch. 3 of this volume.

[12] BVerfGE 123, 267 (353).

Obviously, it can fulfil this role only if it can discern what is at stake in a proposed treaty amendment. The Federal Constitutional Court is well aware, however, that the scope of an authorization via the simplified amendment procedure can hardly be ascertained or predicted. Nevertheless, the Court contents itself with heightening the internal requirements of German approval beyond what the Lisbon Treaty stipulates, although this does nothing to lessen the difficulties of foreseeability or to increase the Bundestag's capacity to fulfil its responsibility for integration.

The German Constitutional Court also expresses concern about the danger of clandestine and subtle amendments to the treaties—a danger that by no means originated with the Lisbon Treaty. The Court has in mind amendments that come about, not by way of agreement among the treaties' signatories, but in the garb of treaty interpretation, and that thus circumvent the safeguards of Article 48 TEU. In this respect, the Court says that the EU must not 'arrogate' to itself the power of *Kompetenz-Kompetenz*.[13] Such 'arrogation' would not be the work of the Member States surrendering the power of *Kompetenz-Kompetenz* through a formal treaty amendment. It would be the work, rather, of the EU taking the power upon itself.

In the Court's view, this risk stems primarily from the ECJ. But here too, if the Court does not want the Lisbon Treaty to fail on these grounds, it can only establish safeguards at the national level. Thus, the Court reaffirms that legal acts, based on treaty-interpretation, that transgress the limits of treaty amendments cannot be applied in Germany. The Court claims for itself the power to decide such questions for Germany in the final instance, since 'otherwise, in the face of advancing integration, the fundamental political and constitutional structures of the sovereign Member States—recognized by Article 48(2)(1) of the Lisbon Treaty—cannot be preserved'.[14] The Court thus

[13] Ibid.

[14] Ibid., 354. Made more concrete in BVerfGE 126, 286 (2010). On this point, see ch. 3 of this volume.

represents the only effective counterweight to the EU's jurisdictional expansion by administrative or judicial means.[15]

2. *The level of implementation*

At the level of implementation, the principle of democracy requires that those entrusted with public responsibility and endowed with public power, as well as their acts, be democratically legitimated.[16] Such legitimation has personal, functional, and factual aspects. In the personal sense, democratic legitimation means that public representatives and administrative officers are integrated within a chain of legitimacy that can be traced back to the people. In a functional sense, it means that their actions are authorized by the citizens. Public authority is always limited authority. An unauthorized action represents not only a breach of such limitations, but an offence against democracy. In the factual sense, the principle of democracy requires that official actions be derivable from the citizens' will. The democratically shaped will of the people must inform official decisions. Precisely how these principles should take concrete shape differs from country to country. There is no unitary model of democratic rule.

When European integration began, democratic legitimacy flowed exclusively from the Member States. There was no provision for an internal European legitimation. The chain of legitimacy for the EEC's institutions ran back to national elections. The governments created by such elections composed the Council. They determined the composition of the Commission and the ECJ. The European Parliament, originally characterized as an 'Assembly,' was composed of members of the national parliaments. It had no powers of decision; its role was merely advisory. The Council was the only European legislature (albeit without the right of initiative, which belonged to the

[15] Cf. Dieter Grimm, ch. 10 of this volume.

[16] Cf. Ernst-Wolfgang Böckenförde, 'Demokratie als Verfassungsprinzip,' in Josef Isensee and Paul Kirchhof (eds), *Handbuch des Staatsrechts*, vol. 2 (Heidelberg: C.F. Müller, 3rd edn, 2004), p. 429.

Commission as guarantor of community interests). The principle of unanimity in Council decisions ensured that the chain of legitimacy from the Member States was never broken. The Commission and the Court were bound by the primary law adopted by the Member States and the secondary law enacted by the Council.

The need for internal democratic legitimacy was first felt in 1987, when the Single European Act (SEA) abolished the principle of unanimity in the Council. Until then, it was impossible for a law that had not previously been approved by a Member State's democratically legitimated and controlled institutions to enter into force within that state. Since then, however, it is possible that a Member State must apply a European law that is not supported by—and might even directly counter—that state's democratic will. Because of the Community's newfound independence from the Member States, the influx of national legitimacy no longer sufficed. If the European legislative authority was to enjoy adequate democratic legitimacy, there must also be an internal legitimation. The most promising candidate, following the nation-state model, was the European Parliament.

As early as 1979, the European Parliament was no longer staffed by members of national parliaments, but instead was directly elected by the Member States' citizens—though, in the absence of a European election law, this was done according to the national election laws of each state. Under the SEA, the European Parliament was granted a limited role in European legislation and was now officially recognized as a parliament tasked with representing the Member States' peoples at the Community level. Subsequent treaties further expanded the Parliament's powers, without however making it coequal to the Council in European legislation. Since the Treaty of Maastricht, the composition of the Commission depends upon the Parliament's approval. Already with the Treaty of Nice, commissioners were no longer delegated by the national governments but were appointed instead by the Council.

In the aftermath of the Lisbon Treaty, the following may be said about the democratic legitimacy of EU institutions and of their legal acts. Only the European Parliament enjoys a direct European legitimacy in a personal sense. The European Council, by contrast, as well as the Council and its president, are legitimated only by the Member States. The Commission relies on a mixed legitimation. The president of the Commission is proposed by the European Council and elected by the European Parliament. The other members of the Commission are nominated by the Council with the approval of the chosen president. The full body of the Council must then be approved by the European Parliament. The European Council appoints the commissioners. The appointment of judges to the ECJ remains the exclusive province of the national governments.

These observations about personal legitimation are not very meaningful, however, unless they are considered in connection with the institutions' respective powers and relative importance. Considered in this light, it becomes clear that the institution with the strongest European legitimacy—the institution whose composition is fully independent of the Member States—the European Parliament, is also the institution with the weakest powers. Despite the increase in its legislative and budgetary powers and its newfound role in staffing the Commission, the European Parliament remains essentially limited to approving decisions made elsewhere—though its veto position allows it to influence the content of decisions and it has the option, through a no-confidence vote, of forcing the Commission to resign.

The limited role of the European Parliament is most obvious, however, in the fact that the policies of the Commission and, still more, those of the other institutions are unaffected by the outcome of parliamentary elections. The great, trend-setting decisions are still reserved for the European Council, the smaller ones for the Council and the Commission. Majority ratios in the European Parliament are not decisive for the activities of other institutions. The fact that national parties compete in European elections, while supranational coalitions of like-minded national parties conduct the business of the European Parliament, makes the very notion of a 'parliamentary majority' seem dubious.

In those institutions composed of national governments, fundamental decisions of European policy are dominated not by party lines, but by national interests, which are balanced, not through deliberation, but by negotiation. The Commission, whose legitimacy is mixed and whose members are not bound by instructions from their states of origin, enjoys a remarkable degree of autonomy thanks to its monopoly on legislative initiative, its independence from the Member States in implementing the programme of integration, its right to hail Member States before the ECJ on charges of treaty violation, and the generally European perspective of its expert staffers.

Under these conditions, is the EU rightly judged to be democratically deficient?

The answer depends, first and foremost, on the standard of measurement. Measured against the standards of nation-state democracies, the EU scores badly. But the EU is not a state and, in the view of the German Constitutional Court, it must not become a state if Germany is to remain one of its members. Hence, the Constitutional Court emphasizes again and again that European democracy need not emulate the model of nation-state democracy, and, therefore, need not be measured by nation-state standards.[17] Instead, because the EU is an association of sovereign states and primarily receives its democratic legitimacy from those states, the required level of legitimacy depends on the quantity of transferred powers and on the autonomy of European decision-making processes.[18] The standard, then, is a variable one. The requirements increase as integration advances. The requirements must not, however, grow indefinitely. The ongoing functionality of Member State democracies and the ban, derived from the Basic Law, on European statehood impose constitutional limits on European democracy.

That the necessary degree of democratization in the EU depends on the scope of its powers, and on the extent of its autonomy from the Member States, should be obvious. The difficulties arise in employing

[17] BVerfGE 123, 267 (344: not to be measured against the concrete characteristics of the democracy principle in nation-states; 347: departures from the organizational principles of national democracies allowed; 365: no structural congruence necessary; 366: not to be realized in the same manner as in the Basic Law).

[18] Ibid., 364.

these criteria. Even if one assumes that the current level of legitimacy suffices, the 'as yet' of the German Constitutional Court signals that, in the ongoing advance of integration, this could change. The decisive questions, then, are how to determine when the democratic requirements must increase and by what means this ought to happen. Where is the threshold, beyond which an increase in the level of legitimacy becomes necessary, and when does the increase collide with the limits of Article 38(1) GG, according to which the German Bundestag must retain enough substantive political powers to make its election politically consequential? This, too, is hard to determine. In any case, the list of legislative matters that, in the *Lisbon* judgment, the German Constitutional Court describes as having a strongly national character does not mark this boundary, but is intended rather as a warning.[19]

It does not seem possible even to obtain reliable information about the current relationship between subject matters regulated by the Community and those regulated by the Member States. Apart from the few exclusive powers of the EU set forth in Article 3 TFEU, the situation is characterized by obscurity and constant flux. A major source of this confusion is the division of powers between the EU and the Member States, not by subject matter (as is usual in national constitutions) but by a final, teleological criterion. According to Article 26 TFEU, the EU may take such measures as are necessary to establish and maintain a common market.

Particularly prominent among such measures is the abolition of national laws that hinder establishing a common market or that restrain competition. Such national laws must bow before the economic freedoms of Article 24(2) TFEU. What constitutes a hindrance can be defined narrowly and limited to laws that discriminate against foreign competitors. But it can also be defined broadly, with the consequence that national laws with no economic motivation at all—to say nothing of a discriminatory motive—are classed as impediments to the free movement of goods, persons, services, and capital. If one chooses this broad interpretation, the norm loses all limits, and can

[19] Ibid., 359 (list); 357 (no ban on transfer).

be applied according to the economic policy preferences of the one applying it.

The Commission inclines towards a broad interpretation—usually with the ECJ's backing.[20] On the basis of this interpretation, numerous norms of national law have become inapplicable, even when they pursued legitimate protective purposes and even when they were passed in fulfilment of constitutional duties to protect. This need not lead inexorably to deregulation. In pursuit of the common market, national law can, under Articles 114–18 TFEU, be replaced by European law. But it is much easier to quash national laws than it is to pass European laws. While negative integration (the abolition of national law) comes about administratively or judicially without the possibility of political intervention by the Council or the Parliament, positive integration (the replacement of national law with European law) requires a political act of the Commission, the Council, and the Parliament, with a high threshold of consensus in each case.[21]

Similar difficulties arise when applying the criterion of the autonomy of European decision-making from the Member States. Without such autonomy, integration could not have progressed—but there would also be no democracy problem. If one wishes to solve this problem, one must ascertain where and how such autonomy comes about. In the European Council there can be no such autonomy. In the European Council, the Member States are represented by their highest exponents, and they make decisions unanimously. Similarly, decisions in the Council are made by representatives of the Member States, though usually by majority vote. This circumvents the democratic will of the outvoted states, but the decision-making procedure is not, vis-à-vis the Member States, autonomous.

[20] Cf. Ulrich Haltern, *Europarecht* (Tübingen: Mohr Siebeck, 2nd edn, 2007), pp. 657–798; Rudolf Streinz, 'Die Rolle des EuGH im Prozess der europäischen Integration' (2010) 135 *Archiv des öffentlichen Rechts* 1.

[21] The book that did the most to draw attention to this asymmetry is Fritz Scharpf, *Governing in Europe: Effective and Democratic?* (Oxford: Oxford University Press, 1999), pp. 43–83.

The European Parliament, by contrast, is the very source of European internal legitimation. It is supposed to close the gaps in the EU's external legitimation. For this reason, the European Parliament is made independent of the Member States institutionally, but not functionally, since in order to legislate it must work together with the Council. Likewise, in staffing the Commission, the European Parliament plays only a participatory role. The European Parliament is truly independent of the Member States only in the case of a no-confidence vote against the Commission. The European Parliament could, however, become autonomous were it to become a true legislature in its own right, and as such override possible participatory rights of the Council. Autonomy would also come about if the European Parliament appointed the Council, in the same way that, in a parliamentary system, the popular assembly appoints the government. In that case the level of European democracy would need to increase.

There remain the institutions that apply and implement law—the ECJ and the Commission. In its decision-making procedures, the ECJ is entirely independent of the Member States. This must be so, however, because otherwise the Court could not fulfil its duty to interpret and implement EU law. That some national high courts reserve to themselves the last word vis-à-vis the ECJ does not make the ECJ's decision-making procedure dependent on the Member States. Similarly, the Commission is supposed to devote itself entirely to the interest of the Community, in contrast to the Member States who, in the Council, pursue their national interests first and foremost. Like the ECJ, then, the Commission must be independent of the Member States in order to perform its functions. Autonomy is particularly relevant where the Commission gives legal recognition to EU law. In this respect, the Commission implements (in the case of primary EU law) the democratic will of the Member States as 'Masters of the Treaties' or (in the case of secondary EU law) the will of the European legislative organs, the Council and the Parliament. The Commission's obligation to law is supposed to compensate for its autonomy.

One must ask, however, to what degree this still holds, in the specific European case, in light of the law's amenability to, and need for, interpretation. With respect to the intentions of lawmakers, interpretations can hit or miss. This is no different with national law than with European law. If the lawmaker believes that a given application runs counter to its intentions or leads to undesired results, it can, by amending the law, redirect the institution that applies it. In this way, autonomy is constrained by legislative institutions with stronger democratic legitimacy. But in the EU, precisely this democracy-reinforcing possibility is sharply reduced. This has to do with a unique feature of European primary law. The treaties (the equivalent, at the European level, of a constitution) are not, like most constitutions, limited to setting forth the Union's goals, powers, organization, and procedures, but also include numerous regulations that, in a Member State, would take the form of statutory law. The entirety of EU competition law is an example. This is one of the reasons that the treaties' bulk far surpasses that of even the lengthiest national constitutions.

Because these regulations have been constitutionalized by the ECJ, the Commission can implement them vis-à-vis the Member States without dispute. Such applications become quasi-constitutional implementation. This has brought about decisive reconfigurations of the economic and social systems of the Member States, the dismantling of numerous public services, the abolition of national safety standards, and the transformation of the relationship between the market and the state.[22] Because it is a matter of implementing the constitution, neither the Parliament, which is legitimated at the European level, nor the Council, which is legitimated at the national level, comes into play. If they conclude that the Commission's measures are harmful, or that they contradict the Member States' intentions upon signing the treaties, they cannot correct the Commission's decisions via statutory amendment, as the legislature of a nation-state could correct

[22] Cf. Martin Höpner and Armin Schäfer, 'Eine neue Phase der europäischen Integration', in Martin Höpner and Armin Schäfer (eds), *Die politische Ökonomie der europäischen Integration* (Frankfurt: Campus, 2008), pp. 129 ss., 135 ss.; Fritz Scharpf, 'The European Social Model' (2002) 40 *Journal of Common Market Studies* 645; Christian Joerges and Florian Rödl, 'Informal Politics, Formalized Law and the "Social Deficit" of European Integration' (2009) 15 *European Law Journal* 1.

its executive. Instead, each correction would require an amendment to the treaty, which is far more difficult than a constitutional amendment at the national level and thus, in most cases, entirely illusory. To a large extent, the European democratic deficit is a product of this imbalance between politics and administration in the EU.

If the Member States maintain that the Commission's actions lack support in the treaties, their only remaining option is an action for annulment before the ECJ. Although its members are chosen exclusively by the individual Member States, the ECJ is autonomous to the highest degree. This autonomy is a product of the ECJ's judicial independence, and of a professional ethos that fosters an integration-friendly self-understanding. It was through the ECJ's jurisprudence that the four economic freedoms—originally conceived of as guidelines for legislation—first became directly applicable. Similarly, it was the ECJ's jurisprudence that first established the supremacy of Community law over national law, including national constitutional law. Without these innovations, the EU would have remained merely one supranational organization among many.[23] In this area, the autonomy of European decision-making reaches its pinnacle—and here the democracy problem is particularly pronounced. The ECJ is freer than any national court.[24]

This opens a gap, inimical to democracy, between jurisdiction and accountability. Jurisdiction over these decisions belongs to the EU's administrative and judicial institutions, the Commission and the ECJ, while the political institutions, the Parliament and the Council, as well as the Member States, play no part and have no power to re-chart

[23] Cf. *Van Gend en Loos v. Nederlandse Administratie der Belastingen*, Case 26/62 (5 February 1963); *Costa v. ENEL*, Case 6/64 (15 July 1964); Joseph H.H. Weiler, *The Constitution of Europe: 'Do the New Clothes Have an Emperor?' and Other Essays on European Integration* (Cambridge: Cambridge University Press, 1999); Karen J. Alter, *Establishing the Supremacy of European Law: The Making of an International Rule of Law in Europe* (Oxford: Oxford University Press, 2001); Alec Stone Sweet, *The Judicial Construction of Europe* (Oxford: Oxford University Press, 2004).

[24] Cf. Fritz Scharpf, 'Das Bundesverfassungsgericht als Hüter der demokratischen Selbstgestaltungsfähigkeit', in Michael Stolleis (ed), *Herzkammern der Republik: Die Deutschen und das Bundesverfassungsgericht* (Munich: C.H. Beck, 2011), p. 186.

the course for the future. The EU's administrative and judicial institutions, however, cannot be held accountable for their actions. They stand relatively independent of the outcome of European elections, and are largely immune, as well, to the pressures of public opinion.

Alongside the difficulty of determining when an expansion of European powers or the autonomy of European decision-making requires an increase in European democracy, there is the additional difficulty of determining what an increased democratization could consist in. The *Lisbon* judgment addressed its criticism of European democracy primarily to the fact that the European Parliament is elected according to national allotments, 'not as the representative of EU citizens as an indistinguishable unity, consistent with the principle of equal voting rights'.[25] As a result, the EU lacks 'an organ of political decision-making, brought into being through an equal election of all EU citizens and capable of a unified representation of the popular will'.[26] This could be read as a call for a change in the voting laws. The Court, however, was only reviewing the Lisbon Treaty for its compatibility with the Basic Law. Accordingly, the Court ultimately condoned the existing state of affairs because the basic rule of electoral equality applies only within a nation, 'not in a supranational representative institution that remains … a representative of nations bound to one another by treaty'.[27]

The *Lisbon* judgment, however, identifies a second deficit. The EU also lacks 'a system for organizing political rule in which a European majority, through free and equal elections, drives the formation of the government, and in which a genuine and, for the citizens, transparent contest between government and opposition can take shape'.[28] This criticism underscores how little is at stake, substantively, in European elections, as well as the lack of any connection between the actions of the Commission and a parliamentary majority. Both factors are responsible for voters' slender opportunities to influence European policy.

[25] BVerfGE 123, 267 (371). [26] Ibid., 372. [27] Ibid., 371.
[28] Ibid., 372.

Here too, however, the Court is not advocating reform but justifying the Lisbon Treaty's acceptability. For 'the formation, from within Parliament, of an independent government vested with the powers typical in states would face fundamental objections'.[29] So long as the EU retains the character of a federation of states (*Staatenverbund*), the organization of European democracy on the nation-state model is unnecessary.[30] Should, however, the EU cross the threshold of a federal state (*Bundesstaat*), it 'must satisfy democratic requirements at a level that corresponds fully to the legitimacy requirements of a polity organized as a state'[31]—but it must do so, in that case, without the Federal Republic of Germany.

The German Constitutional Court does not address the problems that arise from blurring the boundary between constitutional and statutory law at the European level. Nonetheless, by opening up, in the first instance, the possibility of making decisions of great political significance through a non-political mechanism, this represents an important source of Europe's legitimacy deficit. The appropriate remedy for this problem would be to reduce primary law to its quasi-constitutional core and to relegate the treaties' vast remnants to the level of ordinary law. In discussions of reform, however, this solution is not seriously entertained.

There will, of course, be further transfers of powers and increases in institutional autonomy. There will also be constitutional complaints against them. In response, the Constitutional Court will have to work with the standards it has set forth, and in doing so will struggle not only to avoid the impression of decisionism, but to cope with a generally awkward situation. The individual transfer of power, the individual step towards greater autonomy, or even the individual expansive interpretation will always appear too small to justify condemning as unconstitutional the German law approving the change, or requiring a new treaty to increase the level of democracy before the transfer can take effect. The problem is the sum of many individual steps. But the sum is never the object of judicial review.

[29] Ibid., 372. [30] Ibid., 368 s. [31] Ibid., 364.

At the same time, the much-lamented European democratic deficit actually serves to justify the constitutionality of the Lisbon Treaty, since it means that, even after this treaty, the EU will not be a state. As evidence, the Court adduces the difference between the European Parliament and its national counterparts. The Treaty of Lisbon 'decided against the concept of a European federal constitution in which the European Parliament would, as representative of the newly constituted federal people, emerge as the focal point'.[32] The EU satisfies democratic principles 'because a qualitative assessment of its organization of powers reveals precisely that it is not constructed in a manner analogous to that of a state'.[33] The European Parliament 'does not need to honor electoral equality by eliminating differences in the weight of citizen votes that depend on member-state population'.[34]

This, however, presents a dilemma for the programme of integration. On the one hand, the German Constitutional Court deems European democracy deficient; on the other, it warns against curing the deficiency because doing so would give the EU the characteristics of a state and would require Germany to reject it. The bridge between the two positions is the 'as yet'. In the existing state of autonomy and distribution of powers, the deficit is tolerable 'as yet'. The 'as yet' makes clear, however, that the current level of legitimacy will not suffice forever. What then? Because a limit on further transfers of power or increases in autonomy can hardly be defined, this 'as yet' will necessarily persist so long as the EU does not free itself entirely from the aegis of the Member States, thereby assuming the constituent power.

3. *The societal level*

There are, then, sufficient indicators of a European democratic deficit. The deficit does not, however, consist in following a model other than the nation-state model, but rather in the development of autonomous areas reached neither by national nor by European legitimacy. Most

[32] Ibid., 370 s. [33] Ibid., 371 s. [34] Ibid.

proposals for repairing the EU's legitimacy deficit, however, embrace the nation-state model. They begin with the European Parliament. The European Parliament, it is proposed, should assume the central position enjoyed by national parliaments. Towards this end, it should be endowed with those powers that national parliaments traditionally possess. It would thus swap ranks with the Council, which would operate merely as a state chamber of the Parliament, limited in its powers to the right of veto. The Commission would become a parliamentary government. Some reformers complete the model with a European president, popularly elected or otherwise appointed, who would serve as the EU's supreme representative. The only remaining difference between the EU and a federal state would be the latter's possession of constituent power.

It is assumed that this would rid the EU of its democratic deficit, just as it was presumed earlier that transforming the treaties into a constitution would secure for the EU the acceptance of its citizens.[35] But the one assumption is every bit as implausible as the other. The expectation that everything will be taken care of through institutional reform shortchanges the democracy problem. The EU's legitimacy deficit is not ultimately to be found in the structure of its institutions—though there is a need for improvement in those areas where autonomy and legitimacy are incongruent. But in its essential features, the EU's institutional structure is appropriate for a supranational organization. The democratic deficiencies emerge instead—and above all—with respect to the societal preconditions of democracy. The German Constitutional Court alludes to this explicitly.[36]

The Parliament can fulfil its intended function of imparting legitimacy only if it is embedded in a vibrant political process of shaping opinions and articulating interests. This process requires mediating institutions such as political parties, voluntary associations, citizen initiatives, and, above all, communications media. It is the media who

[35] Cf. Dieter Grimm, 'Integration by Constitution' (2005) 3 *International Journal of Constitutional Law* 193.

[36] BVerfGE 123, 267 (358).

first establish the ongoing interplay between voters and institutions, without which democracy remains a purely formal affair, exhausted in periodic elections, and with feeble legitimating force. These preconditions, though with varying efficacy and richness, are considerably better satisfied in the Member States than in the EU.

The EU lacks such a societal substructure, and there is nothing to suggest that this will change any time soon. In particular, there is still no continual, Europe-wide discourse that extends beyond a small circle of experts and elites. Instead, there is only the accumulation of twenty-eight national discourses about European issues. This is true of elections for the European Parliament as well. The combination of legitimacy and accountability that elections ought to impart remains patchy and sparse. Accordingly, the EU will depend for some time yet on the flow of legitimacy from the Member States. Were it to depend solely or primarily on internal legitimation, it would be poorer in democratic substance than it is now. This is the decisive objection against adopting the nation-state model at the European level.

C. The Relationship between European and National Democracy

If one compares the two strands of the EU's legitimacy, it becomes clear that its democratic legitimation still draws, and with increasing force, on the contribution imparted by the Member States. The weaknesses that arise in this respect cannot, without further ado, be offset by Europe's internal legitimation. Under the circumstances, it is in the self-interest of the EU to have functioning national democracies that give citizens the impression of responsiveness to their needs and views. However, the functionality of national democracy does not depend on the Member States alone. Rather, the shortcomings of European democracy affect the Member-State democracies. It places a strain on national democracies when European decisions that encroach deeply into the Member-State structures of long standing are made through the non-political mechanism of treaty implementation.

Because the EU possesses no enforcement agencies of its own, and because the states' monopoly on the legitimate use of force has thus far been unaffected by European integration, the implementation of European laws falls to Member-State institutions. Vis-à-vis European institutions, however, these state institutions are embedded in an essentially more effective combination of democratic legitimacy and accountability, and are not immune to public opinion. As a result, they are held accountable by the people for decisions they did not make, but merely implemented. Meanwhile, the EU faces merely a diffuse sense of discontent. The result is a de-legitimation of Member-State democracies.[37]

De-legitimation through Europe's democratic deficit is not an abstract risk but a concrete danger. It was readily apparent to the German Constitutional Court in the *Lisbon* judgment. One might consider the judgment to be unduly sceptical of European democracy. But it should not be accused of being nationalistic. National democracy and European democracy go hand in hand, but they do not work like communicating vessels. They are not rivals in a zero-sum game. Losses to national democracy are not gains for European democracy. So long as Europe's internal legitimacy cannot replace the legitimacy that flows from the Member States, the functionality of Member-State democracies is in the EU's self-interest. Awareness of this interrelationship still seems to be lacking.

[37] Cf. Helge Rossen-Stadtfeld, 'Demokratische Staatlichkeit in Europa: ein verblassendes Bild' (2005) 53 *Jahrbuch des öffentlichen Rechts* 45; Maurizio Bach, 'Jenseits der Souveränitätsfiktion: Der Nationalstaat in der Europäischen Union', in *Der entmachtete Leviathan* (special issue of the *Zeitschrift für Politik*, 2013), p. 105.

5

The Democratic Costs of Constitutionalization— The European Case

A. Constitutionalism and Democracy

1. *Interdependence*

Democracy and constitutionalism are usually not seen as mutually contradictory. Both emerged simultaneously. The prototypes came into being as democratic constitutions based on the principle of popular sovereignty. Non-democratic constitutions were regarded as a deficient form of constitutionalism. Whenever people fought battles for constitutions, the constitutions they had in mind were democratic. Where nations turned from authoritarian or dictatorial regimes to democracy they started by drafting constitutions. How then can constitutionalization put democracy at risk? Before turning to the European case a look at the idea of constitutionalism as it found expression in the beginnings may be helpful.

Modern constitutions were the product of two successful revolutions against traditional rule: colonial in North America, absolutist in France. These revolutions differed from the many revolts and upheavals of the past in that they did not content themselves with replacing one ruler by another. Rather, they aimed at a different system of rule which they designed before calling individual persons to power. The lack of legitimate public power that the revolution left behind together with the principles that guided the construction of the future regime pointed towards constitutions.

These principles were not invented by the revolutionaries. They had been developed in natural law theory long before.[1] But in spite of its name natural law was not law. It was a philosophical system that did not gain legal recognition before the revolutions. Only after the American colonists and the French middle classes had failed to reach their reform goals—self-rule in North America, removal of feudalism and liberalization of the economy in France—within the framework of the existing legal order did they resort to natural law to justify the break with the old system and to design a new one.

The basic assumptions of natural law theory were two: that government ought to be legitimized by the consent of the governed and limited by the innate rights of the individuals. Yet, these assumptions had only served as a test for the legitimacy of political systems before the revolutions. Political systems were regarded as legitimate if so organized that they could have found the consent of reasonable people. Reason taught that this consent could only be expected if the individuals were not obliged to relinquish their natural freedom when entering into a state. Rather, government was established in order to make natural freedom secure.

In the revolutionary situation these principles became guidelines for political action and thereby transcended philosophical theory. The philosophers themselves were not prepared to design constitutions. They had developed conditions for the legitimacy of government, but not reflected on the means by which they could be implemented.

[1] See from the rich literature Bernard Bailyn, *The Ideological Origins of the American Revolution* (Cambridge, MA: Belknap Press, 1967); Bernhard Groethuysen, *Philosophie de la Révolution française* (Paris: Gallimard, 1956); Wolfgang Kersting, *Die politische Philosophie des Gesellschaftsvertrags* (Darmstadt: Primus Verlag, 1994); Diethelm Klippel, *Politische Freiheit und Freiheitsrechte im deutschen Naturrecht des 18. Jahrhunderts* (Paderborn: Schöningh, 1970); John W. Gough, *The Social Contract* (Oxford: Oxford University Press, 2nd edn, 1957); Ian Shapiro, *The Evolution of Rights in Liberal Theory* (Cambridge: Cambridge University Press, 1986).

With one exception—Emer de Vattel in his *Droit des gens* of 1758[2]—none of the theorists had pushed the ideas to a postulate for formal, legal, and written constitutions. Forced by the task of reconstructing public authority, the revolutionaries did just this. The ingredients of constitutionalism preceded the revolution, the constitutions themselves were a product of the revolution.

Each central element of the new systems—democracy as well as fundamental rights—called for regulation. The problem of democratic government is that the people are the source of all public authority but cannot govern themselves, as the revolutionaries in North America and France understood well when they put their ideas into effect. Democratic rule was necessarily rule by mandate. The mandate had to be conferred and the conditions of mandatory rule had to be fixed. Different from traditional or absolutist rule, democratic rule is in need of being organized before persons are called on to exercise power.

The same is true for limited government. Limits have to be defined and sanctions determined for cases of transgression. Government should be organized in a way that best guarantees individual liberty. As a consequence the revolutionary legislatures in the North American colonies and in France each began with the adoption of a Bill of Rights even before their respective constitutions were enacted. From the perspective of the citizens, they were safeguards on individual freedom; from the perspective of government, they were constraints on public power. Public power was legitimate only if it respected and protected the rights of the citizens.

The rules had to be binding on government. This required their transformation into positive law. Only the law could make them mandatory and enforceable, detaching them from the historical moment of adoption and the persons who formulated them, and extending

[2] Emer de Vattel, *Le droit des gens ou principes de la loi naturelle*, Leiden 1758, § 27. Cf. Heinz Mohnhaupt and Dieter Grimm, *Verfassung. Zur Geschichte des Begriffs von der Antike bis zur Gegenwart* (Berlin: Duncker & Humblot, 2nd edn, 2002), pp. 91 ss., 105 ss.

them into the future. As a matter of fact, the law develops its regulatory potential best where it organizes and limits human behaviour. Law was thus the appropriate means of achieving the revolutionary ends. The contribution of the revolutionaries to a new political order was not the development of the natural law principles, but their transformation into positive law.

A precondition for the norms to fulfil their function was that they enjoyed primacy over all government acts including legislation. Constitutions bring legitimate government into existence and formulate the conditions for the exercise of public power. They thus antedate government and are not at its disposal. The consequence was a distinction between *pouvoir constituant* and *pouvoir constitué*[3] and, accordingly, the division of the law into two parts: one that is attributed to the people and binds government—constitutional law; and one that emanates from the government and binds the citizens—ordinary law. The first part regulates rule-making whereas rule-making itself is left to the second part. This distinction is crucial for constitutionalism.

Democratic government and fundamental rights were the goal of both the American and the French revolutions. Constitutions were the means to make them effective. However, this does not mean that constitutions are necessarily democratic or committed to fundamental rights. Once the constitution had been invented, it became possible to use the form without subscribing to the substance. One can find constitutions with fundamental rights, but without democracy; one can find constitutions with democracy, but without fundamental rights; and one can even find constitutions that lack both rights and democracy.[4]

Even if these constitutions are not mere window dressing, they may have a limited impact. But they then fall short of the achievement of

[3] First formulated by Emmanuel Joseph Sieyes, *Qu'est-ce que le Tiers État?*, Paris 1789. See Pasquale Pasquino, *Sieyes et l'invention de la constitution française* (Paris: Editions Odile Jacob, 1998).

[4] See Dieter Grimm, 'Types of Constitutions', in Michel Rosenfeld and András Sajó (eds), *The Oxford Handbook of Comparative Constitutional Law* (Oxford: Oxford University Press, 2012), p. 98.

constitutionalism.[5] A constitution that is based on a legitimacy principle other than democracy will put the supremacy of its rules at risk since in cases of conflict the legitimacy principle, be it divine, hereditary, or elitist, will prevail over the limits that the constitution imposes on government. Similarly, a constitution without fundamental rights will put the autonomy of the individual—whose protection is the function of legitimate government—at risk. As Jürgen Habermas puts it: democracy and rights are co-equal.[6]

2. *Tension*

If one wants to enjoy the benefits of constitutionalism fully, democracy and rights must coexist. This is not to say, however, that democracy and fundamental rights are always in harmony and can never endanger the constitutional project. Democracy may undermine rights. Rights may overwhelm democracy. There is a tension in constitutionalism itself as it emerged from the two revolutions. Carl Schmitt even saw these two elements of modern constitutions as contradictory so that ultimately a choice between the two would become necessary.[7] Hence the question: is there a tension or a contradiction?

Tension leaves room for accommodation, contradiction excludes it. This raises the question whether each of them could stand by itself. Democracy, to begin with, has some preconditions. It depends on free elections that, in turn, require free citizens. They must be politically free to form and express their opinions, articulate their interests, and associate in order to invigorate their political influence. Free media are an indispensable condition for political freedom of the citizens. But the citizens must also be free in their private sphere, since political freedom will not thrive without private autonomy. Democracy

[5] See Dieter Grimm, *Constitutionalism. Past, Present, and Future* (Oxford: Oxford University Press, 2016), p. 357 ss.

[6] Jürgen Habermas, *The Inclusion of the Other* (Cambridge: Polity Press, 2002).

[7] Carl Schmitt, *Constitutional Theory* (Durham, NC: Duke University Press, 2008); Carl Schmitt, *Legality and Legitimacy* (Durham, NC: Duke University Press, 1997).

itself cannot guarantee these preconditions. They depend on the protection by fundamental rights.

Rights also have preconditions. They do not enforce themselves. They are in need of being protected and they have to be limited in order to make the many liberties or the liberties of the many compatible with each other. In short, they depend on governmental power. Yet, governmental power is in itself a threat to individual freedom. How can the two be reconciled? Among the various forms of government, democracy seems to be the form that best serves the autonomy of the individual because it grounds public power on the will of rights bearers and rejects legitimacy principles that trump rights.

Therefore, Schmitt's asserted antagonism between rights and democracy exists only if they are pushed to extremes. Radical democracy is strictly majoritarian. It recognizes only one fundamental right: the right of every citizen to participate in the formation of the political will of the people. All other limits on government are incompatible with this notion of democracy. The minority is unconditionally surrendered to majority decisions. In a radical democracy, constitutions shrink to a number of rules that regulate political will formation and execution organizationally and procedurally. Majoritarian democracy is formal democracy.

But just as radical democracy tends to minimize legal rules that limit political action, rights foundationalism, as Bruce Ackerman calls it,[8] tends to minimize democracy. The reason is that all matters regulated on the constitutional level are not open to political decision. What has been decided in the constitution is not the object but the premise of political decisions. This means also that elections do not matter as far as constitutional law extends. In the end all politics is reduced to executing the constitution. Public power shifts from the people themselves and their elected representatives to the courts.

[8] Bruce Ackerman, *We the People: Foundations* (Cambridge, MA: Belknap Press, 1991), p. 10.

Both radical versions develop a self-destructive dynamic. Radical democracy may take the form of popular dictatorship. It cannot even defend itself against the abolition of majority rule by majority vote. On the other hand, rights foundationalism reduces the importance of elections and endangers the adaptability of laws to changing circumstances. It therefore risks the constitution hampering democratic change and becoming a barrier to coping with new challenges. The stronger the challenges are, the sooner politics will re-appear on the scene and circumvent or suspend the constitution in order to achieve what politics understand as the common good.

There may be, and often is, too little constitutionalism. But it may also be that there is too much. Both deviations disregard the crucial distinction between the rules for political decision-making and the political decisions themselves, each in its own way. In the first case, the tension is dissolved in favour of politics. The constitution will fail to fulfil its function of guiding and limiting government efficiently. Such a constitution will hardly be able to legitimate the exercise of public power. In the second case, the tension is dissolved in favour of the law. The democratic process is fettered. Politics is reduced to an execution of constitutional prescriptions. The administration and the judiciary marginalize the legislature.

There are no universally applicable principles for determining what belongs in a constitution and what does not. New constitutions react to past experiences and seek to provide for a better future. Every country must decide for itself what it deems so important for a better future that it should be exempted from the wavering will of simple majorities. These questions are not uncontroversial. Agreements between different forces in a convention or a constituent assembly require compromises. Some can only be reached by leaving gaps where one would expect a rule, others may only be reached by accommodating many interests, and thereby inflate the constitution.

However, even if it is difficult to formulate substantive rules for constitution-making, the function of constitutions allows some generalizations that transcend the particular design of political systems, which differs from country to country: federal or unitary, presidential or parliamentary, pluralist voting system or proportional representation, bicameral or unicameral parliament, with or without judicial review, with or without social and economic rights, etc. The function of constitutions is to legitimate and to limit political power, but not to replace it. Constitutions are a framework for politics, not the blueprint for all political decisions.

Where the distinction between a constitution and ordinary law (or dualist democracy in Ackerman's terms) is lost, one will not enjoy the benefits of constitutionalism. The constitution furnishes the basic structure and the lasting principles for politics. Politics concretizes them and fills the space they leave according to changing preferences and circumstances. Constitutions thus provide a durable structure for change. They combine principles that enjoy a broad consensus with flexibility to meet new challenges or changing majorities and thereby enable a peaceful transition of power.

However, the text of the constitution is one thing, its interpretation and application to individual cases is quite another. Even if the text avoids the risks of radicalism, courts may interpret it in a way that increasingly narrows the space for political decisions. To the same extent the power of courts will increase. Constitutionalization of ordinary law by way of interpretation may have the same cementing effect. The more ordinary law is regarded as constitutionally mandated, the less politics can change it if this is required by the circumstances or by a shift of political preferences.

This danger exists especially where courts have the last word on the meaning of constitutional provisions. It is true that constitutions are of little value without judicial enforcement. To be sure, courts should have the power to adapt constitutional law to new challenges. But even though it may be difficult to define, there is a distinction between interpreting law and making law under the disguise of interpretation. When courts overstep this line, the only remedy for politics is to re-programme the judiciary by amending the constitution, which is easy in some countries, but extremely difficult in others. The more difficult constitutional amendments are, the less space remains for democratic re-direction of courts.

B. Europe: Constitutionalization of the Treaties

1. *The cause: Supremacy of EU law*

It is generally accepted that the European Union (EU) suffers from a democratic deficit that affects its legitimacy. But it is rarely noticed that this deficit has a source in the state of European constitutionalism. How can this be true, even though the EU does not have a constitution? After all, the legal foundation of the EU are treaties under international law, originally concluded by six Member States in Rome in 1957, several times amended, and now in force in the form of the Lisbon Treaty of 2010, ratified by twenty-eight Member States after the so-called Treaty on a Constitution for Europe of 2003 had failed in two referenda.

Nevertheless, the treaty fulfils many functions of a constitution. It specifies the purposes of the EU, establishes its organs, determines their powers and procedures, regulates the relationship with the Member States, and contains a charter of fundamental rights just as constitutions do. It differs from a constitution because it does not have its source in an autonomous act of a European constituent power. It is instead given to the EU by the Member States and continues to depend on their agreement. Only they have the power of amendment. They are the 'Masters of the Treaties'.

Although suggested from time to time, the transformation of the treaties into a constitution in the full sense of the concept has not been undertaken up to now. Even the Constitutional Treaty of 2003, the most far-reaching endeavour to form a closer union, did not attempt to change the nature of the Union's legal foundation. If adopted by all Member States, it would still have remained a treaty under international law since the constituent power was not handed over to the EU itself. Rather the Member States reserved this power for themselves so that no transition from hetero-determination to auto-determination has taken place.[9]

Applied to the EU, the word 'constitutionalization' must therefore have a meaning different from the usual one. It neither denotes a process of making a constitution nor the permeation of ordinary law by constitutional law through interpretation, which is characteristic for a number of states with a strong constitutional court. In Europe, the expression is used rather to characterize the result of two groundbreaking judgments of the European Court of Justice (ECJ) that endowed the treaties with effects typical of constitutional law. It was American observers who first described this effect as 'constitutionalization'.[10]

In 1963, the ECJ initially confronted the relationship between European and national law. The traditional answer to that question was clear: since European law is international law, it binds the Member States, but produces legal effects for the individual citizens only after having been incorporated into, or concretized by, national law. This was the position of several Member States when they argued the case in court, and it was equally the position of the Court's Advocate General. In contrast, the ECJ declared European law to be directly applicable in the Member States, to the effect that individuals could derive rights from it and claim them before the national courts without waiting for further concretization by the national legislature.[11]

However, the initial decision did not answer the question what would happen if European and national law conflicted. The answer followed a year later in a second decisive ruling.[12] The Court declared

[9] This distinction separates a treaty from a constitution, see Dieter Grimm, 'Treaty or Constitution?', in Erik Oddvar Erikson et al. (eds), *Developing a Constitution for Europe* (London: Routledge, 2004), p. 69; Dieter Grimm, 'Verfassung—Verfassungsvertrag—Vertrag über eine Verfassung', in Olivier Beaud et al. (eds), *L'Europe en voie de constitution* (Brussels: Bruylant, 2004), p. 279.

[10] Eric Stein, 'Lawyers, Judges and the Making of a Transnational Constitution' (1981) 75 *American Journal of International Law* 1; Joseph H.H. Weiler, 'The Transformation of Europe' (1991) 100 *Yale Law Jounal* 2403.

[11] *Van Gend en Loos v. Netherlands* (1963), ECR 1.

[12] *Costa v. ENEL* (1964), ECR 585.

that the treaties, and European law in general, enjoyed primacy over national law, even over national constitutions. National law that contradicted European law lost its applicability. No national court or other agency was permitted to apply it. In case of doubt, national courts had to refer the question of compatibility to the ECJ, whose decision was binding on them.

The ECJ had opened the door to these judgments by a methodological turn.[13] In its view, European law was neither a part of international law nor dependent on a national order to apply it, but was an autonomous legal order that had emancipated itself from the national sources. This is why the Court did not find it necessary to interpret European law in the cautious manner of international law, emphasizing the will of the contracting parties and limiting the adverse impacts on national sovereignty. Instead, the ECJ began to interpret the European treaties in a constitutional mode, namely as more or less detached from the Member States' will and oriented instead by an objectivized purpose.

Part of this methodological programme was the so-called *effet utile,* which rounds out the direct effect and the supremacy of European law. According to this maxim, European law has to be interpreted in a way that gives the utmost effect to its provisions. If there are several possible interpretations, judges should choose the one that favours the effectiveness of European law and consequently restricts the application of national law. The ECJ understands this maxim not only as guideline for itself but above all as one for the national courts when they decide cases that involve European law.

In hindsight these judgments were perceived as revolutionary. When they were handed down, they remained largely below the threshold of public attention. They appeared as decisions in singular

[13] Stephan Grundmann, *Die Auslegung des Gemeinschaftsrechts durch den Europäischen Gerichtshof: Zugleich eine rechtsvergleichende Studie zur Auslegung im Völkerrecht und im Gemeinschaftsrecht* (Konstanz: Hartung-Gorre, 1997); Jochen Anweiler, *Die Auslegungsmethoden des Gerichtshofs der Europäischen Gemeinschaften* (Frankfurt: Lang, 1997); Carsten Buck, *Über die Auslegungsmethoden des Gerichtshofs der Europäischen Gemeinschaft* (Frankfurt: Lang, 1998).

and non-conspicuous cases, rendered by a court that went more or less unnoticed. Revolutionary they were because neither direct effect nor primacy of European law were explicitly mentioned in the Treaties. Rather, they resulted from a purposive interpretation that was by no means without alternative. They were revolutionary also because, without them, the EU would not have become what it is today, namely an unprecedented political entity somewhere between an international organization and a federal state, but because of the amount of its powers and the density of its organizational structure closer to the latter than to the former.

Yet, they deserve the characterization as revolutionary for still another reason: they radically changed the position of the ECJ itself. Although remaining completely within the framework of its procedural limits, the Court enlarged its own power by the extensive interpretation of substantive law. By re-defining the legal nature of the Treaties, the Court gained a position that by far exceeded the powers of an international court and resembled more that of constitutional courts. Its judgments participated in the direct effect and primacy of European law, not only regarding the organs of the EU but also those of the Member States. It was no longer the exclusive power of the Member States to adjust their laws to European requirements. The ECJ could do this itself by declaring national law inapplicable that it regarded as incompatible with European law.

However, the purpose of this chapter is not to discuss the question of whether these judgments were 'right' or 'wrong' from a legal point of view. They were accepted by the Member States and in principle also by the national courts on whose cooperation the ECJ depends. They are now the law of the EU. The only issue that is contested is the question whether the identity of national constitutions imposes an outer limit to the supremacy of European law and who is authorized to determine whether the EU acted *ultra vires*, the ECJ alone or also the national constitutional courts, as many constitutional courts of the Member States assume. What is of interest here are rather the consequences of these judgments.

2. *The effect: De-politicization*

As an immediate consequence of the two revolutionary judgments Member States were no longer needed in order to establish the single market. Direct effect and supremacy of European law allowed the Commission (as the organ charged with enforcing the treaties vis-à-vis the Member States) and the ECJ (the organ charged with determining the meaning of the treaties in concrete cases) to take the task of implementing economic integration in their own hands. If they declared that national law impeded the common market, the national law became inapplicable without the Member States having a realistic chance to defend their own law in an effective way.

A precondition was, however, that the ECJ had the opportunity to use its expanded power. This depended in particular on the willingness of the national courts to refer to Luxembourg questions regarding the compatibility of domestic law with European law. Lower courts may do this, last instance courts have to do it. In general the national courts cooperated with the ECJ. Only a few judgments of the ECJ, which were difficult to swallow for the national courts, temporarily reduced their willingness to refer further questions to Luxembourg. Once again we owe the explanation of this—by no means evident—behaviour of the national courts to an American observer, Karen Alter.[14]

Everything depended now on how the ECJ would interpret the treaties, favouring uniformity or diversity of the law, market-friendly or regulation-friendly, liberal or social. As it turned out, the ECJ pursued the goal of market integration with considerable zeal, subordinating other concerns to this goal. It was a court with an agenda, as Rainer Wahl has put it.[15] Powers transferred to the EU were interpreted

[14] Karen Alter, *Establishing the Supremacy of European Law* (Oxford: Oxford University Press, 2001). See also Alec Stone Sweet, *The Judicial Construction of Europe* (Oxford: Oxford University Press, 2004).

[15] Rainer Wahl, 'Das Recht der Integrationsgemeinschaft Europäische Union', in *Beharren—Bewegen, Festschrift für Michael Kloepfer* (Berlin: Duncker & Humblot, 2013), p. 233 at 248.

broadly, powers retained by the Member States narrowly. The same can be observed regarding the principle of proportionality. When applied to national laws, the ECJ submitted them to strict scrutiny; when applied to European laws, it used a lenient standard of review.

The main beneficiaries were the four fundamental freedoms, all economic in nature (free movement of goods, persons, services, and capital) and their concretization in the treaties. These freedoms were transformed from objective principles for legislation into subjective rights of the market participants who could claim them against the Member States before the national courts. Their implementation thus became a matter of jurisdiction rather than legislation. There is not enough space to describe this in detail.[16] Three examples for the impact of the Court's jurisprudence must suffice to illustrate this.

(1) The ECJ not only prevented the Member States from upholding protectionist measures in favour of the national economy, as was explicitly mandated by the treaties. The anti-protectionist provisions of the treaties were also interpreted as anti-regulation provisions. Any national law that, in the Court's view, impeded the four economic freedoms as concretized in the treaties became a target for review under the treaty prohibition of customs duties and quantitative restrictions on imports and exports as well as measures having an 'equivalent effect', irrespective of whether the law had a protectionist purpose or even an economic motive and irrespective of whether the market was able to provide the goods or services in the same way. The rule thereby lost its contours since almost every law can be understood as an impediment on the economic freedoms.

The decisive step was an ECJ judgment that insisted that any good lawfully produced in one Member State was marketable in every other Member State, notwithstanding the laws of this state.[17]

[16] For a comprehensive account see Anna Katharina Mangold, *Gemeinschaftsrecht und deutsches Recht* (Tübingen: Mohr Siebeck, 2011).

[17] See the decisions *Dassonville* (1974), ECR 837, and *Cassis de Dijon* (1978), ECR 649. Generally Martin Höppner and Armin Schäfer (eds), *Die Politische Ökonomie der europäischen Integration* (Frankfurt: Campus Verlag, 2008).

The same is true for those subsidies granted by the Member States that distort or threaten to distort free competition. The ECJ did not limit this prohibition to private enterprises but extended it to public services, again regardless of whether the motive behind the subsidies was influencing the competition or pursuing other purposes. In contrast, exceptions for certain impediments or subsidies, which the Treaties allowed in the interest of public morals, public policy, public security etc., were usually interpreted narrowly.

(2) The ECJ's position on European directives reveals the same activist approach. In contrast with EU regulations, directives are binding for the Member States only insofar as they stipulate goals, while it is for the Member States to determine the ways and means of reaching them. However, the space for Member States' decisions has been constantly narrowed. The ECJ ruled that, in the case of non-compliance or insufficient compliance, the directive applies directly within the Member States, provided it is clear and precise enough. As could be expected, this encouraged the EU to make directives more and more detailed.

The Court also required national courts to interpret national law in conformity with directives, regardless of whether the specific law implements a directive or was caused by a directive. Directives are declared applicable even before the deadline for implementation ends. If a directive is not implemented on time or in a deficient way the Member State may have to pay damages to those who can prove damage by virtue of this non-compliance. This non-contractual liability even extends to so-called judicial injustice, i.e. a 'wrong' interpretation of European law by national courts.

(3) The ECJ's most recent step concerns the scope of the European Charter of Fundamental Rights that became legally binding with the Lisbon Treaty. According to its Article 51, the Charter binds all institutions of the EU, whereas the Member States are bound 'only when implementing Union law'. However, for the ECJ implementing Union law includes the implementation of national law, provided that it has

some connection with European law.[18] Due to the degree of entanglement between European and national law, the ECJ has little difficulty to find a connection wherever it wants.

Furthermore, the scope of the European Charter is limited insofar that, according to Art. 53, its interpretation may not lead to a decrease of the national standard of fundamental rights protection in their field of application. Since this field is defined in Art. 51, the value of the limit depends on the Court's understanding of this provision. The problem is aggravated in constellations where two fundamental rights conflict so that the courts have to accommodate them by a process of balancing. Every objection against the result of the national courts' balancing will inevitably lead to a decrease of the fundamental right that enjoyed priority on the national level.

The jurisprudence of the ECJ leaves deep marks on national law and politics.[19] The broad interpretation of the impediments to trade deprives the Member States of the possibility to uphold national standards of consumer protection, workers protection, health protection, etc. The extension of prohibited state subsidies to public services deprives the Member States of the power to determine the borderline between the public and the private sector. The privatization of many public services finds its origin here. The jurisprudence on directives narrows the space for national legislation. The expanded scope of Charter rights and the salience of the four fundamental freedoms impose the ECJ's preference for economic freedoms on the Member States, whose constitutional courts tend to prioritize personal, communicative, cultural, and social rights over economic liberties.

[18] See the decision *Åkerberg Fransson* (2013), EC-617/10. Other decisions show, however, that there is not yet a stable jurisprudence on this matter, see, e.g., Gabriele Britz, 'Grundrechtsschutz durch das Bundesverfassungsgericht und den Europäischen Gerichtshof' (2015) 42 *Europäische Grundrechte-Zeitschrift* 275; Claudio Franzius, 'Strategien der Grundrechtsoptimierung in Europa', id., p. 139.

[19] See Mangold, above n. 16.

C. Democratic Costs

1. *The problem: Over-constitutionalization*

The integration-friendly jurisprudence of the ECJ is usually told as a success story. And a success story it is, at least insofar as the economic integration of Europe is concerned. But the economic perspective is not the only possible one. The economic success has a legitimacy drawback whose deeper reasons are still not sufficiently noticed. The drawback manifested itself when the public became aware of the fact that the object of integration was no longer the economy alone but also the political, yet without the people or their representatives having a chance to influence it.

Due to the jurisprudence of the ECJ, there are now two paths towards integration instead of one. The original path, provided by the treaties, consists in creating European primary law and in enacting European secondary law. This path can be taken by the Member States only—regarding the treaties, by a unanimous decision in the conference of the heads of state and government, followed by ratification in each Member State; and regarding secondary law, by a decision of the Council of Ministers that also required unanimity until the Single European Act of 1987 and has been difficult to achieve to the present day. The new path consists in applying the treaties as understood by the ECJ. This path is open to the executive and judicial powers of the EU.

The two paths towards integration differ considerably. On the basis of the first, powers are transferred by the Member States to the EU. This path is political and involves the democratically legitimated and accountable governments of the Member States and, to varying degrees, the parliaments of the Member States as well as—more recently—the European Parliament. On the basis of the second path, the EU restricts the competences of Member States by a broad interpretation of the treaties. This path is administrative and adjudicative in nature. The democratically legitimated and controlled governments of the Member States, their parliaments as well as the European Parliament, have no share in it. It is integration by stealth.[20]

However, the non-political mode of decision-making in the second path does not deprive the decisions themselves of their political character. It only shifts the power to decide questions of high political impact from the political organs of the EU to non-political institutions. To the same extent, the political means to secure democratic legitimacy and accountability fail to work. In the field of treaty application, the administrative and judicial organs of the EU are uncoupled from the democratic process in the Member States and the EU and enjoy far-reaching independence. This has a number of consequences.

The difference between the political and non-political mode of integration is responsible for the asymmetry between negative and positive integration that was first identified by Fritz Scharpf.[21] Negative integration means deregulation on the national level; positive integration means re-regulation on the European level. As a consequence of the constitutionalization of the treaties, negative integration occurs in a non-political mode by a stroke of pen of the Commission or the ECJ, whereas positive integration requires a political decision where the Member States, the European Parliament, and the Commission must find an agreement. This has worked in some fields, such as protection of the environment, but has failed in other areas.

The asymmetry also accounts for the liberalizing tendency of the ECJ's jurisprudence.[22] This is not to say that the ECJ pursues an agenda of economic liberalism. It rather pursues the treaty goal to establish and maintain the single market. Yet, since the vast majority of requests for a preliminary ruling—which reach the ECJ—has its origin in actions by economic actors who see their interests threatened by national legislation, and since the ECJ can contribute to the

[20] See Domenico Majone, *Dilemmas of European Integration* (Oxford: Oxford University Press, 2005).

[21] Fritz Scharpf, *Governing in Europe: Effective and Democratic?* (Oxford: Oxford University Press, 1999), p. 43. See also Majone (above n. 20), p. 143.

[22] See Vivien Schmidt and Mark Thatcher (eds), *Resilient Liberalism in Europe's Economy* (Cambridge: Cambridge University Press, 2013).

establishment of the single market only negatively, the result is a structural bias in favour of liberalization. This, in turn, affects social policy. Although reserved for Member States, social policy comes under pressure because of the liberalizing effects of the ECJ's jurisprudence, combined with the effects of globalization, while the national social policy comes under pressure because upholding a high standard of social security tends to weaken the competitiveness of national economy.[23]

Why is all this a reason for concern? Are not Member States the 'Masters of the Treaties'? Are they not in a position to stop these judicially created tendencies if they are not happy with them? After all, they decide in the European Council on the direction, extent, and pace of integration and they are the main actors of European legislation in the Council of Ministers. This should give them the opportunity to reprogramme the jurisprudence of the ECJ by explicit legislation if they do not recognize their intentions in the Court's interpretation of the treaties or observe detrimental effects caused by that interpretation.

At this point the special character of the European quasi-constitution comes to the fore. Different from national constitutions, the treaties are not confined to those provisions that reflect the functions of a constitution. They are full of provisions that would be ordinary law in the Member States. This is why they are so voluminous. As long as the treaties were treated as international law this was not a problem. As soon as they were constitutionalized their volume became problematic: in the EU the crucial difference between the rules for political decisions and the decisions themselves is to a large extent levelled. *The EU is over-constitutionalized.* This has two important consequences.

[23] See Fritz Scharpf, *Community and Autonomy* (Frankfurt: Campus, 2010), pp. 221 ss., 353 ss.; Fritz Scharpf and Vivian A. Schmidt (eds), *Welfare and Work in the Open Economy*, 2 vols (Oxford: Oxford University Press, 2000); Christian Joerges and Florian Rödl, 'Informal Politics, Formalised Law and the "Social Deficit" of European Integration: Reflections after the Judgments of the ECJ in Viking and Laval', (2009) 15 *European Law Journal* 1.

First, the over-constitutionalization severely limits the Member States' role as 'Masters of the Treaties'. It exists with regard to formal amendments. But it is undermined at the level of treaty application. The principle of conferral that limits the power of the EU to those competences that have been explicitly transferred by the Member States is undermined. The *Kompetenz–Kompetenz*, which guarantees that only the Member States have the power to determine the allocation of competences, is also undermined. There is a creeping power shift from Member States towards the EU that blurs the borderline between treaty amendment and treaty interpretation and particularly bothers the German Constitutional Court.[24]

Second, the lack of differentiation between the constitutional law level and the ordinary law level, combined with the constitutionalization of the treaties, immunizes the Commission and particularly the ECJ against any attempt by the democratically responsible institutions of the EU to react to the Court's jurisprudence by changing the law. Likewise they immunize the executive and judicial institutions of the EU against public pressure. As far as the treaty extends elections do not matter. The political actors who have to take public opinion into account cannot change anything. The administrative and judicial actors who could change things do not have to pay attention to public opinion.

To be sure, the Member States are not without any means to defend themselves against the creeping power shift towards the EU. They can bring an action for annulment of decisions by the Commission if, in their view, they transgress the competences of the EU. And they can amend the treaties. But the practical use of these instruments is limited. Given the pro-integration attitude of an ECJ that does not understand itself as an umpire between the EU and the Member States, there is little chance of success of an annulment action. Amendments to the treaties are practically unavailable because of the extremely high hurdles they have to jump over to achieve them. It seems almost

[24] See BVerfGE 123, 267(2009); Dieter Grimm, ch. 11 of this volume.

impossible to mobilize this instrument in order to reach a seemingly minor goal such as the correction of a line of jurisprudence.

Thus, the example of the EU confirms the assertion that more constitutional law means less democracy. The confusion of elements of constitutional law with elements of ordinary law in the treaties favours the unelected and non-accountable institutions of the EU over the democratically legitimized and accountable organs. Decisions of great political impact are taken in a non-political mode. The result is a state of integration that the citizens were never asked to agree to, but cannot change either, even if they do not support it.

2. *The remedy: Re-politicization*

Over-constitutionalization is not the only cause of the legitimacy problem the EU faces. But it is the most neglected one. The blindness towards the de-legitimizing effects of over-constitutionalization misguides the search for remedies. The reason for the democratic deficit of the EU is mostly sought in the European Parliament's lack of adequate powers. It does not possess all the competences that national parliaments used to have. Therefore, many believe that the democratic deficit would be repaired if only the European Parliament were endowed with the competences that parliaments in a parliamentary democracy enjoy.

The call for increased powers of the Parliament is by no means unsound. The European Parliament is needed as a counterweight against the dominance of national interests in the Council and the technocratic tendencies in the Commission. But it seems doubtful whether full parliamentarization could solve the deeper problems of European democracy. The reasons are manifold. In general, parliaments are the losers in the growing internationalization of politics. This plays into the hands of the executive. It would be surprising if only the European Parliament would be exempted from this secular trend.

But there are also specific European reasons that contribute to this effect. The European Parliament is much less representative than the national parliaments.[25] The main reason for this is that European elections are not truly Europeanized. The European Parliament is elected according to twenty-eight national election laws. The seats are allocated according to national quotas that do not reflect the size of the national population. The voters can vote only for national parties, which campaign with national programmes. The result of the election is usually evaluated under a national perspective: did the national ruling parties or the national opposition parties win?

Yet, after the elections have taken place, the national political parties (presently 200) do not play a decisive role in the European Parliament. There, European factions, loose associations of ideologically related parties, are decisive, but these factions are neither rooted in society nor do they maintain contact with the voters. This affects the salience of European elections. The parties for which one may vote are not the actors in the European Parliament. The factions that are the actors on the European level do not stand for elections. The legitimacy chain running from the voters to the parliament is thus interrupted.

Finally and most important, the European public sphere and European public discourse is weak compared to the national situation (which, itself, is not always satisfactory). The institutions that mediate between the people and the political organs of the EU are either missing or underdeveloped. There are no European parties. Interest groups, popular movements, NGOs are quite weak on the European level and, most important, there are no European media. The absence of a sufficient societal substructure that is needed for a vibrant democracy makes it unlikely that full parliamentarization would reach its goal, namely to close the gap between the citizenry and the institutions.

Furthermore, the power of the European Parliament cannot be enhanced without decreasing the power of the Council. As a matter

[25] See Richard Rose, *Representing Europeans* (Oxford: Oxford University Press, 2013).

of fact, many reform plans want to reduce the Council to a second chamber of the European Parliament. In turn, the Commission would be upgraded to a genuine European government dependent on parliamentary support. For many, a directly elected European President is the apex of the reform. Yet, the strengthening of the Parliament on the institutional level would add little to European democracy as long as the socio-political substructure of parliamentarianism is missing or underdeveloped.

On the contrary, one must fear that the legitimacy structure of the EU would be weakened rather than strengthened. Originally the democratic legitimacy of European politics emanated exclusively from the Member States. The Council, in which their governments are represented, was the central organ of the EU and its exclusive legislator. A decision of the Council required unanimity. This meant that no Member State was subject to laws to which its democratically legitimated organs had not consented. If the citizens disagreed with their governments, they could voice this in the national election.

The unanimity requirement was given up after a long period of stagnation with the Single European Act of 1987. In certain matters, the Council now decided by a majority. As a consequence it could happen that Member States were subject to laws and legal acts to which their democratically and accountable representatives had not agreed. To the same extent the legitimation chain which ran from national elections over the national parliament and government to the European organs was broken, at least for states that were outvoted in the Council.

This legitimation gap could no longer be bridged by national democracies. As compensation, the European Parliament got a share in European legislation which increased with every treaty amendment. The monistic legitimation of the EU has since been replaced by a dualistic one. The reform project would return to a monistic legitimation, yet one that would not consist in hetero-legitimation but in auto-legitimation. Therefore, the question is whether the EU has sufficient legitimation resources to support itself. This is more than doubtful, given the weak societal substructure of the European democracy. Rather it is likely that a full parliamentarization of the EU would minimize the external legitimation without being able to increase the internal legitimation.

Finally, and most importantly in this context, the parliamentarization of the EU would leave the effects of the over-constitutionalization completely unaffected. In the area that is determined by constitutional law, elections do not matter and parliaments have no say. This source of the democratic deficit can only be repaired by a politicization of the decision-making processes in the EU. If one wants to enhance the legitimacy of the EU the power to decide questions of high political salience must be shifted from the executive and judicial branches to the political organs, the Council and the European Parliament. The only way to achieve this goal is to scale back the treaties to their truly constitutional elements and downgrade all treaty provisions of a non-constitutional nature to the status of secondary law.

This should not be misunderstood as a reversal of the constitutionalization of the treaties and a rollback of the present state of integration. Rather it draws out the consequences of precisely that constitutionalization by giving the constitutionalized treaties the outlook of a constitution. Not a single norm of the Treaties would be sacrificed. Neither would the function of the ECJ as guardian of the Treaties be undermined. This solution would merely open the door for a re-direction of the Court's jurisprudence by the politically legitimated and accountable organs of the EU, if they find it necessary. Legally speaking, this is easy. Politically, it is difficult as long as the democratic costs of over-constitutionalization escape public attention.

6

The Cause of the European Democracy Deficit is Sought in the Wrong Place

Most solutions offered to address the lack of legitimacy of the European Union (EU) at one point or another involve the European Parliament. Once it will have gained the powers national parliaments typically have, the argument goes, the body elected by the Union citizens will move into the focus of the Union. Only then will the Union gain the democratic legitimacy it now lacks. The election of Jean-Claude Juncker to the presidency of the Commission was lauded as a further step in this direction. He was the *Spitzenkandidat* of the group that prevailed in the elections. The Council then reluctantly nominated him for the job. Insofar as fielding *Spitzenkandidaten* in the European election was meant to be an attempt at wresting the power to nominate the president from the Council, the gamble paid off. The election as such has not become more attractive, though. Personalizing the election failed to achieve this aim. Voter turnout in this election was as low as it had been before.

Increasing the clout of the Parliament, however, is only apt as a means to address the lack of legitimacy of the EU, if the reason for this lack is to be found in the weakness of the Parliament. If the reason for this lack of legitimacy is something else, we run the risk of applying the wrong therapy. In other words, the success of an empowerment of the Parliament should not be taken for granted. While democracy is certainly hard to imagine without a freely elected and properly empowered parliament, these elements in themselves merely embody the formal prerequisites of democracy. Whether democracy is lived in actual fact in a community is another question. The answer depends on a number of further standards. Only a full account of these standards allows us to gain certainty about whether increasing the powers of the European Parliament will deliver on its promise.

Representation is first among these standards. A parliament should roughly represent the society for which it stands. Else the binding decisions it takes lack in legitimacy. Most parliaments today struggle to meet this standard. In our highly individualized Western societies traditional ties of family, church, class, and milieu are unravelling, resulting in pluralism of values. This feeds voter fatigue. At the same time ad-hoc protest against specific political measures is easy to organize. There is little to be done against these tendencies of our times. The need for legitimacy remains and it becomes ever harder to meet it. The EU is no exception. Quite the contrary, the fragmentation of national polities in the Union exacerbates the problem. As a result, each and everyone judges the value of the integration of Europe solely by the utility for his or her own country.

The EU unnecessarily complicates matters, though. It reinforces the national fragmentation through its election procedure, rather than mitigating it. As a consequence the European Parliament is not as representative as the national parliaments. This is only partly due to low electoral participation. A more important factor may be that the European elections are not Europeanized. Elections are taking place separately in each Member State, while the national quota in the Parliament do not reflect the number of inhabitants of the Member States. The elections are, moreover, governed by national law and only national parties can be elected—national parties that run national campaigns. These parties, however, do not appear as actors in the European Parliament. Rather, European factions act here. They consist of loose alliances of affiliated national parties. As such they are not rooted in society.

Hence, the European factions fail to act as intermediaries between Union citizens and the European organs. They are not linked to the voters and cannot be held responsible by them. At the same time, the national parties cannot credibly promise that the campaign program they run on will be the program of the European factions in the Parliament after the elections. The link of agency and responsibility between the election and the work in Parliament—a link which is a prerequisite for democracy—is broken. The national parties that can be elected do not direct the work of the Parliament. The European factions that direct the work of the Parliament cannot be elected. Fielding *Spitzenkandidaten* thus promises more democracy than it can deliver.

Even so, some do hope that electoral participation would increase and true European parties would come into existence, if only the European Parliament had the full powers of a national parliament. That is not evident, though. The more powers the European Parliament was awarded in the past, the less Union citizens participated in the elections. Even if the assessment was accurate, not all problems would automatically be overcome. The democratic process does not end once the elections are over. An elected parliament can only fulfil its democratic function if it is anchored in the society which it represents and if it absorbs a society's views, interests, and needs—which it then makes real in between the elections in the decision-making process. Whether this is the case does not so much depend on the powers, but rather on the embedment of the Parliament in a lively public discourse which is inconceivable without the corresponding communication media. The EU comes nowhere near this ideal.

Secondly, an elected parliament must also have influence on political decisions. Yet most parliaments in democratic states see their significance dwindle. Electoral trust is on the wane. In the inter-institutional balance the power shifts away from the legislature towards the executive and the judiciary. The 'scientification' and the internationalization of politics, while discussion and decision are replaced by deals and negotiations, play into the hands of governments. It would be a true surprise if just the European Parliament was spared the consequences. The situation is even exacerbated in the EU where the executive and judicial bodies, i.e. the Commission and the

European Court of Justice (ECJ), are detached from the democratic processes in both the Member States and the EU.

The original conception of the European integration had been different. It was the Council alone that took the key decisions and adopted European legislation. The Member States were represented in the Council adopting decisions by unanimity. As a consequence, no Member State was subject to European legislative acts to which it had not previously consented. The Commission and the ECJ merely enforced the law adopted by the Member States, rather than creating it. In these circumstances the need for European democracy was met entirely by the Member States which were democratic in themselves. The participation of the people on the level of the states was sufficient to legitimize European legislative acts. The European Parliament did not serve to legitimize them. It only had consultative powers.

Two basic changes occurred in the course of time. One of them was the Single European Act which intervened in 1986 after years of political stagnation on the European level. It introduced decision-taking by majority in the Council. Since then it has been possible that a Member State is subject to legislative acts to which it has not consented or which were sometimes even rejected explicitly in the national democratic process. The link of legitimacy from the people over the national government to the EU remained intact only for the treaties, while it was broken for legislative acts. A gap of legitimacy opened which could not be filled on the national level. The second change took place earlier. It did not result from the conclusion of a treaty by the Member States, but from judgments handed down by the ECJ. In 1963, the Court ruled that the European Treaties were directly applicable in the Member States. Hence the market participants were enabled to enforce the Treaties against the Member States. In 1964, the decision was added that the Treaties took precedence over national law.

This did not necessarily follow from the text of the European Treaties. Rather, the ECJ itself paved the way for this conclusion through methodological and theoretical groundwork. According to the Court, the European Treaties were not part of ordinary international law. They rather constituted an autonomous legal order. Hence they were not to be construed like international treaties, namely in the light of the will of the states parties and narrowly where they limited their sovereignty. On the contrary, they were to be interpreted like national law in the light of an objective purpose that is independent from the will of the states. The judgments are reckoned to be revolutionary—and rightly so. Without them, the EU would have remained one international organization among many; it would probably still wield more power and have a denser institutional structure than other international organizations, but it would certainly not be the singular entity we now face, an entity somewhere in between an international organization and a federation.

It was soon noticed that a gap of legitimacy had opened with the Single European Act in 1986. The answer was a continuous upgrade of the European Parliament from the Treaty of Maastricht onward. It had been elected by the citizens of the Member States as early as 1979, but it only then began to participate in legislation, though not on an equal footing with the Council. Thus the exogenous legitimacy resulting from the democratic procedures in the Member States was supplemented by a proper, endogenous European legitimacy emanating from the Parliament. However, that the two judgments were concerned with the European democratic deficit, too, has been largely overlooked. They are normally perceived as part of a success story—which indeed they were with regard to integration, but not with regard to legitimacy and the acceptance of the consequences. The citizens of the Member States and their representatives were neither consulted nor did they have a possibility to intervene.

It was an American scholar, Joseph Weiler, who interpreted the two judgments by reading them as the beginning of a 'constitutionalization' of the Treaties. This means that they functionally transformed the international Treaties into a constitution. The four fundamental freedoms of the Treaties—free movement of goods, persons, services, and capital—profited most from this. While they had originally been conceived as objective standards modifying national law to the requirements of the common market, they were now transformed into subjective rights of the market participants, which could be enforced before national courts. National law that was incompatible with the economic freedoms and their specifics in the Treaties automatically became inapplicable. In case of doubt, the ECJ itself reserved the right to clarify compatibility. National courts had to refer questions as to the compatibility of national law with European Law to the ECJ and were bound by the decision from Luxembourg.

As a consequence of this case law, the parliaments—be they national or European—were no longer needed to establish the common market. The Commission and the ECJ were able to tackle the challenge on their own. It was enough that they disapplied national law which in their view hindered free economic movement. Hence, next to the direct path of integration through political consensus of the Member States an indirect path has emerged through the interpretation of the Treaties by the ECJ. This path the Court trod with missionary zeal. Thus it interpreted prohibitions of discrimination of foreign competitors so widely as to include regulatory bans, because almost any national regulation could be understood as a market access obstacle. The prohibition of market distorting state aid was extended from private undertakings to public service institutions and pushed privatization regardless of the motives for entrusting certain tasks to public services.

As a consequence, the Member States largely lost the possibility to impose their own standards of product safety, consumer protection, work place security, etc. as well as the power to determine the borderline between the private and the public sector, market and state. However, they were unable to defend themselves against the loss of power. The reason for this is again to be found in the constitutionalization of the Treaties. What is laid down on the level of the constitution is removed from political regulation. The results of elections have no influence on it either. Although they were highly political in effect, the decisions of the Commission and the ECJ, legally speaking, came down to implementing a constitution. They were taken in an apolitical, namely administrative and judicial mode, while being immune from corrections by reason of constitutional rank. The democratically legitimized political instances of the Member States and the EU were out of the game. The democratic mechanisms did not play when it came to the Treaties.

The full magnitude of this power shift can only be understood, if the European Treaties are compared to a constitution. Constitutions regulate political decision-making, but leave the political decisions themselves to the political process, so that the outcome of elections has an impact on them. The Treaties, in contrast, take the decisions themselves. They abound with rules that normally are not laid down in constitutions, but in ordinary law. This explains the epic length of the Treaties. Yet, owing to constitutionalization, the interpretation of these rules by the Commission and the ECJ amounts to constitutional interpretation. Even if the political organs, the Council, and the Parliament, are of the opinion that the interpretation goes far beyond their intentions as treaty-making parties, a correction via legislative amendment is beyond their capacities. Only an amendment of the Treaties would achieve the aim, but it is almost always out of reach for such purposes.

Still, the Commission and the ECJ can only disapply national law. They cannot fill the cracks they have ripped into national law with European law. Only the European legislature can do this, which initially meant the Council alone and later the Council in cooperation with the European Parliament. Yet, to make European laws is harder than to quash national legislation. National legislation is invalidated by the stroke of a pen, whereas legislating on the European level requires the Commission's initiative as well as a Council decision and consent by the European Parliament. Fritz Scharpf described this situation as an asymmetry between negative integration—through the cancellation of national regulation—and positive integration—through European regulation. This asymmetry is the root of the liberalizing tendency of the ECJ's jurisprudence—which runs counter to commitments of most Member States to the social state.

This is the heart of the European democratic problem. The executive and judicial institutions of the EU—the Commission and the ECJ—have bid farewell to the democratic processes within the

Member States as well as in the EU and detached themselves. They take decisions of highly political significance in an apolitical mode, while their practice is not subject to political re-direction because of the constitutionalization of the Treaties. They are more independent and freer than any national executive and judiciary has ever been. A parliamentarization of the EU would leave this state of affairs entirely untouched. The Parliament itself is removed from the game to the extent that European law has been constitutionalized. An empowerment of the Parliament would not change anything in terms of detachment of the executive and judicial bodies of the EU.

Thirdly, a parliament has to meet the need for democratic legitimacy in a political entity. Would the European Parliament be up to this task, if its powers were extended to match those of national parliaments? On the face of it, the endowment of the European Parliament with the powers typical of national parliaments seems to bolster European democracy. Yet, it should not be observed in isolation, for the empowerment of one organ always happens at the expense of other organs the contribution of which to the democratic legitimacy of the EU must also be factored in. Indeed, the proposal to strengthen the Parliament is usually embedded in broader plans to reform the EU. According to these plans, the Commission is upgraded to the—parliamentarian—government of Europe, while the Council is downgraded to a second chamber of Parliament.

This is obviously the blueprint of a federation. Indeed, according to this idea the EU would come close to being a state. As per the *Lisbon* judgment handed down by the German Constitutional Court, the transformation of the EU into a federal state is barred by the Basic Law. But even beyond that one wonders whether it would solve the European legitimacy problem. The fact that the democratic deficit is a consequence not so much of the institutions but rather of the societal preconditions of democracy militates against a positive answer, for these preconditions would not be concerned by the reforms. True, the Parliament would have more powers, but it would be as remote from the basis in society as before. The Council would suffer the corresponding loss, be it in the role of the European Council of heads of state and government or the Council of Ministers. The European Council would only continue to be necessary as the organ in charge of Treaty amendment—and some would even like to withdraw this power from it and hand it on to the EU—while the Council of Ministers would remain as the junior part of the legislature without influence on the composition of the government and budget.

Yet, since the Council is the only European organ representing the interests of the Member States which had founded the EU in order to pursue certain common objectives, the removal of the EU from the grasp of the Member States would be pushed further. The chain of legitimacy would be transformed. The chain of legitimacy that originates in the Member States would be weakened. This is by the way the chain that had originally been the only source of legitimacy of the EU and indeed is still the most important source at the moment, because the European Council is the only organ in charge of the guiding decisions writ large and the Council of Ministers is the main part of the legislature. Since the governments of the Member States would be marginalized, the fact that they are democratically legitimized and controlled 'at home' and have to react responsively to elections would not convey democratic legitimacy to the EU any longer or at least not to the same extent as today. The burden of the democratic legitimation of the EU would have to be shouldered to an overwhelming extent by the Parliament.

To put it succinctly, the EU would shift from exogenous legitimation through the Member States which themselves are legitimized democratically to proper, endogenous legitimation through the European Parliament. The question thus is whether the EU has sufficient resources for proper legitimation. In this regard, however, what has been said before about the societal preconditions of a living democracy weighs heavily. These preconditions are underdeveloped on the European level or are missing altogether. The European Parliament would have to bear the weight of legitimation without being able to function as a mediator between the European citizens and the European organs. The conclusion can thus only be that the EU is dependent on a stream of legitimacy from the Member States where the environment for the functioning of democracy is considerably better than in the EU—though, admittedly, it is often far from ideal.

Hence, our stocktaking of democracy reveals that the EU would be weaker after full democratization than before. It would aggravate the problems of legitimacy rather than solving them. This does not militate against further empowering the Parliament, which can act as a counterbalance to the Council where national interests dominate and to the Commission where technocratic and liberal tendencies are prevalent. The best means in this regard is not the extension of powers, though, but rather the enhancement of the representativeness of the Parliament. Key to this is the Europeanization of the European elections and the creation of truly European parties that are in touch with society, campaign on the basis of European electoral platforms, and then feed the views on European policy and the interests of their electorate into the decision processes in Brussels.

It is even more important to put an end to the detachment of the Commission and the ECJ from the democratic processes in the EU and the Member States. Given that the EU will continue to rely on legitimation by way of the Member States, the EU must develop a self-interest in strong democracy in the Member States, rather than undermining it by crippling national powers more and more. Yet only a limitation of the Treaties to a proper constitutional dimension will end the detachment, namely the limitation to the EU's objectives, powers, organs, procedures, and fundamental rights. The extensive provisions on the policies of the EU must be downgraded to the level of ordinary law in order to make possible what is standard in every democratic state, namely to change by way of politics the course of the case law for the future.

The task of the EU thus re-organized of winning the acceptance of the Union citizens would at least be easier. The citizens could develop some awareness of the ability to influence the course of European integration. It would probably not make the EU their emotional home to which they would be tied in the same way as to their Member States. The EU cannot replace the nation-states, but remains a partnership with a special purpose to meet challenges which the nation-states can no longer address effectively in a globalized world. This is its essential and strong rationale. Without the EU the divide between the reach of global economic actors and politics would be much wider than it is today. This rationale is sufficient to sustain a partnership of states. The attempt of the EU, however, to redirect the bond between citizens and their state towards itself seems futile. The EU should abandon this attempt and accept its limitations.

7

The Necessity of Europeanized Elections and Parties

A. Diagnosis

A textbook on the constitutional law of the German Federal Republic that ignored political parties could never paint a realistic portrait of German constitutionalism. The same is true of the other Member States of the European Union (EU). But this does not seem to apply to the EU itself. In textbooks on European law, political parties play no role, though the Lisbon Treaty affords them one. For many authors, political parties do not even merit an index entry; others dispose of them in a few sentences. The question is whether this distorts or reflects the European reality.

The facts lie close at hand. Currently thirteen parties enjoy the status of a European party under Article 10 of the Treaty on European Union (TEU). Most are affiliations of ideologically like-minded national parties. The members constituting these European parties are also national parties, not natural persons. Consequently, under the German law of political parties, these European parties would not be parties at all. Section 2(1) of the Political Parties Act reads: 'Only natural persons can be members of a political party.' The European parties appear primarily at the institutional level—as factions in the European Parliament. Outside of the Parliament, they are barely visible. There the national parties rule the field, even

The Constitution of European Democracy. First Edition. Dieter Grimm. © Dieter Grimm 2017. Published by Oxford University Press.

in matters European. Election law plays a considerable role in this state of affairs. Under Article 14 TEU, the European Parliament represents the citizens of the Member States—not, as before, the peoples of the Member States. But European election law is still rooted in the older understanding. The members of the European Parliament are elected according to national election law. Article 223 of the Treaty on the Functioning of the European Union's (TFEU) charge to create a unified European election law remains, as yet, unfulfilled.

In Germany, members of the European Parliament are elected according to the (German) European Election Act of 1976 and the European Election Ordinance of 1988, both as updated in 1994. Accordingly, parties and other political associations can nominate candidates for the election. 'Parties' here means parties for purposes of the German Political Parties Act—organizations, by definition, with individual membership. For other associations that are allowed to make nominations, individual membership is explicitly prescribed. As a result, European parties for purposes of EU law are usually not allowed to make proposals. This is also apparent in the fact that the candidate list is delivered by the chair of the (German) political party to the (German) election supervisor of each state, at which point the name of a European affiliate may be appended to that of the national party.

The election itself also remains an essentially national affair. During the campaign, national parties compete with one another. They solicit votes on the basis of national platforms, not coordinated European platforms. Substantively, as well, national issues take centre stage. European issues become relevant only in those Member States where parties critical of or hostile to Europe can force established parties into a debate about European politics. Similarly, national considerations and preferences are overwhelmingly decisive for voter decisions. In the media, election results are usually evaluated from national perspectives: Who won—the (national) governing parties or the (national) opposition? What are the consequences for national politics?

The Lisbon Treaty sought to upgrade European elections by directing the European Council to consider electoral outcomes when nominating the Commission's president. In 2014, this led ideologically like-minded national parties to unite for the first time around leading candidates, who then represented the European coalitions during the campaign. This development united three expectations: first, that personalizing the election would increase voter participation; second, that the issues of the election would be Europeanized; and third, that a step would be taken towards the parliamentarization of the EU. The first expectation was disappointed. Voter participation was just as feeble with leading candidates as it had been without them. The second expectation was fulfilled in a limited way through the numerous appearances of leading candidates in the Member States. This depended, however, on the level of interest with which voters received the candidates and their views on European politics—something that varied from country to country.

As far as the third expectation is concerned, the European Council took up, with some hesitation, the parties' plea to nominate the victorious coalition's leading candidate as president of the Commission. Presumably, the European Council will be unable to turn back on this practice after the next election, and the legal duty, under Article 17(7) TEU, to consider electoral outcomes will become a de facto obligation to honour them. But even then, the EU would remain a far cry from parliamentarization. Parliamentarization would require vesting the European Parliament with the powers typically possessed by national parliaments. Many are pushing for this. But it could be achieved only by degrading the European Council and the Council of Ministers. As far as its democratic legitimacy is concerned, the EU would then be freed from its dependence on the Member States and left to its own internal legitimacy. This could come about only by amending the treaty—that is, with the approval of all Member States. Whether the Member States would embrace such a disempowerment is highly questionable.

So long as European election law is not Europeanized, the European Parliament will be staffed by members from national parties.

Following the 2014 election, members from more than 200 national parties entered the European Parliament, in contrast to 160 in the previous election period. Europeanization takes place only after the election, with the formation of factions in the European Parliament. As with the previous election period, this time there are seven factions and a number of members who belong to no faction at all. Only within the European Parliament—not earlier, when it is elected—does the national perspective fade. In the self-understanding of the majority of its members, the European Parliament is a European institution, not an assembly of nations. Voting in the Parliament is mostly determined by party line, not by national allegiance. The Parliament thus serves as a counterweight to the Council, in which Member-State perspectives still dominate.

What this means for the European public sphere cannot be determined without considering the peculiarities of European democracy. Euro-democracy differs starkly from national democracy. The basic principle of national democracy is that state authority flows from the people. The basic principle of European democracy is that the Union's authority flows from the Member States. The Member States not only organized the EU and gave it life; they also retain control over its legal foundation. They are, as the common phrase has it, 'Masters of the Treaties'. With respect to its existence, its objectives, its powers, its institutions, and its procedures, the EU possesses no power of self-determination. Self-determination applies only below the level of primary law.

This difference in the foundation of its legitimacy shapes the EU's institutional arrangement. In such a polity, it seems reasonable that the central institution would not be the popularly elected Parliament, but rather the body in which the Member States are represented: the Council, which today is divided between the European Council, which is composed of the heads of state and government and which determines the broad outlines of European integration, and the Council of Ministers, which serves as the EU's primary legislature. In the original conception, the Council was the exclusive legislature, albeit without the right of initiative, which still belongs to the Commission. In the beginning, the European Parliament was merely an assembly of members of national parliaments and had no decision-making powers. In 1979, its members were directly elected for the first time. Since 1986, its importance has steadily grown.

The reasons for this are to be found in the Single European Act, which abolished, after a long period of stagnation, the unanimity requirement for decisions of the Council. Since then, the Council can make decisions in certain areas by majority vote. This raised the possibility that a law could become applicable within a Member State that had not been approved by that state's democratically legitimated and democratically accountable institutions. As a result, the democratic legitimacy imparted to European legal acts by the Member States no longer sufficed. The chain of legitimacy running from the peoples of the Member States through the national institutions of the Member States to the Council was broken—at least for the outvoted states. The resultant legitimacy gap could not be filled at the national level—only through an internal European legitimacy. Such legitimacy flows from the Union's citizens, who elect the Parliament. It is thus mediated by the Parliament. As a result, it can reach only so far as the Parliament's powers extend.

In the meantime, the European Parliament has acquired extensive powers of participation in European legislation. It determines the EU's budget, and it takes part in staffing the Commission, which it can also depose. The monistic legitimation has been replaced by a dualistic legitimation. But the two pillars are not equally sturdy. The level of primary law is exempted from this duality. And in the creation of secondary law, the European Parliament is not the coequal of the Council. The Parliament is no longer a mere veto player, but neither is it the EU's central legitimating institution. It cannot, in the end, overcome the resistance of other institutions, as can happen in parliamentary democracies. The EU is not a parliamentary system, but neither is it a presidential system. Instead it is something *sui generis*. Of necessity, this affects the role of European parties.

Article 10(4) TEU determines parties' functions: 'Political parties at European level contribute to forming European political awareness and to expressing the will of citizens of the Union.' In what used to be Article 191, the Maastricht Treaty prefaced this with the statement that parties were important for integration. Parties are expected, then, to forge awareness and shape political will. EU citizens form a will, rather than an opinion, only when electing the European Parliament. Citizens' initiatives under Article 11(4) TEU are not acts of will formation by the EU's citizenry, but rather petitions from a number of citizens asking the Commission, in a given matter, to form a will of its own. By contrast, parties are just as indispensable for elections in the EU as they are in a nation-state. By selecting candidates and by reducing the limitless array of opinions and interests to a manageable number of alternatives, parties place citizens in a position to exercise their right to vote.

The current legal situation, however, is at cross purposes with this function: European parties do not stand for election at all. Voters can only elect national parties. Unlike in a nation-state, the groups that stand for election in Europe are not identical with the groups that will later act in the European Parliament. The former are the national parties, the latter the European factions. The European parties, which make no appearance during the campaign, offer the voters no European political platform. The national parties, which wage the campaign, cannot promise their voters that the platform with which they solicit votes will be represented in the European Parliament. They especially cannot promise that, if victorious, their election platform will become the government program. Responsibility for the government program belongs, under Article 15(1) TEU, to the European Council and, within the parameters of Article 17(1) TEU, the Commission.

The difference between the European Union and the Member States is evident at the institutional level as well. The fundamental difference among national parties, the difference that draws the lines of political drama and ensures the media's attention, is the difference between majority and minority, government and opposition. But this difference has no meaning in the European Parliament because there is no government formed on partisan lines and shaped by partisan concerns. The leading governing bodies of the EU do not depend on a parliamentary majority. The Council is not dependent, as an institution, on parliamentary majorities, though in the discharge of its duties it is partly dependent on them. The European Council is not dependent on the Parliament even in drawing the broad outlines of European policy. The Commission depends, as an institution, on the confidence of the Parliament, but this is hardly true of the Commission's performance of its central function—implementing the program of integration—because this function is bound by law.

All of this undermines the European parties' second function: fostering European political awareness. The European parties upon whom this task is laid are trapped in the institutional realm. They are not rooted in European society. They do not emanate from European society, but from national party organizations. Furthermore, they have no personal base in the electorate. They rarely come in contact with society. They operate at the EU level, but not so conspicuously as parties do in nation-states. Even their members' ties to their constituencies is limited by the sheer size of those constituencies. In Germany, a member of the European Parliament represents about 830,000 citizens. The comparable figure for the German Bundestag is 136,000. The mediation of European factions through the national parties from which they stem thwarts any effective contribution to the formation of European consciousness. It reinforces national consciousness.

B. Remedies

That there is a lack of strong European consciousness and that the EU suffers from a legitimacy deficit has become widely recognized. The causes for this deficiency are disputed, and so too are the means of curing it. The cause is most frequently sought in the EU's institutional structure, described above, particularly in the subordinate role of the European Parliament. The only institution fully legitimated at the European level, the European Parliament is also the institution with the weakest powers. Accordingly, many hope to solve Europe's democracy problem by strengthening the European Parliament. On this view, the European Parliament should be vested with the powers typically possessed by parliaments in democratic states. If the elected representative of the Union's citizens were moved to the centre of the EU, the EU would move into the hearts of its citizens.

These proposals amount to a full parliamentarization of the EU. This would not be possible, of course, without consequences for the other institutions. There would need to be a European government established by the Parliament and dependent on it. The only plausible candidate for this would be the Commission, whose importance would increase accordingly. The loser would be the Council, in both its forms—as European Council and as Council of Ministers. It would become a second chamber of the European Parliament. The idea of a European president is also still raised occasionally. This is clearly the model of a federal state, and indeed, if this model were realized, the EU would powerfully resemble a state. If the right to amend the treaties were to be transferred from the Member States to the EU, the threshold of statehood would have been crossed definitively. Whether, under the Basic Law, the German Federal Republic could accede to such a reconfiguration of the EU is a question that cannot be taken up here. The concern here is rather with the prior question of whether the European democratic deficit can be cured in this way.

After all, curing the democratic deficit through parliamentarization would presuppose that the EU's legitimacy is weak because its central legitimating institution is not the Parliament, which is elected by the Union's citizens, but the Council, which is commissioned by the national governments. Only if this is so could the transition from external to internal legitimation solve the legitimacy crisis. But this can by no means be assumed. On the contrary, there is much to suggest that a parliamentarized EU would not be a more democratic one. A link between the powers of Parliament and the acceptance of the EU by its citizens has not, as yet, been proven. Instead, the more the Parliament's powers have grown, the lower voter turnout has sunk. Plainly, then, the cause of EU citizens' minimal excitement for Europe does not lie with the powers portfolio of the European Parliament.

Champions of reform clearly hope that full parliamentarization would change this. A democracy mediated by a parliament does not, however, derive its strength solely from the parliament's powers. Even a parliament richly furnished with powers can fulfils its function only if it is embedded in a continual process of shaping opinions and articulating interests, one that culminates in—but is not exhausted by—elections, and that even in between elections provides a feedback link between the society and its governing institutions. If a parliament is to perform its purported function of mediating between the populace and political institutions, it must be rooted in society in such a way that the public's views and needs are reflected in the parliament and can influence the process of shaping political will.

Even national parliaments struggle with this. On the one hand, the increasingly scientific and international nature of politics works to parliaments' disadvantage. It plays into the hands of executives. On the other hand, public confidence in popular representatives is comparatively slight. Other institutions enjoy much higher rates of approval. It would be surprising if the European Parliament were spared from these trends. Moreover, there are other, Europe-specific challenges. The European Parliament operates under conditions still less favourable than do national parliaments. The most important reason for this is that, in the EU, the societal sub-structure of a vibrant democracy is either weakly formed or lacking entirely. The intermediary forces that contribute indispensably to the feedback link between citizens and Parliament are underdeveloped. Communications media, which sustain political discourse in nation-states, are utterly absent in Europe. A Europe-wide public discourse takes shape only in exceptional circumstances.

Particularly important in this connection is the situation of political parties described at the outset. In contrast to national parties, European parties—which, according to the Lisbon Treaty, ought to help forge European awareness among the peoples of Europe—are limited to internal operations within the institutional apparatus of the EU. This internal operation heightens with every expansion in the European Parliament's powers. But it does not necessarily reach beyond Parliament. Increased powers do nothing to alter the fact that, outside of the Parliament, European parties barely make an appearance. In this respect, the European Parliament is more distant from the EU's citizens than national parliaments are from national citizens. Because of their internal orientation, European parties are also unable to inaugurate or sustain a Europe-wide political discourse. Nor can they offer a reference point for citizen engagement because they lack the necessary personal base. The pan-European perspective that they adopt in the European Parliament has no counterpart in society. The feedback channels are clogged.

National parties cannot fill the gap. They reach only a national, not a European public. But even at the national level they devote little attention to European politics. The ever increasing importance of European politics is not reflected in national party agendas. This is understandable, of course, so long as national elections are about rewarding or punishing national parties. This context thrusts national issues into the foreground. National parties remain obligated to national issues and perspectives because their electoral success depends on them. In Germany, national parties' general reticence about Europe is further strengthened by the fact that established German parties avoid disputes in the realm of European politics, and have been brought still closer to one another by the emergence of Eurosceptic forces.

Change can be brought about, then, only by European parties. They would need to abandon their self-limitation to activity within the European Parliament and establish direct contact with EU citizens. A precondition for this would be to pass legislation in fulfilment of Article 223 TFEU. A European election law for European elections—one that replaced national European election laws and enabled the candidacy of European parties—would redirect the parties' interests towards European issues and a European public. Before entering the campaign lists, the parties would have to reconcile their national interests and outlooks, and coalesce around a European election platform. In this way, voters would be given the opportunity to express their views about European politics—the business agenda of the European Parliament—rather than about national politics.

This would not mean, however, that European parties must be independent of national parties. The interrelationship between national and European politics, between national and European law, is so close as to require correspondence at the party level. This suggests that European parties ought to remain affiliations of national parties, related by interest and ideology, and should formulate their goals accordingly. But because the aim is to open channels of communication and interaction between European institutions and European society, European parties must not remain mere umbrella organizations. Rather, there must be membership-based parties, as they are at the national level. One possibility would be to grant automatic membership to national party members in the corresponding European party, with a multi-tiered delegation from the local to the national to the European level. But another option would be to open European parties to EU citizens with no prior party affiliation.

On the other hand, a unified party platform would not necessarily entail a unified electoral strategy. Elections differ from country to country in format, method, and style. The same is true of the parties' clientele. Even within a Europeanized campaign, emphasis can be placed on different messages in different places. In this respect, parties would need to be able to adapt themselves to national peculiarities. What is more, the provision of European election law that allows national parties to submit a European election list with their European affiliate's name appended to their own would also need to apply in reverse: European parties competing in European elections would have to be able, in each Member State, to append the name of their national affiliate.

The relationship between a Europeanization of the parties and a full parliamentarization of the EU requires an explanation. If the latter were the necessary consequence of the former, one ought, in light of the German Constitutional Court's *Lisbon* judgment, to warn against Europeanization. But in fact the two developments are independent. The Europeanization of political parties and of electoral law would leave the institutional structure of the EU unchanged. It would merely help provide the European Parliament with a societal foundation and thereby enhance its representativeness. The influence of voters would increase. It would be easier for parties to perform their mediating function, and in that way draw the Union's citizens closer to the EU. The powers of the European Parliament would not expand. Similarly, the EU's stock of powers would be unaffected. Transfers of power require treaty amendments—decisions about which are made in the Member States, not in the European Parliament.

Would all of this cure Europe's democratic deficit? This, for various reasons, is improbable. The current structure of European parties is only one cause among many of the EU's legitimacy deficit. There are other causes that can be combatted only with difficulty—or not at all—through institutional reform. These include popular attitudes towards the parties. Parties are essential to democracy. But they are not loved. In an increasingly individualized society, their integrative force is declining. Membership figures have dropped considerably. It is a source of general complaint that political parties have expanded their influence into areas that should operate according to criteria other than those of party politics. Parties pursue control of state institutions, and they employ all means that further this goal. Many regard the state as spoils. They exploit state power for partisan purposes, and they are not always checked by supervisory institutions.

One cannot build a democracy, then, on the basis of parties alone. Democracy requires a significantly broader foundation. There must be organizations and forms of action that counteract the narrowness of parties, that open up political discourse, and that place issues on the political agenda that political parties avoid. The citizen participation envisioned in Article 11 TEU does not achieve this. The Europeanization of political discourse depends in large part on Europeanized media. In all of these respects, Europe is in a bad way.

The most important cause of Europe's democracy problem lies ultimately with the autonomy of the EU's executive and judicial institutions from the democratic processes of both the Member States and of the EU itself. This has come about, in significant part, through the constitutionalization of the treaties, a product of the ECJ's jurisprudence. Constitutionalization means de-politicization. That which is regulated at the constitutional level is no longer open to political decision. Of course, the constitutionalization of the treaties would be unobjectionable if the treaties were limited to constitution-like provisions. This is more or less the case with the constitutions of the Member States. But things are different in the EU. The treaties were not written as constitutions. They are full of what in nation-states would be ordinary law. Thus, for example, the entirety of EU competition law is regulated in the European treaties.

Once these matters—which substantively ought to be ordinary law—have been elevated to the constitutional level through the ECJ's jurisprudence, they are beyond the reach of the EU's democratically legitimated political institutions, the Council and the Parliament. The application of these norms becomes implementation of the constitution. The institutions responsible for that implementation, the Commission and the ECJ, remain essentially unchecked. Their decision-making practice cannot even be redirected by the political institutions via statutory amendment, as is possible in every democratic state. In the EU, because of constitutionalization, this requires a treaty amendment, which appears, for such purposes, to be all but out of the question. Expanding the powers of Parliament or Europeanizing the parties passes over this problem entirely. Europeanizing the parties, then, would make merely a small contribution to alleviating the legitimacy deficit. But it would not reach so far as to necessitate, for legitimacy purposes, making the EU independent and severing the flow of legitimacy from the Member States, which would be the consequence of full parliamentarization.

8

The Significance of National Constitutions in a United Europe*

A. Constitutional Aspirations

The altered significance of national constitutions in a united Europe can be fully appreciated only by recalling their original aspirations. Those aspirations follow from the origins of constitutionalism.[1] The modern constitution[2] developed at the end of the eighteenth century following successful revolutions in North America and France, in which traditional forms of rule were overthrown and had to be replaced by new ones. In this setting, the much older idea that the legitimacy of political rule depends on the consent of the governed acquired practical significance for the first time. Political rule could be derived neither from divine right, nor from the inherent rights of the ruler, nor from a superior understanding of the common good,

* This article was written before the adoption of the Lisbon Treaty, and refers in general to the pre-Lisbon state of EU law. Some particulars of EU law have changed since then. These changes do not, however, affect the general line of the argument.

[1] See Dieter Grimm, *Die Zukunft der Verfassung* (Frankfurt: Suhrkamp, 3rd edn, 2002); Dieter Grimm, *Deutsche Verfassungsgeschichte* (Frankfurt: Suhrkamp, 3rd edn, 1995); Dieter Grimm, 'The Constitution in the Process of De-nationalization', in his *Constitutionalism. Past, Present, and Future* (Oxford: Oxford University Press, 2016), p. 315.

[2] For older conceptions of constitutionalism, see Heinz Mohnhaupt and Dieter Grimm, *Verfassung* (Berlin: Duncker & Humblot, 2nd edn, 2002).

and certainly not from the mere possession of power. It had to be founded in the people.

But the people, as bearers of the right to rule, were unable to exercise this right themselves. As a result, it had to be entrusted to representatives. In accordance with the principle of popular sovereignty, political power became delegated power. Together with an equally venerable and now resurgent idea—namely, that the power to rule should not be bestowed unconditionally or irrevocably, but rather, in the interest of individual liberty, should be divided among different bearers and for specific purposes and limited periods—this conviction led to the formulation of conditions for legitimate rule. These conditions would constrain the individuals who were then appointed to exercise power. Henceforth, endowed with legal validity, these conditions formed the constitution, whose authorship was ascribed to the people and which, in order to fulfil its function, took precedence over the acts of those commissioned to exercise power.

The aspirations of the constitution were thus defined. Constitutions establish legitimate power in the first place, and at the same time regulate its possession and exercise in a manner that is consistent, comprehensive, and binding.[3] This does not mean that every act of governance is defined in the constitution, such that all government would consist merely in implementing the constitution. But it does mean that all government power must be derived from the constitution and exercised in conformity with its requirements. Those in power must neither pursue constitutionally prohibited aims, nor employ constitutionally prohibited means, nor transgress the constitutionally imposed limits of their rule. The modern constitution thus prohibits both the extra-constitutional possession and the extra-constitutional exercise—the ways and means—of political power. Within the polity that it constitutes, the constitution applies universally and exclusively.

[3] On the characteristics of modern constitutions, see Dieter Grimm, 'The Constitution in the Process of De-nationalization', in his *Constitutionalism. Past, Present, and Future* (Oxford: Oxford University Press, 2016), p. 315.

Regulated rule of this sort was impossible unless there was a ruler or ruling body amenable to systematic regulation through laws designed to govern political activity. During the Middle Ages there was no such thing. In medieval society, political power referred to individuals, not territories, and was divided among numerous independent rulers. Furthermore, it was not exercised as an independent function. Medieval societies not only lacked a constitution in the modern sense, they could not possibly have had one. Only the concentration of various powers in a single hand, as well as their consolidation within a unitary, territorially defined public authority—an entity that emerged towards the end of the sixteenth century and was soon christened 'the state'—enabled the regulation of power through a constitution. From a historical perspective, the state necessarily preceded the constitution. The modern constitution was the constitution of a state.

Of course, the fact that constitutionalism's aspirations were already defined in the first constitutions by no means guaranteed that those aspirations would be realized in all subsequent constitutions. Once the modern constitution had emerged and had acquired considerable appeal even in countries that had not experienced revolutions, it became possible to characterize as 'constitutions' documents that fulfilled constitutionalism's aspirations only in part or not at all. From the very beginning, there were constitutions with no serious intention of restraining politics. These are examples of *pseudo-constitutionalism*. Similarly, there were constitutions that did not place political power upon a new foundation of legitimacy, but rather limited in some respects a form of rule older than, and not legitimated by, the constitution. Such 'constitutions' did not constitute political rule; they merely modified it. They are examples of *semi-constitutionalism*.

No constitution subjected state power to foreign rule or recognized acts of foreign powers as binding within its territorial jurisdiction. This was only logical in a world in which nation-states represented the highest level of political authority and asserted within their territories the right of self-determination. This does not mean, however, that the supra-national level was lawless. It was governed by international law. But international law consisted entirely of treaty law or customary law, and its validity was therefore rooted in the will of the states who voluntarily bound themselves under it. Accordingly, the supreme principle of international law was state sovereignty, which secured states' internal autonomy and external independence. The requirements of international law applied only externally. Within states, they were valid only if the state transposed them into national law. Because international law had no executive bodies, states depended on self-help.

National constitutions could regulate public authority comprehensively because it was identical with national authority. There was no supranational public authority. True, there were numerous neighbouring states, but never more than one per territory, and each state's powers ended at its borders.[4] This precondition for fulfilling national constitutions' aspirations became so self-evident as to go unmentioned. That it is a precondition for the comprehensive validity of national constitutions has become apparent only since nation-states started establishing supranational bodies in order to increase their capacity to solve problems. Unlike traditional leagues and alliances, supranational bodies do more than simply coordinate state activities; they have also acquired sovereign rights. These are to be employed in the pursuit of common objectives, and may be validly exercised within nation-states. States cannot resist such exercise by invoking the right of self-determination.

B. The Rise of Supranational Sovereign Power

These are the roots of the altered significance of national constitutions. The shift has been possible because, ever since the rise of supranational sovereign power, public authority and national authority are

[4] The federal state, or *Bundesstaat*, is a special case, in which state power is divided both horizontally and vertically, but conflicting claims of power are averted through a clear hierarchy and division of tasks.

no longer identical. The origins of this development predate European integration. The formation of supranational sovereign power began with the founding of the United Nations (UN) in 1945. The UN's Member States not only renounce the right (except in self-defence) to resolve conflicts by force, they empower the UN, in cases of violation, to enforce this renunciation—by military means, if necessary, but also through civil tools, such as legal proceedings. The UN has thus attained a share of public power that can penetrate national borders. The strict separation between internal and external, upon which the comprehensive aspirations of national constitutions depend, no longer exists.

In the meantime, this development has advanced further. Today, the UN's right to intervene for humanitarian purposes when states abuse their citizens' fundamental human rights is generally recognized. The International Criminal Tribunals of the former Yugoslavia and Rwanda were established on the basis of Security Council resolutions, not treaties, and the activities of these bodies do not depend on the consent of the affected states. Additionally, rules of international law take shape under the UN's aegis that claim validity as *jus cogens*, do not depend on the states' approval, and bind the states when they conclude future treaties. Outside the UN, but involving most nations, the World Trade Organization has acquired authority to enforce trade agreements through a court-like arbitration process, whose binding effect also does not require the consent of affected states.

Nowhere, however, has the development progressed further than in Europe. True, UN interventions, when they come, can have massive consequences. But they do not come often, in part because the vast majority of Member States give no cause for intervention, and in part because the Security Council often decides not to intervene, such as when a permanent member exercises its veto. The UN's sovereign power is not only more substantively limited than that of nation-states, it exercises that power comparatively infrequently and only vis-à-vis the particular state that occasions the intervention. Most nations have never been subject to a sovereign act of the UN. The same is not true of European integration. Although the powers transferred to European institutions do not include the use of physical force, the European Union's (EU) Member States are constantly exposed to the effects of sovereign European acts.

In this respect, however, one must distinguish the Council of Europe from the EU. The Council of Europe affects the states mainly through the European Court of Human Rights (ECtHR), which ensures compliance with the European Convention on Human Rights (ECHR). The ECHR becomes valid within the Member States when they ratify the treaty, and it assumes within a state's legal hierarchy the status the state ascribes to it. The ECtHR can review Member-State acts for their conventionality, but it does not have the power, in cases of violation, to invalidate national acts. The Court's judgments are only declaratory. The Member States' duty to comply is a product of international law, and the Council of Europe cannot compel compliance. In this respect, European human rights protection remains within the framework of traditional international law. That framework is transcended, however, insofar as individuals, and not only states, may assert that Member States have violated their rights under the Convention.

The EU's powers, by contrast, go much further. The Member States have transferred to the EU sovereign rights, which it exercises autonomously. This affects all branches of government activity. The Member States have transferred legislative, executive, and judicial powers. When the EU exercises these powers, its acts, including legal norms, apply directly within the Member States. According to the jurisprudence of the European Court of Justice (ECJ), European law acts take precedence over national law—including the supreme national law, the Member States' constitutions. European law cannot, it is true, invalidate national law: the two flow from independent sources, and the EU lacks a norm, like Article 31 GG, to govern conflicts. But national law that contravenes European law may not be applied so long as the European law remains in force. Although the EU lacks compulsory means to enforce its laws within the Member States, it is still the case that, wherever the writ of European law runs, the Member States can no longer act in a self-determined way.

On the other hand, the EU has not yet acquired the power to determine its own legal foundation. That foundation consists of international treaties concluded unanimously by the Member States. The treaties are not merely the mechanism through which the legal foundation emerges. Unlike federal states, the EU does not control its own legal foundation. Nor is the EU empowered to amend the treaties. That power belongs to the Member States. Furthermore, like the treaties themselves, amendments to the treaties must be adopted by the Member States unanimously. The Member States remain, as is often said, 'Masters of the Treaties.' Even the failed European constitutional treaty did not try to change this. The Member States' control of the treaties means that the Member States determine for themselves which sovereign rights to transfer to the EU and how the EU must exercise those rights. The EU cannot decide unilaterally which sovereign rights of the Member States it wants to assume. The Member States retain the *Kompetenz-Kompetenz*.[5] With regard to its legal foundation, the EU is controlled externally.

This fact distinguishes the EU's legal foundation from a constitution, through which a polity determines independently the purpose, form, and content of its political community. The treaties are nonetheless frequently characterized as the EU's 'constitution'[6]—and rightly so, insofar as the treaties fulfil a number of functions that in a nation-state would be performed by the constitution. The treaties establish the Union, designate its tasks, prescribe its relations with the Member States, erect its institutions, define their powers, and regulate their procedures, etc. What is missing, however, is the constituent element of the constitution—self-determination—and with

[5] It is hard to find evidence for the opposing view set forth, for example, in Ingolf Pernice, 'Multilevel Constitutionalism and the Treaty of Amsterdam' (1999) 36 *Common Market Law Review* 710.

[6] The literature on this has become extensive: see e.g. Anne Peters, *Elemente einer Theorie der Verfassung Europas* (Berlin: Duncker & Humblot, 2001); Armin von Bogdandy (ed), *Europäisches Verfassungsrecht* (Berlin: Springer, 2003); Thomas Giegerich, *Europäische Verfassung und deutsche Verfassung im transnationalen Konstitutionalisierungsprozess* (Berlin: Springer, 2003). For my own position see e.g. Dieter Grimm, 'Does Europe need a Constitution?' (1995) 1 *European Law Journal* 282.

it a link to the EU's citizens as the source of all public authority. This is why the EU has not yet become a state, although it has long since outgrown the legal framework of traditional international organizations. It is a structure *sui generis*—one that transcends conventional forms of cooperation, but for which no suitable name has yet been found.[7]

C. The National Constitution as a Filter for European Primary Law

The fact that the EU's legal foundation derives, not from the EU itself, but from the Member States by way of the treaties is of considerable importance for the role of national constitutions. It means that Member-State constitutions influence primary EU law. This is so because the Member States are bound by their constitutions when they sign or ratify a treaty. On the one hand, the procedural requirements of national constitutions can affect the fate of treaties, as was evident with the proposed European constitutional treaty. The treaty was rejected by referendum in France and in the Netherlands, while it presumably would have been approved by those nations' parliaments. On the other hand, substantive constitutional provisions become significant where national constitutions forbid the ratification of treaties that clash with certain constitutional requirements. In this way, national constitutions provide a filter for primary European law.

This filtering effect cannot, however, prevent every deviation from national constitutions that results from the exercise of sovereign rights by supranational organizations like the EU. A nation-state that insisted on zero deviations would render itself incapable of participating in supranational organizations. As the German Federal Constitutional Court found in its *Eurocontrol* judgment, every

[7] For a list of attempts, see Vivien A. Schmidt, *Democracy in Europe* (Oxford: Oxford University Press, 2006), p. 8 et seq.

transfer of sovereign rights alters the constitutional distribution of powers and amounts, *de facto*, to a constitutional amendment.[8] If a state does not wish to exclude itself from international cooperation involving the transfer of sovereign rights, it must accept some losses to its own constitution and content itself with establishing constitutional conditions and limits for such transfers—and with compensatory shifts in domestic power—as happens in Article 23 (2)–(7) GG.

What this filter allows or inhibits depends on national constitutional provisions. From the very beginning, the German Basic Law (in Article 24) relinquished the German state's claim of exclusive rule and opened the Federal Republic to other sources of law. More recently, in 1992, Article 23(1) expressly authorized German participation in the EU. Most Member-State constitutions contain similar authorizations. In some countries, such as France and Ireland, these are merely ad-hoc authorizations to ratify individual treaties that amend primary European law. These authorizations expire after a single use, and each additional act of transfer requires a new constitutional amendment.

Formally, both Article 24(1) and Article 23(1) GG require a statute for the transfer of sovereign rights. This is the rule in the other Member States as well. Some states permit referenda or, in certain cases, require them. Slovakia, for instance, requires a referendum for accession or exit. Denmark requires a plebiscite if the proposed treaty is supported by less than the required five-sixths majority in Parliament. In the Czech Republic, the Constitutional Court must certify, prior to ratification, that the treaty is compatible with the constitution. If a proposed treaty deviates from the constitution or makes such deviations necessary, some constitutions require ratification by the same majority needed to amend the constitution. Under Article 23(1) GG, the ratification of treaty provisions that alter or expand the Basic Law are subject to Article 79(2)-(3) GG, which makes certain values and guarantees unamendable.

[8] BVerfGE 58, 1 (36) (1981).

The Basic Law also places substantive restrictions on the transfer of sovereign rights to the EU. Article 23(1) GG conditions German participation in European integration on the EU's commitment to principles of democracy, federalism, social justice, and the rule of law. These requirements correspond with the objectives of the German state, set forth in Article 20, and the principles shielded from constitutional amendment in Article 79. Article 23 requires further that the EU provide a level of fundamental rights protection similar to that afforded by the Basic Law, thereby adhering to the unamendable provisions of Article 1 GG. Additionally, the EU must honour the principle of subsidiarity. Such substantive conditions for the ratification of primary European law are less common in the constitutions of the other Member States, but they may be found, for example, in the constitutions of Portugal and Sweden.

The role of national constitutions as filters for the formation of European primary law is particularly pronounced in countries where national constitutional courts, or supreme courts with constitutional jurisdiction, can review treaties for their compatibility with the national constitution. Such review focuses on the national ratification law. In formal terms, this law is the only object of review. But because the ratification law has no independent content, constitutional review centres on whether the treaty itself—the object of the ratification law—conforms with the national constitution. In order to prevent an unconstitutional treaty from becoming binding under international law, the German Constitutional Court permits petitions for review of a ratification law even before the law's promulgation, which is followed by the filing and exchange of ratification documents. The French Constitution, in Article 54, allows review of a treaty even before ratification. If the treaty is unconstitutional, it may be ratified only following a constitutional amendment.

It is not only in Germany that enacting European primary law has depended repeatedly on review for conformity with the national constitution. In Ireland, notwithstanding a constitutional provision intended to prevent conflicts between European and national law, ratification of the Single European Act was reviewed because the constitution did not mention the SEA explicitly.[9] In Germany and other Member States, the Maastricht and the Lisbon treaties were the objects of intense constitutional scrutiny.[10] The Federal Constitutional Court found both treaties to be compatible with the Basic Law, but took the opportunity to mark the limits of integration that follow from German statehood. The Danish Supreme Court issued a similar decision.[11] The French Constitutional Council declared both the Maastricht and Amsterdam treaties incompatible with the French Constitution: the treaties could be ratified only after the constitution was amended to permit them.[12]

D. The Influence of National Constitutions on European Legislation

The influence of the national constitutions does not end with the conclusion and ratification of EU primary law. In attenuated form, it continues with the creation of EU secondary law. This is possible because primary law gives Member States a central role in EU legislation. The EU's peculiar status as a federation of states is evident in the fact (among many others) that the Union's principal legislative body is not the European Parliament, which is elected by the Member States' citizens, but the Council, which is composed of the Member States' governments. The Council, it is true, lacks the right of initiative, which belongs to the Commission. Nor is the Council any longer the sole legislative body. The Parliament's rights of participation have continually expanded, and expand further with the Treaty of Lisbon. But the Parliament can only respond to resolutions of the Council; it

[9] *Crotty v. An Taoiseach*, 9 April 1987 (Supreme Court of Ireland).

[10] BVerfGE 89, 155 (1993); BVerfGE 123, 267 (2009).

[11] *Højesteret*, decision of 6 April 1998, Carlsen u.a. v. Rasmussen, I 361/1997, UfR 1998, S. 800, I 361/1997.

[12] *Conseil Constitutionnel*, decision of 9 April 1992, Rec. S. 55; v. 2.9.1992, Rec. S. 76; v. 23.9.1992, Rec. S. 94; v. 31.12.1997, Rec. S. 344.

cannot lead out on its own. To date, efforts to adjust this arrangement in accordance with a nation-state model have been unsuccessful.[13]

The creation of secondary law differs greatly from the creation of primary law. The latter is enacted through treaties in accordance with the rules of international law, while secondary law is created through resolutions in accordance with the rules of primary European law. The Council, which adopts resolutions, is not a conference of states but an institution of the EU. It wields powers that have been transferred to the EU and is not bound by national constitutions. Unlike all other EU institutions, however, it is composed of members of national institutions, namely the governments of Member States. This arrangement enables Council members to assert their national interests, including the requirements of their national constitutions, in the legislative process. Insofar as national constitutions oblige them to do this, those constitutions indirectly influence European legislation.

Whether such an obligation exists depends on the particular constitution. To answer this question for Germany, it makes sense to focus first on those areas that are not governed exclusively by EU law, but which are merely opened to coordinated action. For the moment, this includes the two EU pillars of joint foreign and security policy, and home and justice affairs. In these areas, collaboration remains intergovernmental. The Member States also have a right to make proposals. Decisions can be made only unanimously. The decision-making mechanism thus resembles that of treaty negotiations under international law. Accordingly, the same rules of conduct apply. The German representatives in the Council must adhere to the requirements of the Basic Law and hence must not agree to any proposal that would violate the Basic Law.

In the communalized policy areas of the first pillar, there was some controversy regarding the German government's constitutional obligations when it participated in Council legislation that, domestically, would have fallen within the jurisdiction of the German states (the

[13] See Dieter Grimm, 'Vom Rat zur Staatenkammer' in his *Die Verfassung und die Politik: Einsprüche in Störfällen* (Munich: Beck, 2001), p. 264.

Länder), who contested the EU's power to regulate in these areas. The German Constitutional Court has held that in such cases the German government must uphold the rights of the Federal Republic against countervailing European legislation, and defend those rights within EU institutions. The federal government may not simply turn a blind eye to the lack of EU powers. The government is justified in relaxing its position only in exceptional cases and for compelling reasons of foreign or integration policy.[14] In an earlier judgment arising from a petition for a temporary injunction, the Court held even more clearly that the government must do everything in its power to prevent the promulgation of secondary EU law that is incompatible with German constitutional law.[15]

These principles can be generalized. But in generalizing them, one must not overlook the peculiar nature of European legislation.[16] Even though secondary EU law emerges by resolution and not by treaty, the Council remains not so much a deliberative as a negotiating body. The Council's members are animated primarily by their national interests and by the political goals of the national parties that form their governments. Legislation in the Council is often the product of negotiated deals, the settling of which requires compromise on all sides. Under these circumstances, national governments can represent their national interests successfully only if they enjoy broad leeway in the negotiations. On the whole, rigid constitutional constraints can disadvantage national constitutions. Still, the Basic Law must remain paramount even when the German government makes compromises. Individual constitutional positions can be surrendered only in the exceptional case that such surrender prevents even greater

[14] BVerfGE 92, 203 (1995)—EG-Fernseh-Richtlinie.

[15] BVerfGE 80, 74 (1989).

[16] See Armin von Bogdandy, *Gubernative Rechtsetzung* (Tübingen: Mohr Siebeck, 1999); Hartmut A. Grams, *Zur Gesetzgebung der Europäischen Union* (Neuwied: Luchterhand, 1998); Stefan Kadelbach and Christian Tietje, 'Autonomie und Bindung der Rechtsetzung in gestuften Rechtsordnungen' (2008) 66 *Veröffentlichungen der Vereinigung der deutschen Staatsrechtslehrer* 7 and 45.

constitutional harms.[17] Approving a European law that violates Article 23(1) GG is never allowed.

Compliance with the national constitution can be guaranteed, however, only insofar as the treaties require unanimity in the Council for European legislation. Accordingly, one must presume that in this area the German government bears a heightened obligation. The unanimity requirement acknowledges that the interests of each Member State possess such weight that each state must be able to assert those interests against every other state. This is possible, of course, only in a negative sense: EU law that is incompatible with the national constitution may be prevented, but EU law that conforms to the national constitution can never be compelled. Thus, the flexibility and willingness to compromise that are needed to influence majority decisions do not justify relaxing constitutional obligations. A combination between legislative proposals that require unanimity and those for which a majority suffices does not occur in practice, so that further exceptions to the government's strict constitutional obligation seem unnecessary.

What is true for the representatives of the German government in the Council, however, applies neither to the Commissioners appointed by Germany nor to the members of the European Parliament elected in Germany. Unlike government representatives in the Council, Commissioners and MEPs are not simultaneously members of an institution of the German state. In the Commission and in Parliament, the levels of European and national activity are not entwined. As a result, decisions in Parliament or in the Commission are not constrained by national constitutional obligations. Although members of the European Parliament are designated in Article 189 EC as 'representatives of the peoples of the States brought together in the Community', and although there is no provision similar to Article 38(1) GG, which says that members of the German Bundestag are representatives of the entire people, MEPs are nevertheless not subject to the constitutions of their respective peoples. Under Article 213 EC,

[17] See also BVerfGE 4, 157 (168 f.) (1955).

commissioners are 'completely independent in the performance of their duties', and must act 'in the general interest of the Community'.

E. The Supremacy of European Law

National constitutions are decisive when it comes to transferring legislative powers to the EU, and they can indirectly influence the Council's exercise of those powers. Once European law enters into force, however, it applies without regard to national constitutions. But this still does not explain how European and national law interact when the two collide. The Treaties of Rome did not regulate this issue expressly. With few exceptions, national constitutions do not regulate the interaction of the two legal orders either. This question was first decided by the EC Justice several years after the European Economic Community was founded, and in a manner quite different from the traditional rules of international law. Only the Court's decision placed the European Community in the special position, which it still occupies today, between an international organization and a federal state.[18]

In 1963, the Court of Justice ruled that European law is directly applicable in the Member States,[19] and therefore (unlike international law) does not need to be transposed into national law. In this way, the national legislature—bound by its own constitution—lost its gatekeeper function vis-à-vis the EU. The decision that European law takes precedence over national law followed a year later.[20] In 1970, the Court of Justice affirmed that this supremacy applies even against national constitutional law.[21] In its decision, the Court maintained

[18] See Karen J. Alter, *Establishing the Supremacy of European Law* (Oxford: Oxford University Press, 2001); Joseph H.H. Weiler, 'The Transformation of Europe' (1991) 100 *Yale Law Journal* 2403; Alec Stone Sweet, *The Judicial Construction of Europe* (Oxford: Oxford University Press, 2004).

[19] *Van Gend en Loos* (1963) Case 26/62.

[20] *Costa v. ENEL* (1964) Case 6/64.

[21] *Internationale Handelsgesellschaft mbH v. Einfuhr- und Vorratsstelle für Getreide- und Futtermittel* (1970) Case 11/70; *Amministrazione delle Finanze v. S.p.A. Simmenthal* (1978) Case 106/77.

that the Community could not fulfil its function if the Member States were free to determine the status of European law and thereby undermine its universal validity. In so reasoning, the Court assumed that European law had freed itself from its origins as international law and had acquired an independent validity. Others continue to derive the supremacy of European law from an authorization by the Member States—the command by the national legislatures to apply EU law domestically.

With respect to the legal consequences of a clash between national and European law, the ECJ initially tended to assume that European law invalidates contradictory national law. If that were so, a Member State would no longer be able to define its own constitution in a sovereign manner. Sovereignty, which in the constitutional state was already limited to the constituent power of the people, would have been extinguished even in this limited sphere. Later, the Court of Justice adopted the view that conflicting European law does not invalidate contradictory national law, but merely renders it inapplicable.[22] The supremacy of European law is not a supremacy of validity but of application. If the contradictory European law were repealed, the national law would automatically revive. Consistent with this view, the ECJ does not invalidate national law,[23] and it allows national institutions to draw their own conclusions from the Court's interpretations of European law.

But even the supremacy of application has far-reaching consequences for national constitutions. The ban on applying national law that contravenes European law gives to every institution responsible for applying national law—whether administrative or judicial—the power to review national laws for their applicability and, in cases of conflict, the power to set them aside. Out of respect for the directly legitimated democratic Parliament, and in order to avoid contradictory statements about laws' validity, the Basic Law denied such a power to ordinary courts and, *a fortiori*, to administrative agencies. The

[22] *Ministero delle Finanze v. IN.CO.GE 90* (1998) Case 10/97.
[23] *Jongeneel Kaas v. Niederlande* (1984) Case 237/82.

Basic Law grants to the Federal Constitutional Court a monopoly on the rejection of German laws, but the ECJ's supremacy jurisprudence has terminated that monopoly. Where European law is concerned, the ECJ has extended the power of review to agencies and courts. By so doing, it has diminished the role that the Basic Law intended for Parliament.

The interpretation of European law acquires a separate significance for the extent to which it displaces national constitutional law through supremacy of application. Above all, as interpreted by the Commission and the ECJ, the four economic freedoms of Article 14 EC and their concretization have set in motion a formidable dynamic that places these freedoms in potential conflict with national understandings of fundamental rights, and puts those national understandings on the defensive. Beginning with *Cassis de Dijon*,[24] the European Court of Justice interpreted Article 28 EC, in the name of the common market, to mean that products that meet the legal requirements of their country of origin may also be sold in every other Member State. As a result, the Member States are no longer able to uphold their own standards of protection, even if those standards were imposed pursuant to positive obligations of national fundamental rights.

In the meantime, the Commission has adopted, with the backing of the Court of Justice, an active policy of liberalization,[25] which has come to target in a particular way the Member States' public institutions. If such institutions have private competitors, the European institutions regard public funding as a state subsidy, which, if it distorts competition, is banned under Article 81 ff. EC. Because the Commission is fixated on competition, no consideration is given to the reasons of general welfare that led to the choice of public organization. The consequence is an asymmetry between negative integration, which removes obstacles to the market, and positive integration,

[24] *Rewe Zentral AG v. Bundesmonopolverwaltung für Branntwein* (*Cassis de Dijon*) (1979) Case 120/78.

[25] See Martin Höpner and Armin Schäfer, 'Eine neue Phase der europäischen Integration', in Höpner and Schäfer (eds), *Die politische Ökonomie der europäischen Integration* (Frankfurt am Main: Campus, 2008), p. 129.

which corrects for market failures. While negative integration takes place through the non-political mechanism of the administrative or judicial implementation of law and can be asserted with a stroke of the pen, positive integration requires legislation and is much more difficult to achieve.[26]

The costs of this asymmetry are borne, in part, by constitutional aspirations towards social justice. True, the Member States are not legally prevented from pursuing such aims. But in practice, the European policy of liberalization drastically reduces their capacity to do so. At the same time, stabilizing the social state at the European level seems all but hopeless in light of the Member States' extremely disparate systems of social welfare.[27] The costs are also borne by national fundamental rights, which are increasingly displaced by market freedoms. At the national level, personal, communicative, and cultural rights are usually afforded stronger protection than economic rights, and constitutional courts tend to review laws that regulate economic activity with a great deal of deference. At the European level, this hierarchy is reversed. Where legislative leeway is greatest under national constitutional law, the interpretation of European law makes it the smallest.

F. The Reservations of National Constitutional Courts

According to the ECJ, the supremacy of European law applies without limits. On this view, the role of national constitutional courts ends with their review of whether a transfer of powers to the EU violates the national constitution. The national constitution has no bearing on how the EU employs its transferred powers. This is true, the ECJ

[26] See Fritz Scharpf, *Governing in Europe* (Oxford: Oxford University Press, 1999), pp. 43–83.

[27] See Fritz Scharpf, 'The European Social Model' (2002) 40 *Journal of Common Market Studies* 645.

maintains, even for the question of whether the EU possesses a certain power in the first place. The ECJ does not deny that EU institutions can exceed their powers. But the treaties provide the sole standard for assessing such violations, and the ECJ itself is the treaties' final interpreter. If a Member State believes that the EU lacks the competence to make a certain decision, it can bring an action for annulment before the ECJ, and national courts may avail themselves of the preliminary ruling procedure. But the ECJ insists that national constitutional courts have no jurisdiction over such matters.[28] They would have to treat a lack-of-competence complaint as inadmissible.

Some Member States accept this without reservation. Slovakia concedes the supremacy of European law in its national constitution. The Irish Constitution, in Article 29, goes so far as to stipulate expressly that none of its provisions may be invoked in opposition to European legal acts.[29] The constitution of the Netherlands, in Article 94, grants precedence of application over national law to the generally binding treaty provisions and to resolutions of international organizations. Other Member-State constitutions contain no such provisions. Although they are open to international law (as is the German Basic Law in Article 24 and, since 1992, and specifically for European law, in Article 23), they say nothing about the question of supremacy. In some of these countries, however, the national supreme or constitutional courts have begun to erect a constitutional barrier against the supremacy of European law.

In its decision in *Costa v. ENEL*, the Italian Constitutional Court was the first to contest European supremacy.[30] It did so by viewing European law's validity from the perspective of international law.

[28] *Foto-Frost v. Hauptzollamt Lübeck-Ost* (1987) Case 314/85.

[29] Art. 29 states: 'No provision of this Constitution invalidates laws enacted, acts done or measures adopted by the State which are necessitated by the obligations of membership of the European Union or of the Communities, or prevents laws enacted, acts done or measures adopted by the European Union or by the Communities or by institutions thereof, or by bodies competent under the Treaties establishing the Communities, from having the force of law in the State.'

[30] *Corte costituzionale*, decision of 5 February 1964, Nr. 14/64, *Costa v. ENEL e soc. Edisonvolta in Foro Italiano* 1964, I, p. 465.

Following the ECJ's seminal decision in the same case,[31] the Italian Constitutional Court backed down, though it reserved to itself, in individual cases of conflict, the right to determine the applicability of national law.[32] This was the practice the ECJ rejected in the *Simmenthal* case.[33] Since then, the Italian Court has retreated to the position that European law generally takes precedence even over the Italian constitution, but insists that the constitution imposes some '*controlimiti*', or counter-limits. On this view, supremacy applies only insofar as fundamental principles and inalienable human rights remain inviolate.[34] In France, it is the *Conseil d'État*, not the Constitutional Council, that supplies sustained resistance.[35]

The German Federal Constitutional Court, by contrast, declined as late as 1967 to review a constitutional complaint against community law, reasoning that even 'such a compelling need of legal policy' could not expand the German Court's jurisdiction.[36] Seven years later, the Court altered course, ruling in *Solange I* that, given the crucial significance of fundamental rights for the legitimacy of political rule, and so long as there was no comparable rights protection at the community level, the Court would review community legal acts for conformity with the Basic Law's fundamental rights provisions.[37] After this decision had prompted the ECJ to develop a more vigorous European rights protection, the German Constitutional Court declared in *Solange II* that, so long as adequate fundamental rights protection was secured at the community level, the Court would no longer exercise its power of review.[38] The Court has not, however, disclaimed this

[31] *Costa v. ENEL*, above n. 20.

[32] *Corte costituzionale*, decision no. 183/73 of December 1973, *Frontini v. Ministro delle Finanze, Foro Italiano* 1974, I, p. 314.

[33] *Amministrazione delle Finanze v. S.p.A. Simmenthal*, above n. 20.

[34] *Corte costituzionale*, decision of 31 March 1994, Nr. 117/94, Fabrizio Zerini in 'Raccolta ufficiale delle sentenze e ordinanze delle Corte costituzionale 1994' p. 785 in (1995) *Foro Italiano* I 1077.

[35] See esp. Conseil d'Etat, decision of 22 December 1978, *Ministre de l'Intérieur v. Cohn-Bendit*, Rec. 1978, p. 524.

[36] BVerfGE 22, 293 (1967).

[37] BVerfGE 37, 271 (1974).

[38] BVerfGE 73, 339 (1986).

power; it has only suspended it. The power of review lies dormant so long as the EU adequately protects fundamental rights. But it can be revived if things change.

Should the EU Charter of Fundamental Rights (proclaimed in 2000 but not yet legally binding) enter into force, it would further strengthen the protection of fundamental rights at the European level. The content of the Charter is not inferior to that of the Basic Law. Indeed, the Charter is closely modelled on the Basic Law, and even embraces concepts that the German Constitutional Court has developed jurisprudentially, enshrining them as independent fundamental rights. In some places, the Charter provides an even higher level of protection than the Basic Law. But, for purposes of the *Solange* decisions, adequate protection of fundamental rights also entails their justiciability and practical implementation by the ECJ. In this respect, the trends described earlier give rise to new doubts. Implementing the Charter would not render the *Solange* decisions moot.

With regard to EU institutions exceeding their powers, the German Constitutional Court has expressly reserved for itself the final word.[39] The Court assumes that European law derives its validity from the command to apply it within Germany that the German legislature issued in the ratification law. Whether such a command has been issued is a question of national law, to be decided by national courts. If EU institutions exercise powers not transferred to them by the national legislature, their acts deprive German national institutions of their constitutionally guaranteed discretion in an impermissible way. Accordingly, the German Constitutional Court can declare that such acts are inapplicable in the territory governed by the Basic Law. The same is true if the ECJ decides a competence question in the EU's favour, but by so doing crosses the line between treaty interpretation and treaty amendment.

The constitutional or supreme courts of Denmark, France, Greece, Ireland, Italy, and Spain have similarly claimed final jurisdiction over

[39] BVerfGE 89, 155 (1993).

questions of competence, and a tendency to follow these examples is apparent in other Member States.[40] Although it is generally acknowledged that the validity of European legal acts within the Member States does not depend on their compatibility with the national constitution, certain core values are nonetheless defended against the claims of European law to universal validity: the Member States' sovereignty or statehood, their reserved powers, their fundamental constitutional principles, their standards of fundamental rights protection. It seems appropriate that the judiciaries of the Member States should erect such barriers, since the claims of European law to unconditional validity are the product, not of the treaties, but of the ECJ's jurisprudence.

G. The Interrelationship between the National and European Judiciaries

As yet, no 'war of the judges'[41] has erupted. National constitutional courts no longer contest the supremacy of EU law. On the contrary, they help to enforce it. In Germany, this effort is furthered by recognizing the ECJ as a 'lawful judge' for purposes of Article 101(1) GG.[42] As a consequence, a German court of last resort that violates its obligation, under Article 234 EC, to refer a question of European law to the ECJ, also violates the Basic Law, and can be challenged before the Federal Constitutional Court. By contrast, national constitutional courts' power to review EU acts is reserved for serious threats to the fundamental relationship between the Member States and the Union,

[40] For a thorough analysis, see Franz C. Mayer, *Kompetenzüberschreitung und Letztentscheidung* (Munich: Beck, 2000), pp. 140–257, 260. Cf. Monica Claes, *The National Courts' Mandate in the European Constitution* (Oxford: Hart, 2006), p. 385 ss.

[41] Claes, above n. 40. This expression is first found in the Cohn-Bendit case: 'Ni gouvernement des juges, ni guerre des juges. Il doit y avoir place pour le dialogue des juges.' See Mayer, above n. 40, p. 154.

[42] BVerfGE 73, 339 (1986) (366 ff.). Yet this leverage works only in the final instance of the deciding courts. See Ulrich Haltern, *Europarecht* (Tübingen: Mohr Siebeck, 2nd edn, 2007), p. 337.

and for the core principles of their national constitutions. In this way, national constitutional courts assert the essential statehood of the Member States and at the same time prevent the EU from becoming a state (though many view statehood as European integration's ultimate goal).

As a result of all of this, the courts in the EU cannot, as in a nation-state, be arranged around a single hierarchical summit. Just as the national and European levels mingle in the creation of norms, national, supreme, or constitutional courts and the ECJ are interrelated, and the question of who has the last word remains open.[43] True, the ECJ can usually assume that the Member States' highest courts will, for the sake of a uniform application of European law, respect the ECJ's decisions. But the ECJ is not in a position vis-à-vis the national high courts to enforce the requirements of European law under all circumstances, as would be possible for a court enthroned at the summit of a judicial hierarchy. If the ECJ wishes to avoid a clash between two opposing decisions of last resort, it must pay close attention to the decisions of the national constitutional courts, and accommodate them in order to avoid insurmountable barriers.

This interplay also characterizes the relationship between national constitutional courts and the ECtHR. Of course, because the ECHR cannot claim supremacy over national law, its position is weaker than that of EU law. But its position is not a subordinate one. The ECtHR's rulings bind the Member State of the Council of Europe against which the complaint was lodged. The German Constitutional Court has confirmed that this is so against the position of German courts that thought they could ignore the ECtHR's judgments. The Constitutional Court held that disregarding ECtHR decisions violated the Basic Law's rule-of-law principle.[44] Like violations of Article 234 EC, failures to acknowledge ECtHR decisions can be challenged before the German Constitutional Court. As the highest national

[43] See Claes, above n. 40; Ingolf Pernice, *Das Verhältnis europäischer zu nationalen Gerichten im europäischen Verfassungsverbund* (Berlin: de Gruyter, 2006).

[44] BVerfGE 111, 307 (2004).

court, the Constitutional Court thus assumes the role of upholding international law within the national judiciary.

But here, too, there are reservations. The German Constitutional Court has explained that consideration does not necessarily mean compliance. National law must yield to the ECHR only insofar as it grants interpretive leeway to the institution applying it. Within this scope, the national courts have to follow the ECtHR, even if doing so means abandoning established national case law. Where such leeway is lacking, however, either because the German legal situation does not grant it or because complying with the ECtHR's decision would lead to a violation of the Basic Law, national law trumps the ECHR. Under the Constitutional Court's jurisprudence, this applies particularly when the relevant national law balances opposing fundamental rights claims and accommodating the ECtHR's jurisprudence would disrupt that balance.

In response, the ECtHR must engage with the national legal situation—particularly national fundamental rights and national rights doctrine—if it wishes to ensure the implementation of its decisions. The ECHR's oft-neglected Article 53 offers one tool for this. Under this provision, the ECtHR may not interpret the Convention in ways that would limit or impair fundamental rights recognized by national law. This rule becomes especially significant when the Court must review national decisions arising from civil-law proceedings in which both parties invoke fundamental rights and the national courts must arrive at a reasonable balance between two rights of equal rank. If the ECtHR grants the petition of the party that loses at the national level, it inevitably diminishes the national rights protection of the party who prevailed in the national proceedings.

The ECtHR has no mandate to unify law in Europe. Its commission is to ensure a minimum fundamental rights standard that is recognized by all Member States in the Council of Europe, not to implement a uniform standard across states. The Court must allow sufficient leeway for national solutions—especially in cases that require courts to balance conflicting rights. The *Caroline* decisions are a good example of this.[45] The various European states reach different results when resolving the conflict between the freedom of the press and the protection of privacy. While in France protection of privacy generally takes priority, the opposite is usually true in the United Kingdom (UK). Guided by the principle of practical concordance between conflicting rights, Germany takes an intermediate position. If the ECtHR resolves the tension in favour of one of the extreme positions, it runs the risk that the affected state will be forbidden by its own constitution to comply with the ruling.

Cooperation between national and international courts in a non-hierarchical system is further promoted by the differing contexts in which these courts operate. National courts are typically embedded in a thicker matrix of participation and accountability than are international courts. Although courts enjoy independence by virtue of their function, this does not remove them from the cultural context within which national law is created and applied, and which informs judges' perceptions of their duties and their craft. Additionally, national judges operate in a considerably thicker deliberative context—both societal and legal—which influences their decision-making and keeps them in touch with the society for which they administer justice. International courts are not similarly embedded in a context that reinforces their obligation to law. As a result, international judges have greater freedom than do national judges, and they must temper that freedom with increased sensitivity to national characteristics.

H. The Role of the National Constitution in the Implementation of EU Law

Finally, national constitutions remain significant when the European legislature exercises its transferred powers in such a way that European

[45] See BVerfGE 101, 36 (1999)—Per contra EGMR, judgment of 24.6.2004, v. Hannover v. Deutschland, complaint no. 59320/00, ECHR 2004-VI, and EuGRZ 2004, p. 404; BVerfGE 120, 180 (2008).

norms do not apply directly in the Member States, but must be transposed or completed by national legislatures. This is the case with framework decisions and directives, which give national legislatures decision-making freedom, or at the very least room to manoeuvre. National legislatures can employ this discretion as they see fit, but they may not violate their national constitutions. Their obligation to the national constitution begins where their obligation to European law ends. National institutions cannot shirk their constitutional obligations under the pretext of implementing European law.

National legislatures enjoy their greatest freedom within the context of framework decisions under § 34 EU.[46] Such framework decisions are part of the EU's third pillar, police and judicial cooperation. Accordingly, they are framed outside of the supranational decision-making structures and constitute international rather than European law—which means that they can be enacted only unanimously. The European Parliament has no right to assist in making framework decisions—only a right to be heard. As acts of international law, framework decisions depend on transposition into national law and are binding only in terms of their ultimate objectives. The choice of format and means belongs to the Member States. National parliaments have the opportunity to reject framework decisions. If they adopt them, they must pass a law that fulfils the objectives of European Law while adhering to the national constitution.

National legislatures enjoy less freedom when implementing European directives. Directives are an instrument of European policy and are governed by the rules of European rather than international law. They do not require transposition into national law. National parliaments are bound by their aims, but free to choose the means of implementation. Insofar as European law affords discretion, however, national legislatures are once again bound by their national constitutions. The decisive factors are the federal allocation of powers, the separation of powers between the legislature and the executive,

[46] See Christoph Schönberger, 'Der Rahmenbeschluss' (2007) 67 *Zeitschrift für ausländisches öffentliches Recht und Völkerrecht* 1107 ss.

and national fundamental rights. These factors can be ignored only insofar as European directives allow the Member States no leeway. In such cases, the national legislature lacks room for discretion in which national fundamental rights could apply.

The German Constitutional Court can review whether national legislative bodies have complied with their constitutional obligations. In the context of the framework decisions, the Court conducted such review in response to a constitutional complaint against the law implementing the European arrest warrant.[47] In that case, the Court concluded that the legislature could not deviate unconditionally from the ban on extraditing German citizens to other EU countries, but must observe the qualified reservation of Article 16(2) GG as well as the principle of proportionality. As a law restricting fundamental rights, the implementation law had to comply with all constitutional requirements and structure the framework decision's fundamental-rights limitation as narrowly as possible. Because the Bundestag in enacting the law was apparently unaware of its own room for manoeuvre, a majority of the justices quashed the law in its entirety, and sent the legislature back to the drawing board.

It has long been acknowledged that laws implementing directives are amenable to judicial review. But the German Constitutional Court has now expanded its *Solange II* holding to clarify that, so long as fundamental rights protection at the European level remains essentially comparable to that provided in the Basic Law, judicial review is not available for directives that give the Member States no leeway in their domestic implementation.[48] Previously, this was recognized only for regulations. But the exception does not apply only to directives that, like regulations, apply directly in the Member States. Whether an implementing law may be reviewed by the Constitutional Court depends solely on whether or not the directive grants discretion to the national legislature.

Insofar as directives of European law grant discretion to the national legislature, the national courts and administrative agencies that apply

[47] BVerfGE 113, 273 (2005).

[48] BVerfGE 118, 79 (95 ff.) (2007).

the implementing law are also bound by fundamental rights. But because the ECJ has ruled that national implementing laws cannot be divorced from the directives—even those not directly applicable—on which they are based, national institutions are limited in this regard. This requirement shapes interpretation, which must conform with the directive.[49] The national law must be interpreted in light of the text and purpose of the directive. The ECJ based this holding on Article 10 EC. The holding, however, also limits review by national constitutional courts. If an interpretation that complies with the directive clashes with an interpretation friendly to fundamental rights, the former prevails, provided that the diminished national rights protection is compensated by rights protection under European law.

None of this would change if the European Charter of Fundamental Rights were to enter into force. True, European fundamental rights do not apply only to EU institutions, but extend as well to all national institutions insofar as they apply European law. But the Charter of Fundamental Rights does not overlap with national fundamental rights in the same way that the Basic Law's fundamental rights, under Article 142 GG, overlap with the fundamental rights enshrined in the constitutions of the German states (*Länder*). When the German state implements European law, it is bound by EU rights. When it concretizes European law, it is bound by national rights. As a result of this rule, state institutions, courts, and administrative agencies must observe different fundamental rights standards, depending on whether they are enforcing European or national law. But no gap may emerge in the protection of fundamental rights.

I. National Constitutions in the Balance

The role retained by national constitutions in the aftermath of the foregoing developments is shaped by the fact that they remain the

[49] *Von Colson v. Land Nordrhein-Westfalen* (1984) Case 14/83.

constitutions of *states*, and as such can be no more relevant within a united Europe than states themselves are. To the degree that nation-states transfer or lose powers to European institutions, the significance of national constitutions declines. In a united Europe, national constitutions are reduced to regulating that portion of public power which remains state power. Even to this extent, however, they can no longer completely fulfil their aspirations of comprehensive regulation. Because the EU largely depends on the Member States' courts and agencies to achieve its objectives, these institutions—though not quite EU institutions—nevertheless act as enforcement institutions of European law.[50] When acting in this capacity, national institutions must—for the sake of a uniform application of European law in all the Member States—surrender their allegiance to their national constitutions.

It would be wrong, however, to look only at the debit side of the balance. Through the communalization of powers formerly exercised only at the national level, the EU's Member States gain influence at the European level and can thereby affect the other Member States. In exerting such influence, the Member States are bound by their national constitutions, the influence of which thus transcends national boundaries. At that point, however, they must confront the similar pretensions of other constitutions, and the influence of any individual constitution is inevitably limited. In areas in which European decisions require the unanimous consent of all Member States, violations of national constitutions can be averted. In the extreme case, no European rule will be adopted. But in these same areas, national constitutional provisions requiring actions rather than omissions can rarely be fulfilled.

The EU's Member States still enjoy their greatest freedom when determining their own fundamental order. The constituent power is subject to no external constraints. It has no legal limits, a fact that

[50] On this view, see J. Temple Lang, 'The Duties of National Courts under Community Constitutional Law' (1997) 3 *European Law Review* 3; Pernice, 'Multilevel Constitutionalism', above n. 5, pp. 710, 718, 724.

distinguishes the EU from a federal state. Certain uses of this freedom, however, would cause a rupture with the Union and lead to a state's withdrawal or expulsion from the EU.[51] If a state wishes to remain in the EU, its constitution can neither annul the preconditions for EU membership nor reverse the state's fundamental relationship with the Union. The former would ensue, for instance, if a Member State were to eliminate democracy or surrender essential elements of the rule of law—though of course variants of democracy and the rule of law are still possible. The latter would ensue if a Member State's constitution were to stipulate (mirroring Article 31 GG) that: 'National law shall take precedence over European law.'

In other respects, too, this freedom is no longer unqualified. Because the Member States' internal organization, as well as the enforcement and implementation of European law, remain largely within the province of national agencies and courts, the structure and jurisdiction of these institutions cannot be a matter of indifference to the EU. The EU imposes requirements on states' internal and national legal orders that are preconditions for the uniform application of European law. The ECJ's *Simmenthal* decision,[52] which dealt with the Italian Constitutional Court's monopoly on annulling laws, is one example of this. In another example, the UK was required to provide interim relief against the Crown in its legal system.[53] Many Member States have had to alter their systems of government liability to ensure the effectiveness of European law.[54] If the relevant national regulations are found in a Member State's constitution, rather than its statute books, the pressure to adapt will be correspondingly great.

With regard to the transfer of powers to the EU, national constitutions can only prescribe the conditions under which, and the degree to which, the state may participate in the supranational community. But the EU's exercise of transferred sovereign rights is no longer

[51] These two positions are not sufficiently differentiated in Pernice, 'Multilevel Constitutionalism', above n. 5, p. 710.

[52] *Amministrazione delle Finanze v. S.p.A. Simmenthal*, above n. 21.

[53] *R v. Secretary of State for Transport, ex parte Factortame Ltd.* (1990) Case 213/89.

[54] *Francovich u. Bonifaci v. Italian Republic* (1991) Case 6/90 and C-9/90.

subject to the constraints of national constitutions. Such constraint would entail nothing less than uneven validity and application across Member States. To prevent this, the ECJ has, in a long line of decisions, continually relegated the influence of national constitutions to their own sphere of application. Although some of the ECJ's decisions have provoked resistance to the clandestine expansion of the EU's powers, on the whole this strand of its jurisprudence offered few opportunities for concentrated efforts to reverse it by legislation. The Court's jurisprudence has the characteristics typical of courts: it has been episodic, gradual, and seemingly apolitical. Its full impact has become apparent only in retrospect. It is this judge-driven development that is commonly referred to as the 'constitutionalization' of the treaties.[55]

National constitutional courts resist only the most extreme consequences of the ECJ's efforts to fully subordinate national constitutional law to European law. But even without this final step, national constitutions can no longer fulfil the expectations to which they originally gave rise. This is true of both their ordering and their legitimating functions. With respect to the ordering function, they can no longer comprehensively regulate state power within their territorial jurisdiction. In spite of this aspiration, there are extra-constitutional bearers of sovereign power and extra-constitutional means of exercising power within the states they constitute. National constitutions regulate the power exercised within their nation-states only in part. Similar phenomena within those states reinforce this trend.[56]

With respect to the legitimating function, national constitutions can no longer guarantee that all power exercised within their territorial jurisdiction derives its legitimacy from the people. True, the powers ceded to the EU do not lack a foundation of legitimacy. That foundation is formed by the treaties that created the Community and that govern it by law. But this law does not originate in the peoples of

[55] See Joseph H.H. Weiler, *The Constitution of Europe* (Cambridge: Cambridge University Press, 1999), p. 19.

[56] See Grimm, *Constitutionalism* (above n. 1), p. 233 ss., 255 ss.

the states that are subject to its rule. The Community's power stems instead from the states themselves. The fact that the states are themselves democratic does not provide a democratic legitimation for this legal foundation in the manner that a constitution would require. It also does not guarantee that a given people are subject only to those acts of rule to which their own state has consented in a democratic process. It guarantees to each Member State the right to participate in the EU's legislative processes, but it forges no link with the people themselves.[57]

J. A European Constitution as Compensation?

The significance that the national constitutions gain through the greater reach of national power in a united Europe does not offset the significance that they lose domestically. The gain in significance is relativized by the need for many states, each bound by its own constitution, to work together, while the loss of significance at home is untrammelled. This does not mean, of course, that the loss in statehood that nation-states incur through the communalization of numerous policy areas is more severe than attendant gains in their power to solve problems and preserve peace. The EU is without doubt one of the greatest and most promising innovations in the realm of political institutions. But that does not dispose of the question whether national constitutions' loss of significance can be compensated on the European level.

For a long time, hopes centred on a European constitution. Following the failure of the constitutional treaty in France and the

[57] These differences are elided in Pernice ('Multilevel Constitutionalism', above n. 5) for whom it is sufficient that in the origins of European integration there was an act of will and therefore one can assert that the decisions of the Community institution are a result of the will of the people. In this way, there can from the outset be no legitimation problem. See Helge Rossen-Stadtfeld, 'Demokratische Staatlichkeit in Europa: ein verblassendes Bild' (2005) 53 *Jahrbuch des öffentlichen Rechts* NF 45.

Netherlands, those hopes have been buried for the time being. But even before the bid for a European constitution, the juridification of the EU's public power was not lacking. This function, which constitutions fulfil at the state level, was performed at the European level by the treaties. To that extent, no constitution was needed. What separates the treaties from a constitution in the full sense of that term is the absence of any connection to the people subject to the treaties' rule.[58] It is the Member States, and not the Union's citizens, who are the source of the EU's public power. The Member States control the EU's legal foundation, while the Union's citizens have nothing to do with it, either as the active agents or as the attributive subjects of European public power. The treaties do not fulfil the legitimating function that is performed in nation-states by the people's constituent power.

This could, of course, be changed. The EU is not unlike the central government of a federal state in terms of its organizational complexity and the fullness of its powers. Unlike a medieval polity, it is undoubtedly 'capable of constitutionalization'.[59] In order to transform the treaties, which currently form the EU's legal foundation, into a constitution, the Member States would have to surrender to the EU their power to control the Union's legal foundation. Following such a surrender, the Member States would no longer be 'Masters of the Treaties.' Instead, the EU could determine its own legal foundation, however pronounced the role of the Member States within the EU's constituent body. If the right of self-determination were to be linked to the Union's citizens as the source of European public power, the treaties would acquire the one feature whose absence currently separates them from constitutions.

But the question remains whether such a European constitution could replicate the achievements of national constitutions—and

[58] See Dieter Grimm, 'Europas Verfassung' in Gunnar Folke Schuppert, Ingolf Pernice, and Ulrich Haltern (eds), *Europawissenschaft* (Baden-Baden: Nomos, 2005), p. 177.

[59] See Grimm, *Constitutionalism* (above n. 1), pp. 4, 45; Dieter Grimm, *Die Zukunft der Verfassung II* (Berlin: Suhrkamp, 2012), p. 227.

thus compensate for their loss of significance—at a higher level. This would depend, first and foremost, on the European constitution's capacity to supply the resources of solidarity and legitimacy that are still at the disposal of nation-states.[60] The preconditions for this, however, are not favourable.[61] Even if one candidly acknowledges the Member States' own democratic deficiencies, the Member States still enjoy comparatively thick structures of civil society, effective means of mediating between states' citizens and their institutions, and a broad array of media that maintain the flow of communication between state and society, and that imbue with life the matrix of legitimacy and accountability envisioned by the constitution. All of this makes it possible to speak, on the whole, of a substantive, and not merely a formal democracy.

In the EU, by contrast, these societal preconditions for a functioning democracy are only weakly developed or are lacking entirely. Political communication as a fundamental condition of democracy is still shaped largely by national interests and habits, and it ends at national borders. The economic conditions for a Europeanized media with a broad reach and a European perspective are unlikely to emerge any time soon. Even if one assumes that Europeanized political parties would emerge swiftly in the aftermath of European statehood, the structures of communication between those in power and their popular base would remain much looser than within the Member States. So too, the willingness to support social programmes out of a feeling of national solidarity, which can still be presumed within a nation-state, will be difficult to foster in an ever-expanding Union.

And yet a self-supporting Union would require much more of all of these things than a Union supported by the Member States—and without any hope of being able to redirect towards itself the states'

[60] See ch. 6 of this volume. Ulrich Haltern, 'Europa—Verfassung—Identität', in Christian Calliess (ed), *Verfassungswandel im europäischen Staaten- und Verfassungsverbund* (Tübingen: Mohr Siebeck, 2007), p. 21.

[61] See Fritz Scharpf, 'Reflections on Multilevel Legitimacy' *MPIfG Working Paper* 07/3.

resources of solidarity and legitimacy. To expect a constitution to supply the lack is to overestimate the power of constitutions. Because the problem's roots are societal, they cannot be resolved through institutional reforms that emulate national models. Indeed, one should worry that an EU liberated from its reliance on the Member States would merely sever itself from the legitimacy that flows from those states, but without being able to replace that flow with a comparable level of internal legitimacy. The result would be a Union more remote from its citizens than ever. To prevent that, the Member States' basic responsibility for the EU should be strengthened rather than reduced. A full-fledged European constitution would have the opposite result.

All of this has consequences for the relationship between national constitutional law and European law.[62] Although national constitutions will never recover their former significance, it is in Europe's self-interest to prevent their sinking to the status of state constitutions in a federal system. In a confederation of states like the EU, all national constitutions are only partial constitutions, and can fulfil their aspirations of comprehensive regulation only in connection with the constitution-like legal foundation of the EU. The two are interdependent. In this sense, it may be appropriate to speak of a 'constitutional compact' (*Verfassungsverbund*).[63] But if the same level of legitimacy cannot be achieved for both sides of this compact—if national constitutions continue to possess greater reserves of legitimacy—then it becomes detrimental to consider the relationship only from the perspective of supremacy.[64] Such a myopic perspective would erode unnecessarily—and beyond the inevitable degree—the achievements of constitutionalism.

[62] See Ingolf Pernice, Peter M. Huber, Gertrude Lübbe-Wolff, and Christoph Grabenwarter, 'Europäisches und nationales Verfassungsrecht' (2001) 60 *Veröffentlichungen der Vereinigung der deutschen Staatsrechtsleher*, pp. 148–415.

[63] 'Verfassungsverbund', see Pernice et al. ibid.; Matthias Jestaedt, 'Der europäische Verfassungsverbund' in Calliess, above n. 60, p. 93.

[64] Christian Joerges, 'Rethinking European Law's Supremacy' (2005) EUI Working Papers, Law, p. 17.

9

The Role of National Parliaments in the European Union

A. General Trends of De-Parliamentarization

The process of European integration leads to a loss of significance for national parliaments and, through them, legislative authority. The beneficiary of this loss of significance is not the European Parliament. Rather, the trend benefits national governments and, through them, executive authority. The increase in powers that the European Parliament requires and receives does not suffice to offset this loss of significance. At the European level, too, Parliament remains weak, even in comparison with national parliaments. One can imagine a better array of powers for the European Parliament, but it would not cure the EU's legitimacy deficit.

This, in compressed form, is the argument of this chapter. Before exploring the argument in greater detail, however, I wish to note that parliaments' loss of significance is not a Europe-specific phenomenon. One can discern, rather, a general trend towards de-parliamentarization. There are structural reasons for this, which dampen hopes that the tendency can be limited or perhaps even reversed. The structural reasons are the result of changed conditions in national politics. The changes are of two kinds. Within states, the changes are triggered by the transition from a liberal state that preserves order to a social state that shapes order. Externally, the changes are products of the transformation of autonomous nation-states into Member States of international organizations, and of the transfer to such international organizations of public authority. Because the European Union (EU) is a highly integrated international organization, the erosion of parliamentary authority is more pronounced here than it is elsewhere.

At the international level, the mechanism of deliberation is replaced by one of negotiation. Parliaments, however, cannot negotiate. It is always the governments that do the negotiating. Parliaments come into the picture, if at all, only to ratify the results of a negotiation. But ratification does not allow as much influence as does legislation. In a legislative proceeding, the parliament determines the content of the decision, even when the proposal comes from the government. This is no mere theoretical possibility, but a practical reality. Rarely does a government proposal become law without alteration. In the case of ratification, by contrast, the content of the decision is fixed. Parliament can only accept or reject it. To reject it, however, would be to disavow the government, which is supported by the parliamentary majority. As a result, the political costs of a 'No' vote are usually too high. The European treaties have failed only where there has been a referendum.

The shift in emphasis from deliberation to negotiation does not, however, depend on external factors alone. It is internally driven as well. The explanation lies with a change in the function of the state that began as early as the late nineteenth century and, despite some minor adjustments, has never been reversed. The state is no longer the mere guarantor of a societal order that already exists and is presumed to be just. Rather, the state develops and revises this order constantly, in an effort to meet shifting challenges and new claims of fairness. Today, the state bears total responsibility for society's preservation and prosperity. Most importantly, the state furthers economic growth and environmental protection, and ensures against risks of every kind.

Many of these functions are no longer fulfilled through the specifically governmental means of command and coercion. In part, such means are factually impossible; in part, they are legally forbidden; in part, they are inopportune. For the fulfilment of its functions, then, the state relies on cooperation with private actors—often the very actors who cause the problems that the state is called upon to resolve. Private actors thus assume a veto position, one that facilitates the transition towards a model of negotiation. If implementing the results of the negotiation require a statute, there is no way to circumvent Parliament. But in that case, Parliament finds itself in a situation similar to the one it faces when ratifying international treaties: it cannot influence the law's content, it can only accept or reject it. If the negotiation leads to an accord by which the government agrees to forgo regulation and the private troublemakers promise to behave themselves, Parliament plays no role at all. With these observations, I turn from the general status of parliamentarism to the particular question of the role of national parliaments in the EU.

B. The Situation in Europe

In describing the European situation, one must distinguish three separate phases:

- The transfer of sovereign rights from the Member States to the EU.
- The exercise of those transferred rights by the EU.
- The implementation of European decisions by the Member States.

In each of these phases, the national parliaments have different functions.

1. *The transfer of sovereign rights to the EU*

The transfer of states' sovereign rights is effected through treaties among the Member States. The content of the treaties constitutes primary European law. As a general rule, the sovereign rights transferred are those that in a state would belong to Parliament—i.e. legislative powers (but also, through the creation of the monetary union, budgetary powers), in sum, the core powers of parliament. Other parliamentary powers, by contrast, such as forming and overseeing the government, are unaffected by the transfer of sovereign rights.

The transfer of sovereign rights requires the unanimous approval of all Member States. The agreement is reached among the heads of government and state. The content is determined by the executives. The result of the negotiations, however, becomes law only after ratification in all Member States according to the provisions of their constitutions. In some Member States, this requires a referendum; in others, a prior constitutional amendment; in most, an approval law passed by Parliament. In the latter case, Parliament faces another Yes/No decision. The content of the Member States' international treaties cannot be altered in the national parliamentary process. Even so, Parliament plays a decisive role. It acts as a filter for the surrender of sovereign rights.

Some national constitutions establish conditions for such transfers. This is particularly true of the German Basic Law. Under Article 23(1) GG, sovereign powers may be transferred only if the EU is bound by principles of democracy, federalism, social justice, and the rule of law, together with the principle of subsidiarity, and only if it provides a level of fundamental rights protection comparable to that afforded by the Basic Law. Because every transfer of powers alters the Basic Law without changing its text, the same rules that apply to constitutional amendments also apply to the ratification of European treaties. They require a two-thirds parliamentary majority and may not run afoul of Article 79(3) GG.

The consequence, of course, is that not everything written in the Basic Law still applies. If one wishes to understand the current constitutional situation in an EU Member State, one cannot rely solely on the text of the national constitution, but must consider the European treaties as well. Thus, for example, Article 73 GG gives the federal power exclusive jurisdiction over monetary matters, currency, coinage, customs, etc. In fact, however, all of these legislative powers have been transferred to the EU. The federal power retains other legislative competences only in part, such as its (ostensibly) exclusive jurisdiction over immigration.

To the conditions for the transfer of sovereign rights established in Article 23(1) GG, the German Federal Constitutional Court has added others, derived from other provisions of the Basic Law. For our purposes, the most significant of these is that the transfer of powers to the EU must not lead to an emptying of the Bundestag's functions. This limitation on transfer is derived from the right to vote under Article 38(1) GG. The Constitutional Court interprets the right to vote in a substantive, rather than a formal sense. It does not give German citizens merely the right to participate in Bundestag elections. Rather, the elected Bundestag must also possess sufficient powers of political decision to enable the implementation of popular will through political action, and to ensure that voter preferences, expressed through the election, have consequences for the political process.

With respect to the conditions for the transfer of powers, the Constitutional Court distinguishes between sovereignty and sovereign rights. The Basic Law, in Article 23(1), allows the transfer of sovereign rights, but not of sovereignty itself. The latter hurdle could not be cleared even through constitutional amendment, since in the Court's view Article 79(3) GG secures the Federal Republic's sovereignty. Consequently, so long as the Basic Law remains in force, the Federal Republic could not take part in the transformation of the EU into a European federal state (*Bundesstaat*).

In the Constitutional Court's view, the Bundestag is also responsible for ensuring that the programmes of integration is determined by the Member States. Accordingly, blank cheque authorizations are completely forbidden. Even in the case of specific authorizations, Parliament may approve only steps towards integration whose scope is foreseeable. This has consequences for the federal government's negotiations in the conference of heads of state and government. It can accept only outcomes that the Bundestag may approve. Hence, the government must exercise caution even at the negotiation phase if it does not want its handiwork to fail later on in Parliament or, ultimately, before the Constitutional Court.

The full scope of a shift in power, however, can be grasped only if one looks beyond the formal transfer of competence to consider as well the subtle erosion of parliamentary powers in the EU's Member States. Such erosion is the product, not of treaty amendments, but of treaty interpretations by the Court of Justice of the European Union (formerly the ECJ, now the CJEU). The CJEU takes as the basis of its treaty interpretation the methodological principle of the so-called *effet utile*. According to this principle, the treaties are to be construed so that the EU may exercise its powers without restriction—which means, at the same time, that national powers must be reduced as much as possible.

The CJEU has pursued this goal with missionary zeal. Through an expansive interpretation of European law, it has, to a remarkable degree, declared laws passed by national parliaments to be inapplicable. The Council, too, has played a role in replacing national parliamentary law with European executive law, and in this respect has profited from the fact that, in the EU, legislative powers are distributed not by subject matter, but according to a teleological criterion. The EU has legislative power to do all that appears necessary to establish or maintain the common market. In this way, the EU can gain a foothold even in areas in which the Member States have transferred no legislative powers at all. The beneficiaries are the four economic freedoms, which thus become (unlike in the Member States) the dominant criterion.

As interpreted by the CJEU, the European Charter of Fundamental Rights has emerged as a new instrument for narrowing national powers. According to Article 51, the Charter of Fundamental Rights binds all European institutions, but binds the Member States only when they are implementing Union law. Expanding EU powers through the Charter of Fundamental Rights is explicitly forbidden, as is (under Article 53) narrowing national fundamental rights protection. The CJEU interprets Article 51 to define the implementation of national law with some connection to Union law as the implementation of

Union law. But national and European law have become sufficiently intertwined that this is the case almost everywhere. On this view, Article 51 loses all contours.

Although, according to Article 51(2), the Charter of Fundamental Rights must not be used to justify any new powers beyond those explicitly transferred, national legislative powers are nevertheless undermined through the Court of Justice's interpretation. Data protection provides a good example. Data protection is not a specialized field; it cuts across subject matters. It must be honoured in all state activity. But because, under the CJEU's jurisprudence, national fundamental rights must already yield wherever they come in contact with Union law, data protection gives the EU access to all sorts of legislative matters that the Member States have never surrendered.

Something similar is true of the guarantee that higher standards of national fundamental-rights protection may not be frustrated through interpretation of the Charter of Fundamental Rights. The CJEU acknowledges this principle only when it does not entail limits on the economic freedoms. Economic freedom thus becomes a supreme freedom. In the case of a tri-polar relationship—when a national court must resolve (usually through balancing) a conflict between two rights-bearing parties—the CJEU, by reversing the national court's decision, diminishes the right that prevailed at the national level and augments the right that had to yield at the national level. When that happens, Article 53's promise becomes an empty one.

National parliaments are powerless against the erosion of their competences. Because the treaties have been elevated to constitutional status through the CJEU's jurisprudence, and because they therefore take precedence over both secondary Union law and all national law, the interpretation and application of the treaties constitutes quasi constitutional implementation. The political institutions of the EU—the Council and the European Parliament—have practically no possibility of corrective intervention. The German Constitutional Court assesses the situation rightly when it maintains that the only counterweight to the expansionist tendencies of the CJEU's jurisprudence comes from national constitutional courts. One of the functions of these courts is to protect national parliaments—and with them national democracies—against further debilitation.

2. *The EU's exercise of transferred powers*

Once national powers have been transferred, their exercise is no longer based on national constitutions, but rather on European law. While European primary law is promulgated by the Member States, European secondary law is enacted by the EU alone. European legislation is the product of cooperation among the Commission, which wields the right of initiative; the Council of Ministers, which determines laws' content; and the European Parliament, which possesses graduated rights of participation. The principal actor is the Council, in which the Member-State governments are represented. The only path through which national parliaments may influence the enactment of European secondary law thus runs through the national governments.

For this there are a number of possibilities, from the usual forms of government oversight to binding mandates for the government, as in Great Britain, Denmark, and Austria. In Germany, Article 23(2) GG governs Parliament's participation in matters of European integration. Specifically, the provision imposes on the federal government a duty to supply information. Parliament is given the opportunity to take a position on European legislation, which the government must bear in mind during further negotiations in the Council. Insofar as European legislation affects matters that within Germany would be governed by the states (*Länder*), the Bundesrat's opinion is to be given 'decisive' consideration. 'Consider' does not mean 'follow,' but deviations require good reasons; in the case of decisive consideration, deviations require compelling reasons.

That there is no binding mandate in Germany seems appropriate in light of the peculiarity of European legislation. By its nature, European legislation is not a matter of deliberation among different political persuasions but of negotiation among different national interests. A government's success in formulating the text of a law depends on its room for manoeuvre in negotiation. A government that cannot respond flexibly, or that must consult with its own Parliament at every step, soon becomes incapable of compromise and wields only the threat of veto. This is often an idle threat, however, insofar as Council decisions are governed by majority rule. One could say, as a general matter, that the influence of an inflexible government on a law's content sinks.

These domestic rules find support at the European level. Article 12 TEU says that 'National Parliaments contribute actively to the good functioning of the Union.' Towards this end, they must be extensively informed. Moreover, the Protocols concerning the role of national parliaments in the EU (Protocol No. 1) and concerning the application of the principles of subsidiarity and proportionality (Protocol No. 2) grant national parliaments the right to submit position statements on questions of subsidiarity, which European institutions must take into consideration. Still further, in order to make the principle of subsidiarity more effective, national parliaments are authorized under Article 5 TEU and Article 8 of Protocol No. 2 to initiate treaty infringement proceedings before the CJEU. This right is additionally strengthened at the national level: Article 23(1a) GG requires that the Bundestag file a complaint whenever a fourth of its members so direct.

3. *Implementing EU law at the national level*

The EU has various forms of lawmaking at its disposal. National parliaments' possibility of influence depends on these forms. European regulations are directly binding on national institutions. There is, in this case, no room for participation by national parliaments. Directives and decisions are binding on Member States with respect to their goals, but accord leeway with respect to the ways and means by which the goal is reached. They depend on implementation through national law, so that in this case national parliaments come into the picture again. A considerable number of national laws are triggered

C. Parliamentarization of the EU as Compensation?

In light of this summary, the question arises whether the European Parliament is capable of compensating at the European level for the erosion of legislative authority at the national level. In answering this question, one must remember, of course, that the EU is not a state, and that its political system is not a parliamentary democracy. It is the creation of sovereign states that have reserved the right to determine the EU's existence, functions, and form. This is apparent in the fact that, despite all amendments to the treaties, the Council remains the EU's central institution. The powers of the European Parliament have continually expanded; it has become more than a mere veto player; but it remains a far cry from becoming the Council's equal, to say nothing of becoming its superior.

It is frequently proposed that this be changed—that the European Parliament be vested with the powers typically possessed by national parliaments. The European Parliament would then move to the centre of the EU, and the Commission would be upgraded into a parliamentary government. Meanwhile, the Council would be demoted into a second chamber of the European Parliament. These proposals are animated by the hope that the European legitimacy deficit will be overcome when at last the destiny of Europe can be determined by the institution that is directly elected by the EU's citizens, the European Parliament, rather than the Council, which is legitimated only nationally and, from the perspective of democracy, only indirectly.

Would these expectations be fulfilled if the EU were transformed into a parliamentary system on the national model? This could be presumed only if the EU's legitimacy problems were a product of the European Parliament's insufficient powers. One can surely doubt that this is the case. Tellingly, participation in European elections has fallen to the same degree that the European Parliament's powers have increased. At the very least, this suggests that insufficient parliamentary powers are not the most important cause of lethargy and even aversion towards Europe on the part of the peoples of the Member States.

Accordingly, one must ask whether the causes of the lack of acceptance do not lie deeper. Some are to be found at the institutional level. The representativeness of the European Parliament is feeble because European elections are not truly Europeanized. This means not only that, despite the injunction of the Lisbon Treaty, there is still no European election law and that European elections are still conducted according to national election law. Rather, the political parties are also not truly Europeanized. In a campaign for the European Parliament, it is national parties that stand for election, and they solicit votes on the basis of national platforms. The election results are assessed through national lenses. Currently no fewer than 200 national parties are represented in the European Parliament.

All the same, national parties as such do not play a decisive role in the European Parliament. Instead, the major players in the European Parliament are the European factions—loose conglomerates of ideologically related parties rooted in no particular society. This gives rise to the odd situation that the parties for which one can vote play no role in the European Parliament, while the parties that do play a role there do not stand for election. The flow of legitimacy from the Union's citizens to their representative institution is diverted. The appointment of leading candidates in the last election did nothing to alter this incongruity.

These institutionally rooted problems could be solved if one were prepared to Europeanize election law and the party system. But one cannot thus hope to solve all the EU's acceptance problems. Parliaments can only fulfil their function as mediators between society and political institutions if they are rooted in the society they represent, and if they are integrated within an ongoing public discourse in which they act as both communicators and auditors. This requirement, however, is not fulfilled when national media simply report on European issues from a national perspective. There would need instead to be Europeanized media, the preconditions for which, however—because of language differences and differing communications practices—are still lacking.

The other mediating institutions that provide a broad structural basis for democratic politics in nation-states are also weakly developed in the EU. As a result, European democracy remains correspondingly weak. Unlike election law or the law of political parties, however, this question is largely resistant to institutional reform and admits of no quick fixes. As a consequence, the values that parliaments promote—transparency, discussion, oversight—are underdeveloped in the EU. Hence the European Parliament is even more vulnerable than national parliaments to the general trends of de-parliamentarization described earlier. The EU has no adequate resources for an internal legitimation. For a long time yet it will depend on the legitimacy that flows to it from the Member States. Full parliamentarization would sever that flow, and is not, therefore, in the democratic interest.

10

The Role of National Constitutional Courts in European Democracy

A. National Constitutional Courts

The constitutional courts of the European Union's (EU) Member States are the guardians of national constitutions. These constitutions, in turn, are addressed to the institutions of national governments. The EU's institutions are not subject to them. If national constitutional courts play a role in European democracy, it is only through their interaction with national institutions. Insofar as national constitutions contain rules governing their states' relationships with the EU, national constitutional courts can enforce these rules against national institutions (provided that national law grants them the relevant jurisdiction). This, of course, can have consequences for EU law, and perhaps for European democracy as well.

Many national constitutions contain provisions dealing with their countries' membership in the EU. The constitutions of France and Austria are particularly detailed in this regard. Others are limited to provisions dealing more generally with international relationships—provisions that usually apply to the EU as well. Most of these provisions deal with the formation of a national will with respect to the European laws in whose creation the Member State takes part. Statements about European democracy, by contrast, are rare. In this

The Constitution of European Democracy. First Edition. Dieter Grimm. © Dieter Grimm 2017. Published by Oxford University Press.

respect Germany's Basic Law, which contains in Article 23(1) a catalogue of principles that must be implemented in the EU if Germany is to participate in European integration, remains an exception.

The requirements that national constitutional courts impose on national institutions (insofar as these institutions help make or enforce European decisions) can have consequences at three different levels: first, the treaty level—i.e. transferring national powers to the EU and regulating how these powers are exercised; second, at the level of the EU's exercise of these powers, so far as national institutions are involved; and third—because the EU lacks its own enforcement agencies and must hence rely on Member-State cooperation—at the level of implementing European law within national legal systems.

1. *The treaty level*

A national constitutional court's sphere of influence is defined by national constitutional law. Insofar as a national constitution regulates how a country accedes to or remains within the EU, or establishes conditions for transferring sovereign rights to international organizations in general or to the EU in particular, the national constitution serves as a filter for the creation of European primary law.[1] This can happen to varying degrees. In every case, national constitutions provide a filter in a procedural sense. They prescribe which institutions take part in the negotiation and ratification of European treaties, and what procedural rules those institutions must follow. Substantive legal requirements are less common.

In Germany, however, Article 23(1) GG (added in 1990) establishes a series of substantive principles that the EU must accept and uphold as a condition of German participation in European integration. These principles include the supreme ordering principles of the Federal Republic set forth in Articles 20 and 28 GG and declared unamendable in Article 79(3). One of these principles is democracy.

[1] Cf. ch. 8 of this volume.

Furthermore, there must be a level of fundamental rights protection at the European level comparable to that provided within Germany. This requirement is also rooted in Article 79(3) GG by way of Article 1(1). Finally, the EU must observe the principle of subsidiarity. Article 23(1) explicitly invokes Article 79 by decreeing that treaty amendments or other regulations that alter or expand the content of the Basic Law are subject to Article 79(2)-(3) GG.

There are limits, then, to enabling further integration even via constitutional amendment. Under Article 79(3) GG, the Basic Law's core identity must not be sacrificed to European unification. The Federal Constitutional Court maintains that the German people have never authorized their representatives and institutions to make such a sacrifice. The Court thus sees in any violation of Article 79(3) GG a simultaneous infringement of the people's constituent (constitution-making) authority. In particular, there is no authorization to surrender the German people's right of self-determination (in the form of Germany's sovereignty under international law) by acceding to a European federal state (*Bundesstaat*). The Basic Law not only assumes German sovereignty, it guarantees it. Accordingly, the decision to incorporate the Federal Republic within a European federal state is 'reserved exclusively to the directly expressed will of the German people'.[2]

There are no indications that the requirements of Article 23(1) GG and Article 79(3) GG are non-justiciable, or that they have been withdrawn from the Constitutional Court's jurisdiction. There is no basis in constitutional law for Jürgen Habermas's view that national courts, 'are not authorized (as the Federal Constitutional Court wrongly assumes) to police the boundaries of transferring national sovereign rights to the European level'.[3] In the same sentence, Habermas approves constitutional judicial review of the 'integrity of those national constitutional principles that are constitutive for the democratic and constitutional development of the respective member states'—suggesting

[2] BVerfGE 123, 267 (347 et *passim*; citation on page 348).

[3] Jürgen Habermas, *Zur Verfassung Europas: Ein Essay* (Berlin: Suhrkamp, 2011) p. 60.

that what he has in mind are not sovereign rights per se, but rather the list of legislative matters deemed to be of a particularly national nature in the Constitutional Court's *Lisbon* judgment.[4]

Whether this list should be understood as a limit on transferring legislative powers, however, seems questionable. The Federal Constitutional Court derives its enumeration from Article 38(1) GG, which guarantees the right to vote in a Bundestag election. In the Court's view, the right to vote is not limited to participation in an election. It also guarantees that the elected institution will possess sufficient powers to give expression to the popular will and to translate that will into political action. Accordingly, the transfer of sovereign powers must not lead to a situation in which the German Bundestag retains jurisdiction over so few matters that the right to vote becomes meaningless. In the Court's view, this danger is particularly pronounced in the areas listed. But there is no mention of a ban on transfers in these areas, nor of any particular legal consequence if the EU were to become active in one of them. On the contrary, the judgment rejects the proposition 'that a certain quantity (definable ex ante) or a certain kind of sovereign rights must remain in the hands of the [nation] state'.[5]

The task of review that the Constitutional Court has set for itself clearly strains the limits of judicial capacity. In such cases as the surrender of constituent authority or the *Kompetenz–Kompetenz* (i.e. the power to define one's own jurisdiction), there might be clear criteria by which to identify the transition to a federal state. But this is not true of other limitations. For instance, the Court derives a ban on the erosion of parliamentary powers from Article 38(1) GG, but it can apply that ban only through a sort of weighted balance, as of the time of decision, between the powers retained by the states and those surrendered to the EU. Assessing the requirements of European democracy drawn from Article 23(1) GG is no easier. Here, too, the required degree of democracy cannot be determined generally and in the abstract. It depends, rather, as the Court itself observes, 'on the

[4] BVerfGE 123, 267 (358 s.).

[5] Ibid., (357).

scope of the sovereign rights transferred and on the degree of autonomy in European decision-making'.[6]

2. *The level of exercising EU powers*

In deciding which powers to transfer to the EU, the Member States are not subject to European requirements, but only to the provisions of their national constitutions. In this regard, no Member State must bow before a majority of the other states. Nor is there such a thing as a necessary consequence. The transfer of powers in one area creates no duty to transfer others. Once a power has been transferred to the European level, however, its exercise by European institutions is governed, not by national constitutions, but by the European treaties. This does not mean, however, that national constitutions are entirely out of the picture. That this is so has to do with the regulation of European legislation.

The promulgation of European secondary law is divided among three institutions: The Commission has the right of initiative, the Council adopts laws, and the European Parliament enjoys various rights of participation. Primary law confers the central role, then, on the Council, an institution composed of representatives of Member-State governments. The Council is not, however, a conference of states but an institution of the Union. Consequently, the legal validity of its actions is determined by Union law. This must be distinguished, however, from the ways in which national governments form their views of Council decisions. As national governments, they are bound by national constitutional law. What this means on the ground, however, cannot be determined independent of the circumstances under which the Council legislates.

Legislation in the Council is not, as in national parliaments, the product of deliberation among different political orientations, but of negotiations among different national interests. This requires that

[6] Ibid., (364).

government representatives have room to manoeuvre, and that they be willing to compromise. A fully fledged constitutional mandate would hinder this, and might actually damage more than benefit the constitution. As a result, the constitutional mandate of the government representatives can only be a graduated mandate. It is stronger where Union law requires unanimity than where it requires only a majority. In no case, however, may the German representatives approve a European law that would be incompatible with Article 23(1) GG. The Federal Constitutional Court can review whether the representatives have complied with these requirements.

3. *The level of implementing law*

It is one of the peculiarities of the EU that the implementation of European law lies primarily in the hands of the Member States—their governments, agencies, and courts. The resulting danger of a non-unitary application of law is not averted by the supremacy of European law over national law. Such supremacy was neither agreed upon nor tacitly assumed in the Treaties of Rome. Rather, the ECJ derived supremacy—over the opposition of the Member States—from the objective of communalization. This objective could not have been achieved in any other way.[7] At its core, supremacy is no longer controversial. In 1997, it was confirmed by the Protocol on the Treaty of Amsterdam. What remains disputed, however, is whether supremacy applies unconditionally or has limits, and who, in disputes about supremacy, has the last word.

Of course, no one disputes that the EU does not possess, as nation-states do, a potentially universal jurisdiction. The EU depends, rather, on the principle of conferral. In this regard, there is no presumption of jurisdiction in favour of the EU. Every EU decision that has consequences for the Member States requires an explicit basis of power. Where such a foundation is lacking, the EU acts *ultra vires*, and its

[7] *Costa v. ENEL*, Case 6/64 (1964).

action is illegal. The only disputed question is who, in case of conflict, finally decides whether a European legal act is supported by Member-State authorization. The ECJ claims this right for itself—but so do several national constitutional courts, including the German Constitutional Court.

In this dispute, the ECJ can invoke the power, conferred by the treaties, to interpret the treaties. The German Constitutional Court can enter the fray because Union law applies in Germany only on the basis of a national order to apply the law. The Court derives from this fact a right to review whether Germany, in its ratification law, issued such an order. To answer the jurisdictional question, both courts must interpret the treaties. One cannot rule out the possibility that the two interpretations will produce disparate results, and that it will not always be clear which interpretation is right and which is wrong. Contradictory judgments on the same issue are at least plausible, even if it has not happened yet.

Should such a conflict arise, there is no legal solution for it. This is so because in the EU, by contrast to federal states, there is no established hierarchy in the relationship between the EU and the Member States. Some potential solutions have nevertheless been proposed. One proposal is to create a specialized court, equally staffed by members of the ECJ and the national high courts, that would mediate conflicts. Another is to allow the Council (on the model of the Canadian override clause) to review ECJ decisions regarding jurisdictional conflicts and, under certain conditions, to set them aside.[8] Both of these proposals, however, would require a unanimous treaty amendment.

[8] Compare, on the one hand, Joseph H.H. Weiler, *The Constitution of Europe: 'Do the New Clothes Have an Emperor?' and Other Essays on European Integration* (Cambridge: Cambridge University Press, 1999), p. 322, as well as Roman Herzog and Lüder Gerken, 'Stoppt den Europäischen Gerichtshof', *Frankfurter Allgemeine Zeitung* (8 September 2008), p. 8; on the other hand, Fritz Scharpf, 'Legitimacy in the Multi-Level European Polity' (2009) 1 *European Political Science Review* 173, 198 *et passim*. See also the discussion in Juliane Kokott, 'Der EuGH—eine neoliberale Institution?' in Christine Hohmann-Dennhardt, Peter Masuch, and Mark Villiger (eds), *Grundrechte und Solidarität: Durchsetzung und Verfahren—Festschrift für Renate Jaeger* (Kehl: Norbert P. Engel, 2011), pp. 115, 132 *et passim*. The override clause reads: 'Parliament or the legislature of a province may expressly declare in an Act of Parliament or of the legislature, as the case may be, that the Act or a provision thereof shall operate

The jurisdictional problem is not, rightly regarded, a question about the limits of supremacy. After all, only Union laws that are in fact lawful enjoy supremacy. The conflict is simply about who has the power to decide questions of lawfulness. This is different from the right claimed by the German Constitutional Court to deny applicability in Germany to European laws that impair the Federal Republic's constitutional identity.[9] Some other national constitutional courts take the same position. In contrast to *ultra vires* review, identity review is not linked to whether European acts exceed the powers of European institutions. The identity problem arises only if, on limitation-of-powers grounds, the European act is unobjectionable.

As a matter of constitutional law, the power of identity review is rooted in the fact that the Basic Law does not authorize German institutions to surrender the state's identity. Article 79(3) GG forbids their doing so. There can be no rivalry between the courts on this point: that questions about the Basic Law's identity can be decided only at the national level is undisputed. What is unclear is whether the identity proviso has a further foundation in European law. Relevant in this regard is Article 4(2) TEU, which declares that the Union honours the national identity of the Member States, as expressed 'in their fundamental structures, political and constitutional'. If the treaties themselves limited the supremacy of Union law, the potential for conflict would vanish. The ECJ would have to retract its unqualified assertion of Union law's supremacy.[10]

The plausibility of a jurisdictional conflict has considerably diminished in light of the German Constitutional Court's *Honeywell* decision.[11]

notwithstanding a provision included in section 2 or sections 7 to 15 of this Charter.' Canadian Charter of Rights and Freedoms (1982), Section 33.1.

[9] Cf. BVerfGE 37, 211 (279 s.); 73, 339 (375 s.); 89, 155 (184); 123 (343 ss., 353 ss.).

[10] Cf. Franz C. Mayer, 'Verfassungsgerichtsbarkeit', in Armin von Bogdandy and Jürgen Bast (eds), *Europäisches Verfassungsrecht: Theoretische und dogmatische Grundsätze* (Munich: C.H. Beck, 2nd edn, 2009), p. 589.

[11] BVerfGE 126, 286 (2010). On this decision, see Dieter Grimm, 'Von Lissabon zu Mangold', in Dieter Grimm, *Die Zukunft der Verfassung II: Auswirkungen von Europäisierung und Globalisierung* (Berlin: Suhrkamp, 2012), p. 178.

But it could revive in the identity realm, even if one excludes, for the foreseeable future, the possibility of a transition to a European federal state. Fundamental rights pose a more immediate possibility of conflict. This might sound surprising in light of the Constitutional Court's 1986 *Solange II* judgment. In that case, the Court declared that the existing state of European fundamental-rights protection was satisfactory; ever since, the Court's power of review has lain dormant, though the power itself lives on.[12] In the meantime, however, a gap has arisen between national courts' interpretation of national fundamental rights and the ECJ's interpretation of the economic freedoms enshrined in Article 26(2) TEU. This gap could fuel the identity question.[13]

B. European Democracy

1. *In the beginning: Monistic legitimation*

The European Community came into being as the purpose-driven creation of nation-states. Their purpose was to create a unified economic market. This creation was coupled with the hope that interconnected economic interests would hinder future wars between European nation-states that had devastated the continent twice in the twentieth century. To achieve this objective, the states transferred portions of their public authority to the Community and furnished the Community with institutions that perceived the Community's interest as independent of the states. This gave rise to a need for democratic legitimacy at the European level—a need that grew with every advancing step towards integration. The institution as a whole needed legitimacy, as did its output—binding decisions that were no

[12] BVerfGE 73, 339 (378 ff., 387).

[13] Cf. Fritz Scharpf, 'Das Bundesverfassungsgericht als Hüter demokratischer Selbstgestaltungsfähigkeit', in Michael Stolleis (ed), *Herzkammern der Republik* (Munich: C.H. Beck, 2011), p. 131.

longer the products of democratically organized national processes, but of supranational processes.

One should distinguish between these two aspects. To say that a supranational polity with sovereign powers is democratically legitimate is not to say that the sovereign acts that flow from that polity also satisfy democratic requirements. That depends, rather, on the design of the polity's organizations and procedures. As an institution, the EU's democratic legitimacy stems from the fact that the states that founded it in 1957, and those that joined it later on, are themselves democratic, and that the decisions to found or join it took place through democratic procedures and in accordance with national constitutions. It was in accordance with the democratic will of the Member States to create a European public authority that narrowed national public authority.

For the exercise of its public authority as well, the European Community originally relied solely on the democratic legitimacy conferred on European acts by the Member States. Until 1986, European secondary law entered into force only through unanimous decisions of the Council. Under these circumstances, it was impossible for a Member State to be subjected to a law that it had not approved through its national government, which was democratically elected and democratically accountable—even for its voting behaviour in the Council—back home. At the level of implementing Community law, there appeared to be no democracy problem: the implementing institutions, the Commission and the ECJ, were strictly bound by the primary law agreed upon by the states, and by the secondary law promulgated in the Council.

2. *Intervening changes*

Over time, this picture changed. The changes, however, did not affect European primary law at the *legislative level*. As before, the EU's legal foundation is determined by the Member States through international treaties. Only for the preparatory phases of treaty amendments did the Lisbon Treaty involve additional actors, whose decisions are not, however, binding on the Member States that sign the treaty. The Member States remain the driving force even in simplified amendment procedures, which are available only under the Treaty on the Functioning of the European Union's (TFEU) third part. Only in *passerelle* procedures—which involve a transition from unanimous- to qualified-majority voting in the Council, as well as from a special to an ordinary legislative procedure—is the European Council responsible, and it requires Parliament's approval while national parliaments wield a potential veto.

Things are different, however, when European secondary law is made. The Single European Act of 1987 softened the unanimity principle in the Council. The Lisbon Treaty made majority voting the rule and unanimity the exception. Consequently, the Member States have the right to participate in legislation, but not the power to block it. It is now possible for a Member State to be subject to a law that its elected representatives explicitly rejected. As a result, the legitimacy imparted by the Member States no longer sufficed. The advent of majority voting entailed the need for internal European legitimation. Accordingly, the European Parliament, which had been directly elected since 1979, was increasingly involved in promulgating European secondary law. The original monistic legitimation gave way to a dualistic legitimation.

At the *level of legal implementation*, the changes came much sooner, and they came through the jurisprudence of the ECJ. In the beginning were two fundamental decisions: *Van Gend en Loo*- (1963) on the direct effect of community law in the Member St-es and on the transformation of the four economic freedoms -om legislative guidelines into subjective individual rights, an- *-osta v. ENEL* (1964) on the supremacy of community law over -ional law, including national constitutional law, as later -ed in *Internationale Handelsgesellschaft* and, pointedly, in *S-enthal.*[14] These judicial decisions launched a development thr- -hich the

[14] ECJ, Slg. 1963, I; 1964; 1970, 1125; 1978,

European Community has assumed a special status among international organizations.

The significance of this development went unnoticed for a long time, and precisely because it came about through judicial means—i.e. in the form of judicial decisions applying existing law to a particular case. Of course, between a norm and its application there is always the judge's interpretation. General and abstract norms can never be applied to a concrete case without first bridging this gap through interpretation. The level of judicial interpretation rarely receives the attention it deserves because it is regarded merely as the implementation of decisions made long before. But interpretation involves much more than uncovering meaning already lodged in the text. Instead, interpretation helps constitute meaning. In this respect, interpretive method is an independent factor. In the choice of method lie the pre-choices of outcome.[15]

3. *The consequence: A democracy problem*

Thus, law's implementation, and not just its creation, is of democratic interest. Courts are granted independence so that they can resolve legal conflicts free from the influence of extra-legal criteria or pressures. In the discharge of their duties, courts are removed from the democratic matrix of political elections and political accountability. This is democratically acceptable because courts do ot make freestanding political decisions, but are bound strictly by la But if it turns out that being bound by law constrains courts' dis etion in only a limited way, and that courts generate, at least in t, the meaning of the norms they apply, then the result is a de cratic gap. The problem is exacerbated when courts are emp ed to invalidate the decisions of a democratically elected major

15 Cf. Di m, 'Methode als Machtfaktor', in his *Recht und Staat der bürgerlichen Gesell* nkfurt: Suhrkamp, 1987), p. 347.

The problem, of course, is not specifically European; . general. In most cases, the problem is softened by the fact th. political actors no longer recognize their intentions in a court's . pretation, they can reverse the court's interpretation by amendı the law. The possibility that a line of jurisprudence can be corrected politically is thus a necessary corollary to the imperfect legal constraint of judicial power. It is, of course, more difficult to correct a constitutional court politically than it is to correct an ordinary court. Constitutional jurisprudence, unlike the application of ordinary law, cannot be reversed through a statutory amendment enacted by a bare majority. It requires a constitutional amendment, which usually requires a heightened majority.

The obligation to law, moreover, is not the only obligation that constrains courts that apply law. The context in which jurisprudence typically unfolds also helps soften the democracy problem. Two factors play a role here. First, courts operate in the environment of a legal culture governed silently, but therefore all the more enduringly, by collective understandings about the limits of judicial power, the division of labour between courts and legislatures, the rationality criteria of legal application, the justification of judicial decisions, etc. These understandings do not shift from one day to the next. They flank the obligation to law, and narrow the discretion that this obligation leaves open.

Second, jurisprudence unfolds before the steady scrutiny of the general public and a special public of legal experts. The general public's reactions to legal decisions might well be overwhelmingly result-oriented. But even so they give voice to dominant legal sensibilities. The expert public—especially legal scholars—understand their task to be the systematic development and explanation, beyond the individual case, of the legal materials with which courts work, as well as the case-oriented discussion of pending legal questions and the criticism of judicial decisions and their rationales. In similar, but hard-to-measure ways, both discourses help keep courts in contact with the societies for which they administer justice. In this way, they promote acceptance of court decisions.

[redacted]ion in Europe

. makes the EU special is that, on the one hand, the sphere in ich courts can be corrected politically is considerably smaller than n nation-states, and that, on the other hand, the mechanisms that in a nation-state soften the democratic dilemma of jurisprudence are largely absent. In this respect, the ECJ is considerably freer than national courts. This is the product of many factors rooted partly in the peculiarities of Union law, partly in the methods of its interpretation by the ECJ, and partly in the context of European jurisprudence. In the EU, then, the jurisprudential problem is especially acute. Because the problem is often overlooked and its importance underestimated, it must be examined more closely before taking up the relationship between national constitutional courts and European democracy.

The point of departure is the ECJ's foundational, methodological watershed. Traditionally, there are differences between the interpretive methods of international and national law. In international law, applying a norm's meaning to a concrete problem depends primarily on the intentions of the treaty's signatories. Norms that restrain sovereignty are construed narrowly. In national law, by contrast, norms are construed predominantly in terms of their objective purpose. Thus, the application of national law tends to be more strongly liberated from the political lawgiver than the application of international law, but it is also more powerfully dependent on the national, legal-cultural context and the possibility of political correction. Although by nature the European treaties are international treaties, the ECJ has, from the very beginning, construed them in accordance with the canons of national rather than international law.

The significance of *Van Gend en Loos* is not limited to its holding that community law is applicable in the Member States without transformation into national law. This could have been derived from the treaties themselves. The true novelty was that the Court interpreted the four economic freedoms (the free movement of goods, persons, services, and capital), which in the treaty were framed as binding legislative guidelines, as directly applicable, subjective righ vate economic actors, who could invoke these rights in com against their Member States. This did not preclude legislative m ures, but it made them unnecessary for the establishment of an inte nal market. Through the preliminary ruling procedure, the ECJ could determine alone how the economic freedoms were to be understood, and which national laws infringed them.

The significance of *Costa v. ENEL* was that national law became immediately inapplicable if the ECJ found that it contradicted community law. There was nothing national legislatures could do about it. This holding undermined the German Constitutional Court's monopoly, under Article 100 GG, on invalidating legislation. Out of respect for the democratic legislature, the Basic Law had reserved to the Constitutional Court alone the right to determine that a democratically promulgated law clashed with higher law. Now, on the basis of European law, every court—indeed every agency—could make that determination. The development launched by the ECJ was quickly characterized as the constitutionalization of the treaties. Although the treaties originated as international law, thanks to the ECJ's jurisprudence they functioned as a constitution. And the ECJ did not shy away from describing them as such.[16]

This process gained its full weight, however, only in connection with an additional circumstance: the scope of the treaties. True, the treaties now function like a constitution, but they do not look like a constitution. While at the national level the constitution is precisely that law that regulates legislation, but leaves decisions about the content of laws to political institutions, and in this way makes them dependent on electoral outcomes, at the European level many matters are already regulated comprehensively in the treaties themselves and thus immunized against legislative intervention. At the same time, the legislature cannot correct the ECJ's treaty interpretations—even if the

[16] Cf. Eric Stein, 'Lawyers and Judges and the Making of a Transnational Constitution,' (1981) 75 *American Journal of International Law* 1. Joseph H.H. Weiler, 'The Transformation of Europe' (1991) 100 *Yale Law Journal* 2403; Joseph H.H. Weiler, 'A Quiet Revolution' (1994) 26 *Comparative Political Studies* 510; ECJ, *Les Verts*, Slg. 1986, 1339 (1365).

thinks the interpretation runs counter to the intentions of no originally adopted the regulation.

us, thanks to the treaties' constitutional stature, together with eir scope and content, the ECJ is much more powerfully immune to democratic influences than are national courts. Correcting the ECJ's jurisprudence requires amending the treaty. For that, however, a qualified majority is insufficient. In the Member States, a qualified majority—which usually requires cooperation among a few national parties—would suffice. But in Europe, amending the treaties requires unanimity among all twenty-eight Member States. Because the contextual conditions are also weak—in light of the encounter among many legal cultures and a rudimentary European public sphere—the judicial democracy problem in the EU is greater than in any nation-state—including the USA, which is all too obsessed with this problem.

5. *The non-political mechanism of decision*

In light of the current scope of primary law, however, this is not the end of the consequences of the treaties' constitutionalization. Those consequences also affected the mechanism of decision. Everything that is already regulated by primary law no longer requires statutory implementation. But neither can it be amended by statute. This is merely a question of legal implementation, in which the EU's non-political institutions—the Commission and the Court of Justice—are entirely independent. By contrast, the institutions that depend on democratic elections—the Council and the Parliament—have nothing to do with the interpretation and application of Union law. Thus, the only Union institution that represents the interests of the Member States has no say when it comes to the application of primary law. Decisions with far-reaching consequences for the Member States are thus made through administrative and judicial avenues and a non-political mechanism.

This non-political mechanism of decision is not limited to matters of slight political weight. On the contrary, many decisions made in this way were of extraordinary political consequence. After accomplishing the first stage in establishing an economic community—the customs union—the Commission moved on to the common market. Its most important tool in this endeavour was the former Article 28 TEEC (now Article 34 TFEU), which banned quantitative restrictions on exports between Member States, and 'all measures having equivalent effect'. The ECJ interpreted these words, not in their original, anti-protectionist sense, but in an anti-regulatory sense. The Court found that any measure capable of hindering intra-Community commerce—directly or indirectly, potentially or in fact—had an effect equivalent to export restrictions.[17] The provision thus lost nearly all limits.

By contrast, the Court interpreted narrowly, and subjected to a strict proportionality test, the provisions exempting measures that promote legitimate government purposes. The most important consequence of this jurisprudence was that products legally manufactured in their country of origin had to be allowed entry into all other Member States, regardless of those states' local regulations.[18] The Member States thus lost the power to implement at home their own standards of protection, whether in environmental law, hazard prevention, or consumer protection. True, they could have maintained these standards for goods produced and distributed domestically. But they would then be guilty of internal discrimination, and would place domestic firms at a competitive disadvantage.

In a third phase of integration, after the completion of the internal market, the Commission's policies focused primarily on the fullest possible implementation of the principle of competition. Its principal tool was the ban on subsidies contained in the former Article 80 TEEC (now Article 107 TFEU). This provision banned state subsidies of every kind, insofar as they distorted competition by promoting certain enterprises or branches of production and thereby inhibiting interstate trade. Here, too, an expansive definition of 'subsidies' prevailed, such that even broadcasting fees, to take one example, counted as subsidies. Understood thus, the ban reaches not only private

[17] ECJ, *Dassonville*, Slg. 1974, 837.

[18] ECJ, *Cassis de Dijon*, Slg. 1979, 649.

enterprises that receive state aid, but increasingly also public institutions that provide services to residents. As long as there are private competitors, public financing or risk mitigation counts as a subsidy and requires justification.

Which services should be provided publicly and which privately depends powerfully on national traditions and varies, as a result, from one Member State to another. The reasons for public services are legion. Often the decision to make a certain sector public is made in the light of experience. At some point, the good in question was either not provided by the market at all, or not provided in the desired, or in some cases constitutionally required way. There are, however, exceptions to this rule. And yet the Member States' reasons of general welfare are in danger of withering before the EU's fixation on competition. Thanks to the treaty interpretations of the Commission and the ECJ, the decision of which services to leave to the market and which to provide under public aegis has been taken out of the Member States' hands.

6. *Structural promotion of liberalization*

The effects are not limited, however, to making politically weighty decisions through a non-political mechanism. Structurally as well, the non-political mechanism favours economic liberalization. The explanation for this lies in the difference (which pervades community law) between positive and negative integration.[19] Negative integration—i.e. deregulation at the national level for the sake of opening the market—advanced inexorably through the non-political mechanism. Positive integration—i.e. re-regulation at the European level to correct market failure—depended on political decisions. Thanks, however, to the consensus requirements in the Council

[19] Cf. Fritz Scharpf, *Governing in Europe: Effective and Democratic?* (Oxford: Oxford University Press, 1999), pp. 42–83; Susanne K. Schmidt, 'Europäische Integration zwischen judikativer und legislative Politik', in Martin Höpner and Armin Schäfer (eds), *Die Politische Ökonomie der europäischen Integration* (Frankfurt: Campus, 2008), p. 101.

(particularly before enactment of the SEA), such decisions were hard to come by.[20] As a result, there was often no compensation at the European level for the abolition of national standards of protection.

In the public sphere, European over-regulation is often perceived as a problem. But European *under*-regulation, in those areas that used to be regulated at the national level for public welfare reasons, is no less problematic. The privatization of services that used to be provided publicly—a privatization achieved through non-political means—also leads in the direction of market control rather than public services, but without improving conditions of supply in every case. Even if in some areas consumers are better off financially than before, comprehensive services rooted in the social contract are endangered without public guarantees. And public guarantees, for their part, risk falling within the European Commission's line of fire.

Above all, however, liberalization worsens the conditions for Member-State policies that promote social justice. True, even after the Lisbon Treaty social policy is largely reserved for the Member States. But the EU's economic policies, which focus on competition, together with the effects of globalization, have narrowed the scope for national social policy. The more intensively a Member State pursues its social policies, the more competitive disadvantages it brings for domestic industries. In consequence, national social policy comes under pressure. Compensation at the European level faces two obstacles: not only are the legal preconditions lacking, but so too (thanks to the pronounced disparity among the Member States' social insurance systems) are the political possibilities. What might appear to be socially responsible in the ECJ's jurisprudence—such as including within national social security systems persons who do not belong or contribute to the community of shared risk—contributes in the long run to the disintegration of such systems.[21]

[20] On the not fundamentally different situation after the transition to majority decisions, see Gerda Falkner (ed), *The EU's Decision Traps: Comparing Policies* (Oxford: Oxford University Press, 2011).

[21] Cf. Fritz Scharpf, *Community and Autonomy: Institutions, Policies, and Legitimacy in Multilevel Europe* (Chicago: University of Chicago Press, 2010) especially pp. 221 ss.

Finally, the liberalization promoted through non-political decision-making often results in the need to balance the European treaties' economic freedoms on the one hand (which have been exalted through interpretation into fundamental rights), and national fundamental rights on the other. At the European level, the economic freedoms tend to outweigh the personal, communicative, social, and cultural rights of national constitutions, which within the Member States are usually given greater weight than are economic rights. An uneven application of the principle of proportionality—strict with respect to national law, generous with respect to Union law—reinforces the trend.[22] Taken together, this goes far beyond a discrimination-free common market and aims at a general system of economic freedom, which national constitutional law wanted to prevent.[23]

7. *Diminishing democracy*

Meanwhile, the design and function of European primary law not only produce a structurally based, economic liberalism; they also undermine democracy. Insofar as decisions of the Commission and the Court come in the guise of treaty interpretation, they are removed from the democratic process. The democratically legitimated institutions take no part in these decisions, nor can they correct them through legislation. In the latter case, the treaties' constitutional stature prevents their doing so. It is possible, on the other hand, to enact new, European regulations in the place of national regulations that have been declared incompatible with Union law. But such replacements face enormous hurdles in the Commission's exclusive right of initiative and in the high requirements of consensus for European legislation.

and 353 ss.; Christian Joerges and Florian Rödl, 'Informal Politics, Formalized Law and the "Social Deficit" of European Integration' (2009) 15 *European Law Journal* 1.

[22] Cf. Christian Calliess, 'Europäische Gesetzgebung und nationale Grundrechte' (2009) 64 *JuristenZeitung* 113.

[23] Cf. Scharpf, 'Bundesverfassungsgericht' (above n. 13).

The causes of Europe's democratic deficit are overwhelmingly sought at the institutional level. Those seeking explanations note that the legal foundation of the EU is established without citizen participation, or that the European Parliament is not the centre of EU decision-making, but rather lags behind the governmentally staffed Council. Transforming the treaties into a constitution via constitutional referendum, vesting the European Parliament with the powers typical of national parliaments, and downgrading the Council into a second chamber of Parliament are the commonly proposed remedies. But it has long been objected that the roots of Europe's democratic deficit are to be found less in the EU's institutional structure than in the absence or inadequacy of the societal preconditions for democracy and constitutionalism.[24] And that cannot be changed in the short term.

At the same time, the democracy problem stemming from the gap between democratic legitimation and political power has been neglected. As has been shown earlier, in areas regulated by the European treaties the decision-making power of the democratically legitimated institutions, the European Parliament and the Council, is slight. By contrast, the decision-making power of institutions with considerably weaker democratic legitimacy is much stronger. Thus, legitimacy and accountability part paths. The gap could be reduced to some degree through institutional reforms, such as augmenting the powers of Parliament. But reducing the gap would also require, and much more crucially, a structural modification of the treaties.

The content of the treaties, just like that of a constitution, is removed from the realm of political decision-making. In this sense, elections are of no avail. Accordingly, it is a requirement of democracy to maintain the boundary between constitution and statute, and not to overload the constitutional plane with matters fit for legislation. If the treaties

[24] Cf. Dieter Grimm, 'Does Europe Need a Constitution?' (1995) 1 *European Law Journal* 282; Rainer Wahl, 'Die Rolle staatlicher Verfassungen angesichts der Europäisierung und Internationalisierung', in Thomas Vesting and Stefan Korioth (eds), *Der Eigenwert des Verfassungsrechts: Was bleibt von der Verfassung nach der Globalisierung* (Tübingen: Mohr Siebeck, 2011), p. 355.

are already constitutionalized, they should be organized like a constitution: they should be relieved of matters that in a nation-state would be addressed through legislation. Of course, this is probably just as improbable as Scharpf's suggestion that the Member States convened in the Council be given defensive possibilities beyond filing actions for annulment, which actions have proven (thanks to the ECJ's relative insensibility to the rights of Member States) largely ineffectual.[25]

C. European Democracy and National Constitutional Courts

The role of national constitutional courts for European democracy cannot be determined without regard to the peculiarity and current conditions of this democracy. In this respect, one must not saddle the EU with false expectations. For one thing, the EU is not a state, and European democracy will not, therefore, be the same as national democracy. The nation-state model serves nonetheless as the basis for many descriptions of the European democratic deficit and many prescriptions for curing it. In such cases, European democracy will inevitably receive poor marks. For another thing, one must not forget that national democracies have deficiencies of their own. Comparing European realities with national ideals would be methodologically dubious, and its results of little use.

European democracy was originally transmitted by the Member States alone. Today it rests on two pillars. To the democratic legitimation imparted by the Member States as 'Masters of the Treaties' and as the decisive actors in the European Council and in the Council, there has been added an internal legitimation, one that flows from the Union's citizens and operates through the European Parliament which those citizens elect. But even if one does not deny Parliament's representativeness, the legitimacy imparted by Parliament remains,

[25] Cf. Fritz Scharpf, 'Individualrechte gegen nationale Solidarität', in Höpner and Schäfer (eds), *Politische Ökonomie* (n. 19), p. 96 s.

in many respects, inferior to that imparted by the Member States. The two pillars are not equally sturdy.

Internal legitimacy does not extend to the EU's legal foundation, only to acts issued on the basis of that foundation. Jürgen Habermas's construction of a European popular sovereignty notwithstanding,[26] the Union's citizens have no part in the EU's 'constituent authority' because the European Parliament, their representative, plays no role in creating or ratifying the treaties. The EU's internal legitimacy suffers further from the fact that the European Parliament is elected under conditions that do not enhance Europe-consciousness. The vote is divided by Member State and governed by national election law. The campaign is conducted by national parties and dominated by national themes. The results are evaluated in terms of their national significance.

Furthermore, the democratic legitimacy imparted to the EU's decisions by its citizens can only develop within the framework of the European Parliament's powers. Europe's internal legitimacy cannot reach areas where Parliament is not involved. The European Parliament now enjoys extensive rights to participate in legislation, but it is still not the coequal of the Council. The same is true of setting the budget. On the other hand, Parliament's influence now does extend to the Commission: Parliament appoints the Commission's president upon a proposal from the European Council, and the Commission's membership as a whole requires Parliament's approval. Through a no-confidence vote, Parliament can force the Commission's members to resign. To this extent, the Commission takes part in the EU's internal legitimacy. This does not, however, mean that in its general operations the Commission must account for European elections, as a national government would have to do. For the Commission's general policies, electoral outcomes are more or less inconsequential.

Thus, comparing the two strands of legitimacy, even without considering the differing societal preconditions for democratic governance,

[26] Habermas, *Verfassung Europas* (n. 3), p. 62 ss.; in response, see ch. 3 of this volume.

reveals that European democracy still draws more powerfully on the legitimacy imparted by the Member States. Under these circumstances, it is in the EU's self-interest to promote functional national democracies capable of giving citizens the impression that politics are responsive to their needs. But this is not apparent in the EU's policy of liberalization. That policy trenches deeply into national structures—and precisely those structures with deep and venerable roots in the societies' conceptions of solidarity, the provision of public services, the production of public goods, etc. The emaciation of national politics is an essential source of Euro-scepticism.[27]

National democracies are further burdened by the fact that decisions about liberalization are made without Member-State participation through the non-political method of treaty implementation. In the absence of European executive agencies, these decisions must be implemented by the governments of the Member States. In general, the public holds these governments accountable for such decisions, even though the governments played no role in making them. By contrast, the European institutions that *do* make the decisions—the Commission and the Court of Justice—cannot be held democratically accountable, nor are they the target of organized protest within the Member States. The resulting de-legitimation of Member-State institutions affects not only the government that happens to be in power, but the democratic system as a whole.

When European decisions are made through a non-political mechanism, the Member States can defend themselves only by filing an action for annulment. Experience has shown, however, that the prospects of such actions are dim. There are a few exceptions in the ECJ's jurisprudence, but not enough to reverse the general trend.[28] By contrast, the Commission often avails itself of treaty infringement proceedings to enforce its policies vis-à-vis the Member States. Because

[27] Cf. Fritz Scharpf, 'Reflections on Multilevel Legitimacy' (2007) 20 *EUSA Review* 2.

[28] Cf. Rudolf Streinz, 'Die Rolle des EuGH im Prozess der Europäischen Integration' (2010) 135 *Archiv des öffentlichen Rechts* 1.

the Commission prefers to proceed against one Member State at a time, and because the ECJ always decides only the individual case, there is usually no common grievance of an entire group of Member States. 'Thus, a unified reaction among all member states, or even among those with similar institutional arrangements and preferences, is all but out of the question. Before the Commission and the Court, each state stands alone, and each state loses for itself.'[29]

In considering the dangers posed to national democracy by the interpretation and application of Union law, one must look beyond the creeping accumulation of EU powers. The ECJ's very fundamental rights jurisprudence, once called for by the German Constitutional Court, tends now to oppose Karlsruhe's highly developed understanding of fundamental rights—an understanding rooted in individual, not economic freedom, and that has decisively shaped the identity and legitimacy of Germany's constitutional order. Recently, the EU's Charter of Fundamental Rights has adopted many strands of Karlsruhe's jurisprudence. Furthermore, the Charter does not supplant national fundamental rights; it merely—under Article 51(1)—binds the Member States when they enforce Union law. Enforcing Union law, however, is not a minor element of the Member States' legal activity. Even more important, Article 51(1)'s limitation does not apply to the TFEU's economic freedoms—and it is unclear whether the ECJ will feel obligated by the Charter to modify its economic freedoms jurisprudence.

One must keep all of this in mind when considering the role of national constitutional courts in European democracy. In the current constellation, national constitutional courts are the only available counterweight to the democracy-diminishing mechanisms at work in the EU. The weakening of national democracy is not an abstract risk, but a concrete danger. The German Constitutional Court's concerns about democracy in the *Lisbon* judgment should not be mischaracterized as an obsession with sovereignty. National and European democracy are interdependent, yet not in the form of communicating

[29] Scharpf, 'Individualrechte' (n. 25), p. 97.

vessels. They are not rivals in a zero-sum game. Losses for national democracy are not gains for European democracy. So long as Europe's internal legitimacy cannot replace the flow of national legitimacy, the EU must come to terms with this.

Under current conditions, national constitutional courts' most crucial contribution to European democracy is to constrain the undermining of national democracy through European law, and to urge European institutions towards greater respect for the results of national democratic processes. This should be understood not merely as a threat to integration but as a contribution to democracy. Competence review and identity review are the constitutional courts' tools. Whether the courts rightly claim such powers must also be considered in connection with democracy, for every assumption of powers in violation of the treaties weakens democracy. This holds, of course, in both directions. The German Constitutional Court tried to account for this in its *Honeywell* decision. The world is still waiting for the ECJ's reciprocal step of giving teeth to Article 4 TEU's reaffirmation of limited self-authorization and its command to honour national identities.

11

The Basic Law as a Barrier against a Transformation of the EU into a State

Comments on the *Lisbon* Judgment of the Federal Constitutional Court

A. Ambivalent Reception

The message of the German Constitutional Court's (*Bundesverfassungsgericht*) decision on the Lisbon Treaty[1] is that European integration will not be brought to a halt by Germany but finds its limits in the German Constitution, the Basic Law. The first aspect of the judgment was received with much relief, the second has brought a mixture of consent and disapproval. However, the judgment does not emerge *ex nihilo*. It is the continuation of a long line of precedents. Therefore, an isolated examination would fail to show where it breaks new ground and where it merely builds on earlier judgments. Likewise, it would be misleading to isolate it from the context of the development that the European integration has taken over the last twenty years, not only by the amendments to the Treaties but also through their interpretation and through the practices of the institutions of the EU and the Member States.

[1] BVerfGE 123, 267.

B. The *Lisbon* Judgment in the Context of its Precedents and the Progress of European Integration

1. *The precedents*

Ever since its beginnings, ten years after the establishment of the European Economic Community, the jurisprudence of the German Constitutional Court in European matters[2] has been determined by a number of basic assumptions. It starts from the premise that the Treaties have not established a European state but a community *sui generis*,[3] later described by the Court as a confederation (*Verbund*) of sovereign nation-states that is supported by these states and has to respect their national identity.[4] It was not sovereignty that has been transferred, but only a number of powers (*Hoheitsrechte*), insufficient to turn the Community itself into a sovereign entity.[5] The sovereignty retained by the Member States is protected by the principle of conferred powers; they enjoy the *Kompetenz-Kompetenz*.[6] It is for them to decide which powers they want to transfer to the Community instead of the Community deciding which powers it wants to take from the states. They are the 'Masters of the Treaties'.[7]

From this premise several conclusions were drawn. National law and Community law are independent legal orders. Community law is neither a part of international law nor of domestic law.[8] It flows

[2] Decisions of the Federal Constitutional Court (BVerfGE) 22, 134 (1967); 22, 293 (1967); 31, 145 (1971); 37, 271 (1974)—Solange I; 45, 142 (1977); 52, 187 (1979); 58, 1 (1981); 73, 339 (1986)—Solange II; 75, 223 (1987); 89, 155 (1993)—Maastricht; 102, 147 (2000).

[3] BVerfGE 22, 293 (295 s.); 37, 271 (278); 75, 223 (242); 89, 155 (181, 188).

[4] BVerfGE 89, 155 (181, 186, 189, 190).

[5] BVerfGE 22, 293 (296); 37, 271 (279 f.); 73, 339 (374 s.)—1986 (Solange II); 89, 155 (183). In the *Maastricht* decision one can find the argument that the Member States founded the EU to jointly discharge part of their tasks and to that end to jointly exercise their sovereignty (p. 188 s.). But in so doing, they did not transfer their sovereignty to the EU, cf. BVerfGE 75, 223 (242)–1987.

[6] BVerfGE 75, 223 (242); 89, 155 (189 ss., 192–98).

[7] BVerfGE 75, 223 (242); 89, 155 (190).

[8] BVerfGE 22, 293 (296); 31, 145 (173 s.); 37, 271 (277 s., 280).

from an autonomous source. Community law, therefore, is not valid in Germany of its own accord, but because of Germany's order to apply it domestically (*Rechtsanwendungsbefehl*).[9] It derives its legal force within Germany from a domestic act. This act 'opens' the German legal order for law from a source other than the state.[10] As such, Community law differs from international law, which is in need of transformation. The order to apply Community law domestically, in turn, is given wholesale by way of ratification of the European Treaties. This means that secondary Community law that has been enacted in accordance with primary law does not need to be ratified. It takes direct effect within Germany.[11]

In principle the same is true for the supremacy of Community law. The supremacy had been established by the European Court of Justice (ECJ)[12] before the *Bundesverfassungsgericht* first dealt with the relationship between European law and domestic law. The German Constitutional Court rejected the assumption that the supremacy follows directly from Article 24 Basic Law.[13] It likewise rejected the assumption that the supremacy was inherent to Community law, for otherwise it would be unable to fulfil its function. In the German Court's view, the legal validity of Community law is not put into question by a lack of supremacy. The Court nevertheless conceded the supremacy, but derived it, like direct effect, from the national order to apply Community law domestically.[14] This order is regarded as constitutive for the applicability of Community law in Germany.

However, Article 24 Basic Law does not empower the German government to open the German legal order without limits. German

[9] BVerfGE 45, 142 (169); 52, 187 (199); 73, 339 (375); 89, 155 (190).

[10] BVerfGE 37, 271 (279 s.); 73, 339 (374).

[11] In its first case on Community law, in which the question of compatibility of Art. 189(2) EEC with the Basic Law arose, the Court ducked deciding BVerfGE 22, 134 (1967) at a time when the ECJ had already ruled on this matter from the perspective of Community law in *Van Gend en Loos* (Case 26/62, ECR 1963, 1). Since BVerfGE 22, 293 (295 s.) the immediate validity of regulations is also recognized in Germany.

[12] *Costa v. ENEL*, Case 6/64, ECR 1964, 1253.

[13] BVerfGE 37, 271 (278 s.); 73, 339 (374 s.).

[14] BVerfGE 73, 339 (375); 89, 155 (190).

state institutions may not permit a transfer of powers by which the identity of the German Basic Law would be affected.[15] Further limits result from the democratic principle of the Basic Law.[16] Since the democratic legitimation of the EU emanates from the peoples of the Member States, mediated by their parliaments, these parliaments need sufficiently significant fields of activity of their own in which the people can articulate their ideas and interests and thus influence the formation of the political will. As the people exercises its prerogatives mainly by electing representatives, it must be guaranteed that Parliament can decide about Germany's membership in the EU, its existence, and further development.[17] In the Court's view, this is only possible if the programme of integration is clearly and predictably regulated in the Treaties. In no case does the Basic Law permit an indefinite authorization of the EU.[18]

The *Bundesverfassungsgericht* is, however, aware that every transfer of powers to the EU entails a democratic loss on the national level. Due to the openness of the Basic Law to integration, this loss does not amount to a violation of the democratic principle. Yet, the Court requires that the loss on the national level be compensated by adequate democratic legitimation on the European level. This legitimation is mainly provided by the national parliaments, which ratify the transfer of powers and control the national executive that is active on the European level. The growing power of the EU makes it necessary, however, that a legitimation by the European Parliament be added, although it is not deemed capable of replacing the national parliaments since the societal preconditions of democracy are underdeveloped on the European level.[19] In addition, the democratic principle requires that Community powers are exercised by an organ in which the national governments are represented that are subject to democratic control at home.[20]

[15] BVerfGE 37, 211 (279 s.); 73, 339 (375 s.); 89, 155 (184).
[16] BVerfGE 89, 155 (186). [17] BVerfGE 58, 1 (37)–1981; 89, 155 (187 s.).
[18] Ibid. [19] BVerfGE 89, 155 (184). [20] Ibid., (187).

Transferred powers can only be exercised within the framework of the Treaties. Amendments to the Treaties are reserved for the Member States as the 'Masters of the Treaties'. A change of the integration programme by organs of the EU is not covered by the German ratification law.[21] Should the EU claim a power that has not been transferred by Germany, acts based on that power will not be valid in Germany. This would be against the constitutive force of the German order to apply Community law domestically.[22] Furthermore, the position of the Member States must not be allowed to erode through interpretation of the Treaties. Thus, the space for an extensive judicial interpretation is limited.[23] Interpretations that are *de facto* changes to the Treaty are not within the legal power of the Community's institutions. Legal acts based on this kind of interpretations cannot bind the German authorities.[24]

Similarly, there is a long tradition of jurisprudence regarding judicial review of Community law. The *Bundesverfassungsgericht* distinguishes between Community organs and Community law. Already at an early stage it declared inadmissible constitutional complaints which directly challenge decisions of Community organs since these organs are not bound by the Basic Law. No interest, however pressing it may be, could justify such an extension of the admissibility of constitutional complaints.[25] Yet, the German Court left the door ajar on the possibility of Community powers being measured against the standard of the Basic Law in cases of admissible constitutional complaints (i.e., against actions by German state authorities). In the Court's view, this depended on the answer to the question of whether Germany, when transferring sovereign powers according to Article 24 Basic Law, may free the Community institutions from the Basic Law's obligations.[26]

[21] BVerfGE 58, 1 (37); 89, 155 (187 s.).
[22] BVerfGE 58, 1 (30 s.); 75, 223 (235, 242); 89, 155 (188).
[23] BVerfGE 73, 339 (376); 75, 223 (240 ss.); 89, 155 (187 s., 199, 209 s.).
[24] BVerfGE 37, 271 (282); 89, 155 (188).
[25] BVerfGE 22, 293 (298).
[26] BVerfGE 22, 293 (298 s.).

The answer to that question followed suit seven years later as part of the *Solange I* decision. Accordingly, the identity of the Basic Law, which may not be surrendered by any legal act, includes an adequate and effective protection of fundamental rights against public authorities.[27] The Court announced that, as long as this protection is missing on the European level, it will review Community acts according to the standard presented by the German Bill of Rights. Hence, references by German courts to the *Bundesverfassungsgericht* are admissible and necessary if these courts deem Community actions to be incompatible with the Basic Law. However, this presupposes that the domestic courts have sought a prior decision by the ECJ on the interpretation of the relevant Community laws and that their judicial reservations are not cleared by the Court of Justice's ruling.[28]

Five years after the judgment, the *Bundesverfassungsgericht* left it still open whether the situation had changed.[29] Yet, in 1986, after a thorough analysis of the ECJ's jurisprudence on fundamental rights protection, the *Bundesverfassungsgericht* reached the conclusion that by then sufficient legal protection had been established on the European level. Thus, in *Solange II* the German Court declared that it would no longer exercise its power to review Community law as long as this state of fundamental rights protection is maintained.[30] The Court, however, left no doubt that the transfer of powers to supranational institutions finds its limits in the identity of the German constitutional order, part of which is the existence and effective protection of fundamental rights. Therefore, the judicial power to scrutinize Community acts may be taken up at any moment. The *Bundesverfassungsgericht*'s judgment on the Treaty of Maastricht did not change anything with regard to these matters. It is not a *Solange III* judgment.[31]

However, it was only with the *Maastricht* judgment that the *Bundesverfassungsgericht* drew the procedural consequences from

[27] BVerfGE 37, 271 (280); confirmed in 73, 339 (375 s.). [28] Ibid., (285).
[29] BVerfGE 52, 187 (202 s.). [30] BVerfGE 73, 339 (387).
[31] BVerfGE 102, 147 (163)–2000 (Banana market regulation).

the earlier statement that Community acts without a basis in the Treaties do not apply in Germany. It extended the right of scrutiny to the question of whether Community law is covered by German implementation order or whether it 'breaks out' of the competence frame determined by the Treaties.[32] It is this extension that brings the German Court into a conflict with the ECJ that the *Solange* opinions had avoided. While they require only an interpretation of the Basic Law, followed by an appraisal whether the contested Community act is compatible with it, the determination whether a Community act has broken out of the Treaty framework requires an interpretation of the Treaties (if only in their capacity as integral part of the German ratification law), which the Court of Justice claims exclusively for itself.

In sum, Community law is, on the one hand, not applicable in Germany without due regard to the Basic Law. On the other hand, not all Community law that is incompatible with the Basic Law is categorically denied applicability in Germany. To the contrary, it is recognized that the authorization to delegate powers to the Community level entails a deviation from the Basic Law's legal demands.[33] This does not, however, impede the primacy of Community law. Exceptions are limited to identity infractions of the German Constitution and *ultra vires* acts by the Community institutions. So far there is no case in which a legal act by the Community has been denied applicability. Yet, there are decisions in which the *Bundesverfassungsgericht* protected the primacy of Community law against conflicting German courts.[34]

2. *Baseline of the* Lisbon *judgment*

The new judgment takes all this jurisprudence on board. Since the *Bundesverfassungsgericht* has ruled that the ratification law, and as a

[32] BVerfGE 89, 155 (188). The term 'break out' can already be found in BVerfGE 75, 223 (242).

[33] BVerfGE 58, 1 (36); 89, 155 (183).

[34] BVerfGE 75, 223 (1987).

consequence also the Lisbon Treaty, are compatible with the German Basic Law, it can confront the dangers that, in its view, nonetheless threaten the German constitutional order, only on the domestic level. This takes place in three ways. First, the Court marks the limits for the German institutions when attempting future extension of Union competences or other structural changes. Second, it prescribes parliamentary cooperation on the national level, even in cases where the European Treaties do not require a national ratification process to extend Union competences. Finally, it confirms the constitutional limits of the applicability of Union law in Germany and insists on its own right to review whether the Union institutions have adhered to these set limits.

As with the *Maastricht* judgment the *Bundesverfassungsgericht* derived the standard of scrutiny from the individual right to vote in Article 38 Basic Law. It was this individual right that allowed citizens to launch the procedure for a constitutional review of the Lisbon Treaty in the first place. The review extends to Article 20 Basic Law because elections are the main mechanism to implement the principle of democracy. The principles laid down in this article are not subject to constitutional amendments, which, in turn, brings the eternity clause of Article 79(3) Basic Law into play. This clause is interpreted as the protection of the Basic Law's very identity. It is from this identity of the Basic Law that the *Bundesverfassungsgericht* connects to the issue of sovereignty, which, however, is not explicitly mentioned in the Basic Law. Yet, according to the Court the Basic Law not only presupposes the 'sovereign statehood of Germany', it also guarantees it.[35]

This chain of reference from the right to vote to state sovereignty can only be made if Article 38 Basic Law is interpreted in a substantive way. Were it limited to the mere right of citizens to participate in elections, it would not be evident how it could have been infringed by the ratification of the Lisbon Treaty. However, the *Bundesverfassungsgericht* never adopted such a formal understanding of the right to vote. In its view, Article 38 Basic Law guarantees, among other things, that

[35] Lisbon judgment, para. 216.

the elected body has sufficient opportunities to make policy choices in sufficiently important subject matters. An election of a body without substantial political power would deprive the voters of their most fundamental democratic right. That is why not only the democratic principle but also the right to vote is curtailed if the decision-making powers of the *Bundestag* as the only organ that enjoys direct democratic legitimation are significantly reduced.[36]

A certain curtailment of the German Parliament's power to make policy choices is, however, an inevitable consequence of the transfer of powers from the national to the international level, which Articles 23 and 24 Basic Law permit. It is likewise inevitable that the exercise of transferred competences will not follow the requirements prescribed by the Basic Law for acts of the German authorities. This is a natural consequence of the European integration process that the Basic Law not only permits but in fact requires, as the Court states for the first time in the *Lisbon* judgment. State sovereignty therefore exists only within the limits of the Basic Law's receptiveness for international and European law (*Völkerrechtsfreundlichkeit und Europarechtsfreundlichkeit*).[37]

At the same time, Germany's 'sovereign constitutional statehood'[38] (*souveräne Verfassungsstaatlichkeit*) forms the limit of integration. According to the judgment, the Basic Law does authorize the German authorities to give up the national sovereignty. This could not be done even by a constitutional amendment. Such an amendment would fail at Article 79(3) Basic Law. It excludes any changes to the Basic Law's identity. Crossing this line would therefore constitute an assault on the constituent power of the German people. Permission to transform the EU into a federal state can only be given by the people through a new constitution. As long as the Basic Law is in force the EU may not be turned into a state with German consent. It has to remain an association of states (*Staatenverbund*). By this the Court means:

[36] Ibid., para. 210. [37] Ibid., para. 225. [38] Ibid., para. 226.

a close long-term association of states, which remain sovereign, an association that exercises public authority on the basis of a treaty and whose fundamental order is subject to the disposal of the member states alone and in which the peoples of the states, i.e. the citizens of the states, remain the subjects of democratic legitimisation.[39]

The characteristics of an association of states, to which the Basic Law's amendment ban applies, include that the EU receives its legal foundation from the Member States by way of concluding treaties. The EU is not permitted to constitute itself. This has direct implications on the way the EU is endowed with competences. These competences are transferred according to the principle of conferral and may be withdrawn through the same procedure. A transfer of the *Kompetenz-Kompetenz* to the Union is impermissible. If the Union were to rid itself of its legal dependence on the Member States and become a self-supporting entity, Germany would have to make use of the exit clause and leave the EU. This possibility must be guaranteed in the Treaty.

Insofar as the Treaties provide for amendments of the Treaties by EU institutions, i.e., without conclusion of a new treaty and consequently without national ratification procedures, legal compensation has to occur at the national level in compliance with the requirements of Article 23(1) Basic Law. To this extent German constitutional organs hold a 'permanent responsibility for the integration process' (*Integrationsverantwortung*),[40] which can only be discharged by law. In order to ensure the 'integration responsibility', an act of Parliament is necessary for every textual change to the Treaties. This includes changes under the simplified revision procedure, the 'lacuna filling' procedure of the Treaties and changes to the EU's decision-making procedure. The discharge of the integration responsibility must be subject to judicial review by the *Bundesverfassungsgericht*.

These limits may not be undermined by way of treaty interpretation. The 'integration programme'[41] has to be determined by the Treaty. Just as the German government is constitutionally prevented from consenting to blanket empowerments, the effect of such

[39] Ibid., para. 229. [40] Ibid., paras. 245, 236. [41] Ibid., para. 236.

empowerments may not be created by treaty interpretations. Treaty interpretations that tend to maintain the *acquis communautaire* and to guarantee an effective use of the competences (*implied powers, effet utile*) must be tolerated. An interpretation that expanded or changed the primary law would, however, violate the principle of conferred powers and could ultimately lead to a disposal in the hands of the EU over its legal foundations. This is why there have to be control or break mechanisms, at least for extreme cases, that are able to prevent the Union from ridding itself of its legal dependency on the Member States.

As the EU institutions exhibit a 'tendency to political self-empowerment'[42] it is not sufficient that the ratification laws and domestic accompanying laws to further integration steps maintain the principle of conferral and make sure that the EU does not avail itself of the *Kompetenz-Kompetenz*[43] or violate the integration-resistant identity of the German constitution. Rather, the possibility of an external control by the *Bundesverfassungsgericht* is indispensable in order to determine in concrete cases whether the EU has remained within its contractual boundaries and respected Germany's constitutional identity:

> With progressing integration, the fundamental political and constitutional structures of sovereign member states, which are recognised by Article 4(2) sentence 1 TEU Lisbon, cannot be safeguarded in any other way.[44]

Finally, the *Bundesverfassungsgericht* derives from Article 23(1) Basic Law on the one hand that the EU, when acting autonomously, has to follow democratic principles and on the other hand must not erode democratic rule in the Member States. As far as European democracy is concerned, the Court sees no need that the nation-state model is adopted. The EU's democratic requirements are rather dependent on the 'extent and the weight of supranational power'.[45] If this power increases, the level of democratic legitimacy also has to rise if the

[42] Ibid., para. 237. [43] Ibid., para. 239. [44] Ibid., para. 240.
[45] Ibid., para. 262.

increase is to secure German consent. Considering the current development of the EU, the Court finds the level of legitimation sufficient. However, should the development of the EU take a state-like direction, Germany would be forced to demand changes to the Union's democratic legitimacy. If these demands were to be unsuccessful, Germany would have to leave the Union.

With regard to national democracy, the *Bundesverfassungsgericht* derives further limits from the Basic Law regarding the transfer of sovereign powers to the EU, even if the threshold of the constituent power of the German people and the sovereignty of the state have not yet been affected. Germany has to retain sufficient room for shaping the economic, cultural, and social circumstances of domestic life. In particular, it must have the decision-making power in areas 'which affect the citizens' circumstances of life, especially the private space of individual responsibility and of personal and social security, which is protected by the fundamental rights, as well as for those political decisions that particularly depend on cultural, historical and language preconditions and which unfold in a discursive manner in a public sphere that is organised by political parties and Parliament'.[46]

In subsuming the Lisbon Treaty under these criteria, the *Bundesverfassungsgericht* detects a democratic deficit in the EU in comparison to the level of legitimacy within nation-states. The reasons behind this deficit are found mainly in the unequal election procedure for the European Parliament. European democracy is said to be caught in a 'contradiction of values'[47] (*Wertungswiderspruch*) and 'over-federalised'[48] (*überföderalisiert*), because its electoral procedure for the European Parliament emphasizes the equal representation of states and thereby reduces the equality of the voters. The European Parliament is therefore not regarded as the representation of a European people but rather a representation of the Member States'

[46] Ibid., para. 249, a specific listing of the areas of lawmaking competence that in the Court's view are called 'especially sensitive for the ability of a constitutional state to democratically shape itself' in ibid., para. 252.

[47] Ibid., para. 287.

[48] Ibid., para. 288.

peoples. This deficit is not balanced out by other provisions in the Lisbon Treaty, such as the citizens' initiative, the double majority voting system in the Council, or the participation rights of the national parliaments: 'The Treaty of Lisbon does not lead to a new level of democratic development.'[49]

However, under present conditions of the allocation of powers and the degree of autonomous decision-making, the standard of legitimation is 'still' considered sufficient, provided that the principle of conferral is guaranteed domestically in a way that goes beyond the guarantee given by the Treaties. It is crucial for the Court's approval of the Treaty of Lisbon that it does not transform the EU into a state and thus leaves Germany's sovereignty untouched. The principle of conferral is seen as the most important protection of the Member States' statehood. They remain the 'constitutionally organised primary political area' (*verfasster politischer Primärraum*).[50] The EU is but of additional and secondary importance and limited to those tasks that have been conferred to it. Furthermore, it is obligated to respect the national identity of the Member States and bound by the principles of subsidiarity and proportionality and the early-warning system.

The special treaty amendment procedure that is introduced or extended by the Lisbon Treaty is only accepted under the precondition of a domestically regulated compensation, countering the procedure's potential threat to German sovereignty. The simplified procedure according to the new Article 48(6) TEU has to be treated domestically like a transfer of powers, which requires a ratification law according to Article 23(1) sentences 2 and 3 Basic Law. Similarly, for the so-called passerelle clause according to the new Article 48(7) TEU, a ratification law, according to Article 23(1), sentence 2 and, if applicable, sentence 3 Basic Law, will be necessary. Also the 'lacuna-filling' competence in Article 352 TEU requires a domestic ratification law supported by a parliamentary majority necessary to amend the constitution. Only if and when these conditions are met may the German representative in the Council declare Germany's support.

[49] Ibid., para. 295. [50] Ibid., para. 301.

Yet, the *Bundesverfassungsgericht* is not at issue with the confirmation of the primacy of EU law, added to the Lisbon Treaty in Declaration 17. It only confirms the current state of law. The Lisbon Treaty does not change its nature as an institution transferred to the Union by an international treaty. Its legal validity in Germany still depends on the national order to apply it domestically. Consequently, it is effective only within the scope of this order. In the Court's view, the Treaty does not prevent the Member States from denying legal acts of the EU domestic applicability if they are not covered by the order to apply the law. The *Bundesverfassungsgericht* claims the power to review EU acts as to their compatibility with this order and to verify that they do not violate the constitutional identity of the Basic Law. The 'right to review adherence to the integration programme'[51] by the EU remains with the Court.

An abandonment of the territory of Germany does not occur through the Lisbon Treaty. The EU has no territorial sovereignty. Similarly, there is no Union-specific territory. Neither is the citizenry of the Member States transformed into a European citizenry by the Lisbon Treaty. In fact, EU citizenship does not constitute a European people with the right to self-determination about its political community formation. EU citizenship is rather derived from state citizenship and added to it. New rights for EU citizens comprised in the Treaty, such as the citizens' initiative, also do not constitute an 'independent personal subject of legitimation at the European level'.[52] Finally, the extension of EU competences does not lead to an erosion of the statehood of the Member States. The German *Bundestag* maintains sufficiently large sphere for policy choices.

3. *Evaluation of the Lisbon judgment*

If this substantial judgment is reduced to its core, it appears that the *Bundesverfassungsgericht* is concerned with maintaining the current

[51] Ibid., para. 334. [52] Ibid., para. 349.

structure of the EU as a political entity created and supported by the Member States, without being a state itself, and to prevent its open or creeping EU transformation into a state. This is why, on the side of the EU, the German Court puts so much weight on the treaty character of the EU's legal basis, the fact that its public power is not original but derived from the Member States, the hetero-determination of its competences and the principle of conferred powers. Conversely, the Court is determined to defend the statehood of the Member States and their responsibility for the basic legal structure of the EU. This is why, on the side of the Member States, much emphasis is placed on sovereignty, their status as 'Masters of the Treaties', the order to apply Union law, the *Kompetenz–Kompetenz* and constitutional identity. Both sides are connected by the necessity of democratic legitimacy, which has to be maintained also in the process of European integration.

Thereby the *Lisbon* judgment exceeds previous case law without deviating from it. In fact, it relies on it. The premises of the decision regarding the validity of Union law and its relationship to national law are based on previous case law, and the same is true for the *Bundesverfassungsgericht*'s power to review Union law in view of the Basic Law. This applies also to the identity review, which is already part of the core of the *Solange* case law. It is here that the protection of fundamental rights is already referred to as a substantial part of constitutional identity. Previous case law is, however, extended and differently accentuated. More emphasis than before is placed on German sovereignty. Nevertheless, the core statement that Germany has not transferred its sovereignty, but only relinquished some of its sovereign powers, already characterizes the previous judgments.

What is new are the domestic provisos, which the Court summarizes under the 'integration responsibility' of the German *Bundestag*. They extend the prerogative of the German Parliament to consent to Council decisions beyond the limits set by Article 23 Basic Law. Yet, they were instigated by the new or extended possibilities in the Lisbon Treaty to expand competences and alter the decision-making procedures by Council vote and thus without participation of domestic parliaments. The subsequent power of the *Bundesverfassungsgericht* to review these decisions of the *Bundestag* also comes as a novelty. The most conspicuous innovation, however, lies in the judgment's prospective character. It does not content itself with stating the compatibility of the Lisbon Treaty with the Basic Law, but develops limits to future integration steps that are neither taken nor envisaged by the Lisbon Treaty.

The preventive character of the decision modifies the function of some basic principles of the integration project, such as the mastery of the Member States over the Treaties, their *Kompetenz-Kompetenz* and the principle of conferred powers, all of which had already played a prominent role in the Maastricht decision. Yet, in this decision the *Bundesverfassungsgericht* was satisfied with stating their recognition in the Maastricht Treaty so that it could be declared compatible with the Basic Law, whereas in the *Lisbon* judgment, they have become conditions for the constitutionality of future treaty amendments and thus for the participation of Germany in future integrational steps. The preventative statements culminate in the negative answer to the question of whether the Basic Law permits the transformation of the EU into a federal state—a question that had been left open in the Maastricht decision.

The main line of the *Bundesverfassungsgericht*'s reasoning that supports the results of the judgment cannot be criticized from a constitutional perspective. The Court follows consistently the premise that Union law enjoys direct effect and primacy in Germany only because of the state's order to apply it domestically, and that this order does not extend to turning the EU into a federal state. This proves neither Euroscepticism nor nationalism. The sovereign statehood of the Member States is understood and accepted from the outset as statehood within a larger community of states. The promise of the Basic Law's Preamble that the German people is determined 'to promote world peace as an equal partner in a united Europe' is not revoked by the judgment. The meaning of this promise is explained in Article 23(1) Basic Law. According to this article, the EU is a means to the end of a united Europe. That is why Germany is constitutionally permitted to transfer sovereign powers to the EU level, provided that the Union fulfils certain conditions, on which, according to the Basic Law, the legitimacy of public power depends.

Whether the Court was right to refer in this context to the term 'sovereignty' or whether that led to a narrowing of the judges' mindset with a view to the judicial results, depends on the notion of sovereignty. Yet, whatever notion one adopts, the assertion that the decision should not have been based on sovereignty because the term does not feature in the Basic Law[53] is rather strange. If it were true that legal interpretation may rely solely on terms that appear in the text of the norm, the fundamental European Court of Justice decision of *Costa v. ENEL* on EU law primacy would not be less illegitimate than the *Lisbon* judgment. However, this is not the case, unless the interpreter of the law is methodologically committed to the crudest form of literalism, or even attempts to make this method binding for national courts only, while international courts are exempted from it.

The Basic Law empowers the Federal Republic to transfer sovereign powers in general and from the very beginning in Article 24(1), and with special reference to the EU in the new Article 23(1). Indeed, if by sovereignty one understands the possession of the entire range of public powers in a specific territory, there would be no longer sovereignty at all. Sovereignty perceived as the quintessence of public power would already be given up with the relinquishment of but one single power. This concept of sovereignty was the predominant one for a long period of time. Since the end of the Second World War and the development of an order of international law starting with the foundation of the United Nations (UN), it is no longer sustainable.[54] Using the term 'state sovereignty' nowadays always includes a compatibility with the existence of supranational public power. This is clearly expressed in the *Lisbon* judgment.[55]

[53] Cf. Carl Otto Lenz, *Frankfurter Allgemeine Zeitung* (8 August 2009), p. 7.

[54] Cf. in this context Dieter Grimm, *Sovereignty* (New York: Columbia University Press, 2015).

[55] *Lisbon* judgment, para. 223.

It is, however, controversial whether the level of public power that is left to the states, including Member States of a supranational organization, can still be classified as 'sovereign'. The question is whether sovereignty in the post-1945 era has been dissolved into its elements, the various powers, or whether sovereignty can be sustained as a concept even if several autonomous actors exercise sovereign powers on one territory. This controversial question cannot be fully discussed here—suffice to say that the majority of authors tend to agree with the latter interpretation. They recognize the remaining function of sovereignty in the guarantee of the self-determination of a political unity under the conditions of an increasing transfer of public power to the international level where democratic legitimacy is either weak or completely absent.

If this is accepted the *Bundesverfassungsgericht*'s differentiation between the notions of sovereignty (*Souveränität*) and sovereign powers (*Hoheitsrechten*) is not unsound. Sovereignty is then no longer a question of 'all or nothing', but of 'more or less'. It remains true that a community without the right to determine its own basic political order cannot be referred to as sovereign. Apart from that, the answer to the question who is sovereign in the context of multi-level governance depends on who decides about the allocation of sovereign powers and how they are allocated in terms of quantity. Sovereign in a multi-level system of governance is the entity that holds the *Kompetenz–Kompetenz* and does not use this power in a way which leaves but a marginal portion for itself. A few scattered powers are not sufficient to constitute sovereignty.

The *Bundesverfassungsgericht* has been widely criticized for its statement that the EU, in spite of the improvements through the Lisbon Treaty, still lacks a sufficient level of democratic legitimacy, compared to democratic standards of states.[56] As a matter of fact, precisely because national democracy is chosen as the relevant yardstick, the Court pays little attention to the strengthening of the EU's democratic legitimacy by the Lisbon Treaty. Here the reasoning is indeed

[56] Cf. e.g. the contributions of Christoph Schönberger and ten other authors in (2009) *German Law Journal* No. 8 (Special section: The Federal Constitutional Court's Lisbon Case).

somewhat irritating. In the earlier parts of the judgment, the question seemed to be whether the expanded public powers granted to the EU by the Lisbon Treaty are sufficiently democratically legitimated. Now it looks as if the EU had to reach the level of legitimacy of a democratic state. This would indeed be a trap. The lack of a democratic standard equivalent to that of a nation-state puts the EU into the muddy zone of potential incompatibility with the Basic Law. Should it reach a level of democratic legitimacy equivalent to a nation-state, Germany would be unable to remain in the Union. However, the judgment clarifies towards the end that this is not a relevant concern because the EU is not a state nor may it ever become one.

According to the *Bundesverfassungsgericht* this impediment cannot be overcome because the Basic Law prohibits amendments that touch upon the constitutional principles named in Article 79(3). As a matter of fact, the provision protects the identity of the Basic Law against the amending powers of the legislature. This so-called 'eternity clause' is a result of the German experience from 1933. However, it does not mean that the sole function of this clause consists in preventing a return of the national-socialist dictatorship. The basic principles are protected against every enemy of the free democratic order. Yet, it is not as certain whether Article 79(3) Basic Law also excludes steps towards integration that do not abolish the identity principles of the Basic Law but rather re-establish them on a higher level.

The question discussed here is not whether a federal European state, especially from a democratic perspective, is desirable. Rather, it is whether Germany would be allowed to join such a state if its democratic legitimacy were at the level required by Article 79(3) Basic Law. The Court connects the unchangeable principle of democratic rule with a prohibition of Germany's membership in a European federal state with a simple 'with it': *with* Article 79(3) Basic Law Germany's sovereignty is not only presupposed, but also guaranteed.[57] This conclusion would be unassailable if democracy could only be realized within the nation-state. The democratic preconditions may be less

[57] *Lisbon* judgment, para. 216.

favourable on the European level than on the state level. The EU may even be unable to attain the democratic standard realized under the Basic Law for a long time to come. Yet this does not mean that it may never reach this standard. Therefore, the judgment should have been more elaborate on this point.

Still, Germany's incorporation in a European state would be a step of such magnitude that it could not be done via the routine amendment procedure of the Basic Law. It would mean that the Member States of the EU ceased to be the 'Masters of the Treaty' und lost the *Kompetenz-Kompetenz*. The EU would emancipate itself from the Member States and would become a self-supporting entity. It would gain the right to self-determination about its legal foundations while the Member States would by the same token lose this right. The EU would then be permitted to determine which powers it leaves for the Member States. Such an abandonment of national sovereignty would indeed require the direct and explicit consent of the people as the ultimate holders of all state authority (Article 20 Basic Law). To that extent, the *Lisbon* judgment is certainly correct. Currently, the Basic Law does not provide for a referendum on this matter. But it could easily be created through an amendment to the Basic Law. A new constitution, as the Court thinks, would not be indispensable.

Somewhat unclear is the reasoning behind the list of legislative fields that the Court regards to be 'especially sensitive for the self-determination ability of a constitutional state'. They are discussed in connection with the substantive competences the *Bundestag* must retain for any ratification law to meet the conditions set in Articles 38 and 20 Basic Law. However, it is neither said that these areas are prohibited for the EU nor are legal consequences mentioned should the EU become intensively engaged in these areas. On the contrary, the Court admits that 'a definable number or certain types of powers' which are reserved for the Member States,[58] cannot be derived from the principle of democracy. Under these circumstances the

[58] Ibid., para. 248.

list fulfils the function of a warning sign: touching these matters implies a danger to the identity of the Member States, as guaranteed in the new Article 4(2) TEU, which, in turn, will be guarded by the *Bundesverfassungsgericht*.

The *Bundesverfassungsgericht* is able to accept the Lisbon Treaty precisely because in this sense it does not contest Germany's sovereignty. Sovereignty is, however, challenged by the simplified treaty amendment and 'lacuna-filling' procedures that feature in the Lisbon Treaty and affect legal positions that Germany may not surrender. To be sure, the Member States are protected from being outvoted because the respective Council decisions have to be taken by unanimity and, hence, cannot take legal force without German approval. Still, they are not decisions taken by the 'Masters of the Treaties' but by an EU organ and as such constitute a self-empowerment of the EU. However, in spite of the justified concerns that these provisions might become a backdoor to a state-like development of the EU, the Lisbon Treaty does not fail. Rather the Court resorts to precautions on the domestic level against such a development.

In parts, the Court reassures itself with a treaty interpretation in conformity with the constitution that, of course, cannot be binding on the Union level. But mainly, the Court requires domestic safeguards that prevent a German Council vote on the aforementioned procedures from being taken on the basis of a government decision alone. The potential veto power for the national parliaments, as established in the new Article 48(7) TEU, is not sufficient in this context as it does not require explicit action by the *Bundestag*. The Court rather demands that this kind of treaty amendments are treated in the same way as the transfer of sovereign powers. The loss of domestic democracy that occurs when formal treaty ratification procedures are circumvented must be compensated through the participation of the *Bundestag* in these simplified procedures.

This demand has been interpreted by critics of the judgment as patronizing to the German Parliament. Their argument is that, after all, the Parliament already holds the competence to render the decisions that the Court is now calling for. If Parliament decides not to use powers it has this must be taken as an expression of its political will.[59] Of course, the right to act does not equate to the duty act. However, a duty to act is not alien to the Basic Law. There are certain responsibilities that the German Parliament may not relinquish. Thus, the experience of the Weimar Republic and the Empowerment Law of 1933 have led to severe restrictions on the possibility to delegate legislative competences. And the *Bundesverfassungsgericht*, through its case law, has further extended the areas to which a restriction of legislative delegation applies. Parliament has to act in cases in which fundamental rights contain a duty to protect. The transfer of powers from the national to the EU level is added to this line of argument.

It is quite normal that constitutional duties of a state institution can be enforced by the *Bundesverfassungsgericht*. Without a possibility for the Court to control whether the *Bundestag* discharges its responsibility for the integration process, a gap would appear in the German rule of law system. In the same vein, it is difficult to find fault with the Court's claim regarding to exercise *ultra vires* and identity control. This is a direct consequence of the constitutive effect of the 'order to apply the law'. Yet, even after the *Lisbon* judgment, the Court's aforementioned competence claim remains limited to extreme cases and is far from bringing European integration 'under Karlsruhe's total control'.[60] In any case, the legal plurality, which is a direct consequence of the concurring competence claims, is no longer regarded solely as a negative development.[61]

[59] Christoph Möllers, 'Was ein Parlament ist, entscheiden die Richter', *Frankfurter Allgemeine Zeitung* (16 July 2009).

[60] As the title went of a critique of the decision by Christian Callies ('Unter Karlsruher Totalaufsicht') in *Frankfurter Allgemeine Zeitung* (27 August 2009), p. 8.

[61] Cf. e.g. Monica Claes, *The National Courts' Mandate in the European Constitution* (Oxford: Oxford University Press, 2006); Neil Walker, 'The Idea of Constitutional Pluralism' (2002) 65 *Modern Law Review* 317; and 'Late Sovereignty in the European Union', in N. Walker (ed), *Sovereignty in Transition* (Oxford: Hart, 2003), p. 11; Miguel Poires Maduro, 'Contrapunctual Law', in the same volume, p. 502; Stefan Oeter/Franz Merli, 'Rechtsprechungskonkurrenz zwischen nationalen Verfassungsgerichten, Europäischem Gerichtshof und Europäischem Gerichtshof für Menschenrechte' (2007) 66 *Veröffentlichungen der Vereinigung der Deutschen Staatsrechtslehrer* 361 and 392. The Court did not fail to note that the ECJ is using the same instrument with regard to UN decisions (para. 340).

The constitutional ban on German state institutions to participate in attempts to transform the EU into a federal state, just like the list of 'sensitive areas', is one of the many *obiter dicta* contained in the judgment. They do not contribute to the solution of the case at hand and are therefore not necessary for the decision. It is easy to rebuke the Court for this practice. However, here the context of the judgment comes in. The transformation of the EU into a state is not just a purely theoretical possibility. Many politicians and academics can imagine the completion of European integration only in the form of a European federal state and orient their ideas on institutional reform accordingly. However, it appears to be even more significant that important changes in the integration programme were not effectuated by way of treaty amendments but through interpretation and application of EU primary law by the Commission and the ECJ, hence without involvement of the Member States and the political organs of the EU, solely on administrative and adjudicative paths.

That is facilitated by some peculiarities of Union law that are not always sufficiently taken into consideration. It seems particularly noteworthy that the European treaties have been 'constitutionalized' by the jurisprudence of the ECJ, but, by contrast to state constitutions, do not only contain the basic principles of the Union order and the norms that regulate the EU organs and their competencies and procedure. Rather numerous fields that would be ordinary law in the Member States are regulated on the Treaty level and consequently participate in the constitutionalization. The implications of this difference are considerable. What has been regulated on the treaty level no longer needs to be regulated on the statutory level, nor can it be changed by legislation. The executive and judicial actors of the EU are able to impose what they consider to be the right interpretation without the political actors, Council and Parliament, being able to re-programme that interpretation if they consider its results to be harmful.

However, the implications of the constitutionalization also extend into the area that is open to legislation, and make their presence known in the form of the familiar asymmetry between positive and negative integration.[62] While negative integration, i.e. deregulation on a national level in order to implement the internal market, can be accomplished in the administrative mode, positive integration, i.e. re-regulation at the European level in order to correct market failure, relies on the political mode, law-making in the Council and the Parliament, for which the threshold of consensus is considerably higher and the chances of success are correspondingly smaller. In practice, this results in a bias towards liberalization, which extends its effects even into the weakly communitarized field of social policy. To be sure, the Member States continue to be legally free in this area, but in practice they cannot maintain their level of social policy without damaging their national economy.[63]

The tendency towards a creeping evisceration of state legislative authority is promoted by the way in which competences are distributed in the EU. Unlike federal states, the European Treaties do not allocate legislative competencies according to subject matters, but according to a teleological criterion. The goal, the establishment and the maintenance of the Common Market, has the effect of blurring boundaries. Since every national law can reveal itself to be a hindrance for the four freedoms of the old Article 14(2) EC, divorce law as well as the educational system, penal law as well as monument protection, it depends largely on the Commission's interpretation of Union law and its initiative to enforce it vis-à-vis the Member States and on the attitude of the ECJ to what extent national rules are overridden by Union law. Even the Member States' discretionary space and the boundary between communalized and inter-governmental lawmaking is now coming under pressure.[64]

[62] Cf. Fritz Scharpf, *Governing in Europe* (Oxford: Oxford University Press, 1999), p. 43 ss.

[63] Cf. Fritz Scharpf, 'The European Social Model' (2002) 40 *JCMS* 645.

[64] Cf. for the first alternative e.g. the decisions of the ECJ in the cases *Viking*, Case C-438/05, and *Laval*, Case C-341/05 of December 2007. A striking example for the

The effects also extend to fundamental rights. The Union and the Member States do, to be sure, share a common basis of values. However, among the various guaranteed fundamental rights and freedoms, contradictions do arise. These contradictions tend to be resolved differently on the European level and on the national level.[65] On the state level, economic rights are consistently the ones that are most weakly protected, and national measures to regulate the economy are scrutinized less vigorously by the constitutional courts than limitations on personal fundamental rights. On the European level, it is the other way round. Here, the economic rights tend to prevail over personal, communicative, social, and cultural guarantees. Where national constitutional law grants the national legislature the most freedom, European law grants it the least.

Therefore, risks to identity and evisceration of competences are not just a threat on the treaty-making level, but also on the treaty-application level. The only way to counter them would be treaty revisions. There are admittedly few prospects of such revisions being made. In the last treaty revision process, the problems mentioned here were not even an issue. Since on the European level, the ECJ forms the keystone of the system and has tended to use this position in a Union-friendly way,[66] only the highest national courts, particularly the constitutional courts, can potentially counterbalance it. Admittedly, that alone would not allow them to make use of their power if there were no legal grounds for them to act. However, the *Bundesverfassungsgericht* has provided plausible grounds for how its position and controlling authority result from the very premises of Union law and are demanded by the national constitution.

second one is the Data Retention decision, Case C-301/06, which was published during the oral hearings of the German Constitutional Court on the Lisbon Treaty on 10 February 2009. The interpretation and application of the competition rules of Art. 81 ss. EC has a similar effect on the public services of the Member States.

[65] Cf. ch. 8 of this volume; Christian Callies, 'Europäische Gesetzgebung und nationale Grundrechte' (2009) *Juristenzeitung* 113.

[66] Cf. e.g. Karen J. Alter, *Establishing the Supremacy of European Law* (Oxford: Oxford University Press, 2001).

C. No Halt to Integration

The view that the *Lisbon* judgment of the German Constitutional Court has brought European integration to an end can only be maintained if a European federal state is seen as the ultimate goal of integration. The question whether this is something worth striving for is debatable. Even if it were something worth striving for, it would not be something that can be quickly accomplished. However, as long as the EU is a community of states whose identities are to be protected, then their position as 'Masters of the Treaties', *Kompetenz-Kompetenz* and the principle of limited and specific power transfer all have their well-deserved places. Below these tenets, particularly in the secondary lawmaking process, nothing is changing anyway, as the Court's endorsement of the Lisbon Treaty shows. At best, the decision will increase the EU's mindfulness that its legitimacy depends largely on the democracy of the Member States and that it should be hesitant to exhaust this capital.

12

Europe Needs Principles, Not Pragmatism

A. The Open Finality of European Integration

In the current debt crisis, lack of clarity regarding core questions of European integration is particularly detrimental. The European Union (EU) has long since become more than an economic community. But there is no answer to the question of its ultimate goal. At the end of the integration process, should the EU become the United States of Europe, or should it remain a community of Member States who unite for specific purposes in areas that they can better address unitedly than separately? Equally unclear are the questions of membership in Europe—the questions of inclusion and exclusion—and the relationships between unity and diversity, market economy and social justice.

The treaties say nothing about these questions, contenting themselves with a dynamic prescription for an 'ever closer union among the peoples of Europe'. How close they are to be in the end must eventually be decided politically. But politicians shun discussions of finality, and they react to calls for explanations of principle with reassurances that these questions will be discussed when it is time to decide them. This gesture towards the future, however, does not stop politicians from making decisions today that, while suppressing the question of ultimate goals, will have consequences tomorrow and will prejudice the answers to the ultimate questions. When the consequences materialize, it is usually too late to discuss their desirability.

The current crisis provides the best example of this. Twenty years ago, when the Treaty of Maastricht founded the European Monetary Union, there were ample warnings that a monetary union among states of greatly unequal economic strength presupposed a readiness among those states either to embrace common financial and economic policies or to make strong states liable for the debts of their weaker siblings. Discussions of whether such a readiness actually prevailed among the Member States were, at the time, strictly avoided. Today, the admonishers have been proven right, but it is too late to make up for the missed discussion of readiness. The omissions of 1992 compel the actions of today—at least if one maintains that there must be no backward steps on the path towards integration.

The prospects for change are slim, as avoiding discussions of finality has been a condition of success for the advance of integration. If the consequences of proposed decisions had been openly discussed in light of ultimate goals, the democratic process in the Member States would likely have led to the decisions' being rejected. Integration would have lagged far behind what it has since achieved. It is a mistake, however, to think that the progress purchased by shunning principles comes without cost. The EU pays the price in the form of its legitimacy deficit. The advance of integration lacks societal support. The Member States pay the price in the form of citizen distrust, as citizens are confronted by ever more requirements, about whose necessity they have been left in the dark.

What is true of the monetary union is also true of calls for a European constitution, which are now being issued again—by the German foreign minister, among others—just a few years after the failure of the constitutional treaty. A constitution—if it deserves the name, and is not merely a new international treaty bearing a constitutional label—prejudices the finality question. The difference between a treaty and a constitution is that, under a constitution, it will no longer be the Member States, but rather the EU itself, that determines the EU's legal foundation. In other words, the Member States will no longer decide which powers to transfer to the EU, but rather the EU will decide which powers to take from the Member States. In that case, the step towards a European state would have been decisively taken, whether the Member States' governments and peoples are aware of the fact or not.

The transformation of European institutions in accordance with a nation-state model—a transformation increasingly championed during the debt crisis—would also lead towards a European state. The Council would become a second chamber of Parliament, the Commission would become the government, and enthroned above all would be Europe's president. But the Council owes its privileged position in the EU's goal-setting and law-making precisely to the fact that the EU is a conglomeration of states, not a self-sustaining polity. To the degree that the Council is demoted, the EU becomes independent of the states' support—without, however, being able to replace the legitimacy that currently flows from the states with a commensurate internal legitimacy.

One cannot, then, transform the institutional structure of the EU on the nation-state model and at the same time defer to a later date the question of European statehood. Following such a transformation, the EU would be so altered that discussions of statehood would be superfluous. Politicians tend to praise as pragmatism their own timidity regarding first principles—as Wolfgang Schäuble, Germany's finance minister, did in December 2013. In reality, it is a clandestine means of cloaking questions of principle. And it becomes a legitimacy problem when so-called pragmatism presents the peoples of Europe with *faits accomplis* about which they had no opportunity to form or express an opinion, and which they therefore perceive as being dictated to them rather than authorized by them.

B. The Judicial Limitation of European Integration

There is a need, then, for greater orientation to principle and more explanations of consequences. But where are these to come from, if they seem to complicate rather than simplify the task of politicians? Where are they to come from, if politicians think that the advance of integration is better promoted by avoiding final questions than by discussing them, and if politicians can assume, moreover, that the consequences of their decisions will be felt only years later, after they have left the political stage? If one looks around for an answer, one's glance falls yet again on the German Constitutional Court. Just as, in national questions, the Court has increasingly assumed the role of reminding short-sighted politicians of the polity's enduring values, the Court also calls, in questions of European politics, for greater attention to principle.

In contrast to national questions, however, the Court's influence on European questions is limited. It can express itself only defensively; it cannot point the way forwards. This is because the Basic Law is silent about the construction of Europe. It must be silent, because the construction of Europe does not depend on Germany alone, but on the other Member States as well, for whom the Basic Law is not binding. The Basic Law imposes only a few conditions and limitations, which must be observed if the Federal Republic is to be part of a united Europe—e.g., that the EU must honour democratic principles and respect fundamental rights. The Constitutional Court enforces these conditions and limitations vis-à-vis German politicians. But it cannot impose objectives on Europe.

According to the Court's *Lisbon* judgment, the absolute outer limit of European integration is to be found where German statehood is surrendered and the Federal Republic is incorporated within a European federal state (*Bundesstaat*). In the Court's view, there is no constitutional path towards this destination. The obstacle cannot be removed even by constitutional amendment, since European statehood would affect the foundations of democracy, which Article 79(3) GG insulates from constitutional amendment. Accordingly, anyone who sees European statehood as the final goal of integration must be prepared to sacrifice the Basic Law and embrace a new constitution that explicitly allows such a step. Obviously, politicians cannot do this alone. They must involve the people. When it comes to the

Federal Republic's existence as a self-sufficient state, the people have the last word.

The Constitutional Court has been heavily criticized for drawing this conclusion because it was unnecessary to answer the question at all. The Lisbon Treaty, after all, does nothing to promote European statehood. Whether the Basic Law established European statehood as the outer limit of integration, then, was irrelevant to whether the Lisbon Treaty was compatible with the Basic Law. The Court's observations about European statehood were obiter dicta; they contributed nothing to the resolution of the case at hand, but served rather as a warning for a case that might arise but had not yet. Obiter dicta are usually deemed a judicial vice. But in light of the *political* vice of avoiding final questions about European integration while nevertheless taking steps that prejudice those questions, the judgment appears in a different light.

The Constitutional Court is well aware that the threshold of European statehood need not be crossed openly and in one fell swoop. It can also be reached clandestinely through many small steps that, in the aggregate, have precisely the same effect. For this reason, the Court insists on preserving those elements of the EU's basic order that distinguish it from a state. Decisions about the EU's basic order—its quasi constituent authority, that is—must remain in the hands of the Member States and must not be surrendered to EU institutions, though Minister Schäuble recently declared such surrender to be inevitable. As a result, the Constitutional Court struggled with the new rules concerning treaty amendments.

The principle of conferral must also be preserved. The *Kompetenz-Kompetenz*—the power to determine the division of powers between the EU and the Member States—must not be relinquished to the EU. Likewise, the EU institution in which the Member States are represented—the Council—must remain the central institution of the (non-state) EU and must not be subordinated to the other institutions. Moreover, as an EU Member State, the Federal Republic and its Parliament must retain political powers sufficient to make Germany's elections more than mere formalities, and to ensure that the election results have consequences for decisions that affect German citizens.

Still further, the Court establishes a link between the scope of EU powers and the autonomy of European decision-making on the one hand, and European democracy on the other. The more powers the EU acquires, and the more independent it becomes in the exercise of those powers, the greater the constitutional requirements for European democracy. Internal democratic legitimacy flows to the EU through the European Parliament. Parliament's powers, however, remain small, and European elections are merely a sum of national elections. Europe's internal legitimacy is correspondingly weak. As a result, the best that the German Constitutional Court could say was that, in the circumstances created by the Lisbon Treaty, the level of democratic legitimacy sufficed 'as yet'.

Of course, treaty amendments are not the only source of danger for the limits imposed by the Basic Law. Indeed, it is possible that the EU's institutions—primarily the European Court of Justice (ECJ)—will interpret the treaties in a manner that amounts to a treaty amendment. For this reason, the Constitutional Court reaffirms its authority to review whether EU legal acts are based on powers transferred by the Member States. If a European law lacks a basis in a transferred power, it cannot be applied in Germany. Even laws that respect the limits of the EU's powers, however, cannot be applied in Germany if they infringe upon the Basic Law's identity. Germany's constitutional identity is not at Europe's disposal.

C. The Limits of the "Yes but" Jurisprudence

Despite these constitutional concerns about the development of European integration, the Constitutional Court has never annulled the ratification of a European treaty or declared that a European law could not be applied in Germany. Instead, the Court has helped to heighten the domestic requirements for German approval of treaty amendments. Even in cases where the European treaties do not require ratification in the Member States, shifts in power from the Member States to the EU and similarly fundamental steps towards integration must be approved by a Bundestag majority sufficient to amend the constitution. The Bundestag bears the 'responsibility for integration', and it must not shirk that responsibility through inaction.

The Court's 'Yes, but' approach—approving the European treaties while overcoming reservations by raising the bar on German approval—seems, however, to have reached its limits. It is hard to see how parliamentary participation in the transfer of sovereign rights could be strengthened further. Thus, in the case of new transfers of power or institutional reforms, the national 'but' drops out of the picture. Does this mean that only the European 'yes' remains? If so, the Court's review would be limited to whether a treaty transgresses the constitutional threshold of statehood. Beyond that, it would have to content itself with assessing the soundness of the national ratification procedure.

It is unlikely, of course, that there will be a treaty on the subject of EU statehood any time soon. Additional shifts in power, by contrast, are all but certain, and one must also be prepared for treaty interpretations that stretch—and perhaps overstretch—the EU's powers. In such cases, there are sure to be constitutional complaints. What then? It is hard to imagine that the Constitutional Court will quit the field—that it will abandon its responsibility for integration and render meaningless the requirements, under Article 23 GG, for Germany's ongoing participation in European integration, and the limits on integration derived from Article 79.

In fact, if the Lisbon Treaty is merely compatible with the Basic Law 'as yet', one must assume that the constitutional limits of further integration are not far off. Then comes the stress-test of the criteria the Court has established for assessing whether the limits have been transgressed. It will be a test less of the criteria's correctness than of their workability. It might still be possible clearly to identity the transition to European statehood if that transition is agreed upon by treaty. But where is the threshold beyond which the EU's level of democratic legitimacy must increase before Germany may transfer further powers to the EU? And how can one increase the level of legitimacy without reorganizing the EU on the statehood model? At what point are the Bundestag's powers so undermined that national elections become meaningless?

If the Court is called upon to decide such questions, it will struggle not only to avoid giving the impression of decisionism, but will find itself in an awkward situation more generally. For crying 'Halt!' after this of that single step on the path towards integration will always seem somewhat exaggerated: no individual step will ever be responsible for the changes that make crying 'Halt!' seem plausible. By contrast, the sum of the individual steps that lead surreptitiously to statehood is never the subject of judicial review. The upshot is that the Constitutional Court is drawn into the maelstrom of EU-political peculiarity described at the outset—that of ostensibly avoiding questions of principle while making decisions whose dimly foreseen consequences, when they arise, prove irreversible.

But if the Court lacks opportunities to implement its positions of principle in concrete decisions, the pattern of 'acceptable as yet' is likely to endure. Under these circumstances, the Court could continue to provide small course-corrections in the realm of treaty implementation. It could thwart manifest transgressions of competence or serious discrepancies of fundamental rights interpretation. The first of these would require revising the *Mangold* decision, under which a European act, even if it obviously exceeds the EU's powers, becomes inapplicable only if it leads to a shift in the division of powers between the EU and the Member States. The second would require activating the *Solange* jurisprudence, under which, if the EU fails to provide adequate fundamental rights protection, the Court may review European acts for conformity with national fundamental rights.

This power is currently dormant, because the German Constitutional Court held in 1986 that European fundamental-rights protection was essentially comparable to German fundamental-rights protection. As integration advances, however, more and more disparities emerge. The ECJ tends to review national law strictly and European law generously. In its jurisprudence, economic freedoms tend to weigh more heavily than personal or communicative freedoms. In the jurisprudence of the German Constitutional Court, the reverse is true. Whether this will change following the EU's adoption of a Charter of Fundamental Rights or its accession to the European Convention on Human Rights (ECHR) remains to be seen. For now, this continues to be a field in which the German Constitutional Court must go on to play a guardian's role.

References

1. 'Europa ja – aber welches?' in (2014) 68 *Merkur* 1045–1058.
2. 'Auf der Suche nach Akzeptanz – Über Legitimationsdefizite und Legitimationsressourcen der EU' in (2105) 43 *Leviathan* 1–13.
3. 'Sovereignty in the European Union' in J. van der Walt and J. Ellsworth (eds.), *Constitutional Sovereignty and Social Solidarity in Europe*, Luxembourg Legal Studies 1, (Baden-Baden: Nomos, 2015), p. 39–54.
4. 'Zum Stand der demokratischen Legitimation der Europäischen Union nach Lissabon' in H.M. Heinig and J.P. Terhechte (eds.), *Postnationale Demokratie, Postdemokratie, Neoetatismus*, (Tübingen: Mohr, 2013), p. 105–122.
5. 'The Democratic Costs of Constitutionalisation: The European Case', in (2015) 21 *European Law Journal* 460–473 (extended Version).
6. 'Die Stärke der EU liegt in einer klugen Begrenzung', *Frankfurter Allgemeine Zeitung* of August 11, 2014, p. 11.
7. 'Die Parteien als Akteure einer europäischen Öffentlichkeit' in J. Krüper et al (ed.), 50 *Parteienwissenschaften, Schriften zum Parteienrecht und zur Parteienforschung* (Baden-Baden: Nomos, 2015), p. 303–314.
8. 'Zur Bedeutung nationaler Verfassungen in einem vereinten Europa' in D. Merten and H.-J. Papier (eds.), *Handbuch der Grundrechte* vol. VI/2, (Heidelberg: C.F. Müller, 2009), p. 3–32.
9. 'Die nationalen Parlamente in der Europäischen Union' Unpublished speech in Rome on Mai 12, 2015.
10. 'Die Rolle der nationalen Verfassungsgerichte in der europäischen Demokratie' in C. Franzius, F.C. Mayer, and J. Neyer (eds.), *Grenzen der europäischen Integration* (Baden-Baden: Nomos, 2014), p. 27–47.
11. 'Das Grundgesetz als Riegel vor einer Verstaatlichung der Europäischen Union' in (2009) 48 *Der Staat* 475–495.
12. 'Es geht ums Prinzip', *Frankfurter Allgemeine Zeitung* of February 6, 2013, p. 28 (original version of the slightly shortened text in FAZ).

Index

acceptance (of European integration) 1, 10–12, 14, 18, 21, 23, 78, 109, 114, 124, 179, 193
action for annulment 7, 74, 100, 149, 202, 204
amendment
  constitutional 46, 63–64, 74, 88–89, 139–141, 170–171, 183, 193, 214–216, 225–226, 236
  of treaty 10–11, 23, 26, 28, 32, 36, 47–50, 54, 60–65, 74, 89, 100, 103, 111, 113, 119, 124, 128–129, 137, 151, 172, 178, 183, 187, 190, 196, 207, 211, 216, 219, 222, 227, 229, 237–238
  statutory, of laws 9–10, 36, 73, 111, 129, 193
application, implementation of law 7–8, 10, 32, 50, 54, 73, 79–80, 88, 91, 95–96, 98, 100, 129, 146–149, 151, 153–154, 156–157, 159–161, 169, 172–173, 175–176, 186, 191–194, 196–197, 200, 204–205, 213, 229, 231, 240
asymmetry (of integration) 6, 29–30, 98, 111, 147–148, 230

Basic Law 4, 46, 57–58, 62–64, 69, 75, 112, 124, 139–143, 146–147, 149–154, 157–158, 170–171, 182–183, 188, 195, 207, 209–223, 225–226, 228, 236–239

Charter of Fundamental Rights 30, 89, 95–96, 151, 158, 172–173, 205, 241
citizens 2, 10, 12–17, 19, 21–24, 26, 32, 34, 36, 47–48, 50–52, 57–61, 64, 66–67, 75, 77–79, 83–86, 90, 101, 103, 105–107, 109, 113–115, 118, 121–128, 135, 138, 141, 157, 163–165, 171, 178–179, 202–204, 214, 216, 218, 220, 234, 238
citizens' initiatives 58, 78, 122, 219–220
Commission 3, 6–7, 9, 12, 15, 17, 25, 32–33, 50, 52, 66–69, 71–75, 78, 93, 98, 100–101, 103, 105, 107–108, 110–112, 114, 119–124, 129, 132, 141, 144, 147, 154, 174, 178, 185, 190, 196–200, 203–205, 229–230, 235
common market 3, 5, 10, 14, 18, 22, 34–35, 70–71, 93, 109–110, 147, 172, 197, 200, 230, *see also* single market
community law 4, 26–27, 74, 150, 190–191, 194–195, 198, 208–209, 211–213, *see also* Union law, law, European
competence, power 2, 6–8, 12–15, 17–18, 23–29, 31–37, 40–49, 51–55, 58, 60–70, 73–78, 82–83, 86, 88–89, 92–94, 96–98, 100–102, 104–110, 112–114, 119–121, 123–126, 128–129, 132–137, 139, 142–143, 145–147, 149, 150–152, 156, 159, 161–165, 167, 170–173, 176–178, 182, 184, 186–191, 193, 201, 203–206, 208, 210–217, 219–228, 230–231, 235, 237, 238–240
  erosion of 35, 173
  loss of 6–7, 110, 159, 197
  restriction of 97
  transfer of 6, 18, 28, 33, 36–37, 42, 46–47, 50, 52–54, 62–63, 69, 76–77, 88, 93, 97, 100, 128, 136, 142, 145, 148, 151, 155, 159–160, 170–174, 182, 184–185, 208, 210–212, 215–216, 218–219, 223, 227–228, 232, 235, 238–240
competition law 73, 129
confederation 39, 52, 165, 208
conferral, principle of 7, 54–55, 100, 186, 216–217, 219, 237
constituent power 47–49, 51–53, 63–64, 77–78, 89, 146, 159, 163, 215, 218, *see also* pouvoir constituant

constitution 4–5, 9–12, 14, 23, 27–28, 31–32, 36, 40, 42, 49–50, 53, 57, 59–61, 63, 71, 73, 77–78, 81–90, 99, 104, 109–111, 129, 131–133, 136–142, 144–146, 149–150, 155, 158–159, 162–165, 181, 186, 195, 201–202, 207, 213, 215, 217, 219, 226–227, 234, 236, 239
  national 7, 27, 30, 53, 60, 70, 73, 91–92, 99, 131, 134–135, 138, 140–146, 148–149, 152–153, 155–156, 158–163, 165, 170, 174, 181–182, 185, 190, 200, 231
  partial 165
  state 60, 159–160, 162, 165, 170, 229
constitutional
  amendment, *see* amendment, constitutional
  court 4–5, 15, 27, 31, 40, 46, 53–55, 57–58, 62, 64, 69–70, 76–78, 80, 90, 92, 96, 100, 112, 127, 138–141, 143, 147–154, 157–158, 160–161, 171–173, 176, 181–184, 186–189, 193–195, 202, 205–209, 231–232, 236–241
  identity 188, 217, 220–221, 238
  implementation 32, 73, 173
  state 146, 226
  treaty 11, 23, 60, 89, 137–138, 140, 162, 234
constitutionalism 9, 31, 81, 83–85, 87–89, 117, 131, 133, 165, 201
constitutionalization (of the Treaties) 5, 10, 28–32, 35–37, 54, 81, 88, 90, 98, 100, 104, 109–112, 128–129, 161, 163, 195–196, 229
Council 3, 6, 8–11, 15, 17, 25–26, 32–33, 36, 47, 50, 52, 58, 61–62, 66–68, 71–74, 78, 101–105, 108–109, 111–114, 120–121, 123–124, 129, 141–145, 172–175, 178, 185, 187, 190–191, 196, 198, 201–203, 219, 221, 227, 229–230, 235, 237
Council of Europe 10, 136, 153–154
Council of Ministers 3, 15, 17, 30, 97, 99, 113, 119–120, 124, 174
courts
  international 13, 43, 155, 223
  national 4, 26–28, 90–96, 110, 149, 151, 154–155, 157, 183, 189, 194, 196, 223, 231

data protection 173
decision making 9, 11, 16–17, 71, 74–75, 87, 98, 111, 155, 185, 201, 219, 238
  power 3, 121, 201, 215, 218
  procedure 71–72, 216, 221
deliberation 9, 17, 69, 168, 174, 185
democracy, democratic 15–17, 31, 56, 58–59, 64, 66, 69, 74, 76, 78–79, 81, 83–88, 101, 102, 105–107, 112–114, 125, 128, 140, 160, 164, 170, 178, 182, 184, 200–202, 205–206, 210, 214, 225–227, 232, 236
  European 49, 57–58, 64, 69, 72, 75–77, 79–80, 101, 103–104, 108, 112, 120, 180–181, 184, 194, 202, 204–206, 217–218, 238
  deficit, problem 10, 12, 58, 71, 74, 77–78, 80, 89, 101, 104, 109, 112, 124, 128, 199, 193, 196, 201–202, 218
  national 59, 79–80, 120, 202, 205–206, 218, 224
  parliamentary 101, 178
  transnational 49
de-legitimation 204
de-parliamentarization 167, 180
de-politicization 35, 128
deregulation 71, 98, 198, 230
directive 25, 95–96, 156–158, 175–176
discourse, public 16, 102, 107, 125, 179
discrimination, prohibitions of, ban on 5, 110

economic
  freedoms 5, 26, 70, 74, 94, 96, 110, 147, 172–173, 189, 191, 194–195, 200, 205, 240
  policy 30, 34, 71
economy 30, 82, 94, 97, 99, 230–231, 233
effet utile 91, 172, 217
election 8–9, 12, 15–16, 24–25, 31–33, 35–37, 56, 59, 66, 68, 70, 75, 79, 85–87, 100, 102–107, 110–111, 113–114, 118–120, 122, 125–127, 171, 178–179, 184, 192, 196, 201, 203, 214–215, 237–238, 240
electoral law, election law 16, 24, 36–37, 67, 102, 118–119, 126–127, 179–180, 203

EU law, European law 4–6, 10, 27–30, 36–37, 44, 53–54, 64, 67, 71–73, 80, 90–96, 110–112, 117–118, 127, 136, 138–140, 142–153, 156–161, 165, 169, 172–174, 176, 181–182, 186, 188, 195, 206, 209, 215, 220, 223, 231, 238, 240, *see also* Community law
European Coal and Steel Community (ECSC) 2, 22
European Convention on Human Rights (ECHR) 136, 153–154, 241
European Council 15, 17, 30, 50–51, 57, 61, 63, 68, 71, 99, 112–113, 119–120, 122–124, 191, 202–203
European Court of Human Rights (ECtHR) 136, 153–155
European Court of Justice (ECJ) 3–10, 13, 25–30, 32, 36, 52, 54, 61, 65–66, 68–69, 71–74, 90–100, 104, 108, 110–111, 114, 128–129, 136, 146–153, 158, 160–161, 172, 186–191, 194–199, 202, 204–206, 209, 212–213, 223, 229–231, 238, 240
European Defense Community (EDC) 2, 3, 22
European Economic Community (EEC) 2, 3, 5, 21, 66, 145, 208
European election 16, 24, 32–33, 35, 56, 68, 75, 102, 105–106, 114, 119, 126–127, 178–179, 203, 238
European federal state 171, 183, 189, 225, 229, 232, 236
European Parliament, *see* Parliament, European
European Political Community (EPC) 2–3, 22
excess of powers 7, 27, 92, 149, 151, 188, 221, 240, *see also* loss of competence, *ultra vires* action
executive 74, 101, 107, 112, 125, 156, 170, 210

factions 16, 23–24, 102, 107, 117, 120, 122–123, 179
Federal Constitutional Court 15, 46, 53, 57, 62, 64–65, 138, 141, 147, 150, 152, 171, 183–184, 186
federal state 5, 15, 35, 45–46, 52, 76, 78, 92, 112, 124, 137, 145, 160, 163, 171, 183–184, 187, 189, 215, 222, 225, 229–230, 232, 236
federalism 45, 140, 170
finality 233–234
financial crisis 12, 18, 34, 61
fundamental rights 5, 30–31, 36, 83–86, 114, 147–148, 150–151, 154, 157–158, 173, 176, 189, 200, 205, 228, 231, 236, 240–241
fundamental rights protection 30, 86, 96, 140, 150–152, 157–158, 170, 172–173, 183, 189, 212, 221, 240

globalization 34, 56, 99, 199
government 3, 8, 10–12, 15, 17, 24–26, 32–33, 49–52, 56, 58, 60–63, 66–68, 72, 75–76, 78, 82–87, 97–98, 103, 108, 112–113, 122, 124, 132, 141–144, 160, 163, 167–171, 174–175, 178, 181, 185–186, 190, 203–204, 209–210, 216, 235

hetero-determination 90, 221
human rights 135, 150

identity 23, 27, 45, 53, 92, 183, 188, 205, 208, 210, 212, 214–215, 217, 219–221, 225, 227, 231, 238–239
independence 17, 67, 69, 98
infringement proceeding 175, 204
integration
  economic 3–4, 22, 28, 93, 97
  European 1–2, 10, 15, 21–23, 34, 41, 46, 62, 66, 80, 108, 114, 120, 135, 140, 153, 167, 174, 176, 182, 207, 215, 221, 228–229, 232–233, 236–239, *see also* unification, European
  negative 29, 71, 98, 111, 147–148, 198, 230
  positive 29, 71, 98, 111, 147–148, 198, 230
intergovernmental 4, 142, 230
internal legitimacy 17, 60, 80, 119, 165, 203, 206, 235, 238
international law, *see* law, international
international/supranational organization/institution 5, 13, 40, 43, 45, 55–56, 74, 78, 92, 109, 138, 145, 149, 168, 182, 192, 224
internationalization 13, 56, 101, 107

interpretation of treaties, *see* treaty interpretation
ius cogens 43

judicial independence 7, 74
judicial power, institutions 18, 44, 74–75, 97, 100, 111, 128, 136, 146, 152, 193, 212
judiciary 5, 87–88, 107, 112, 154, *see also* judicial power
jurisdiction 18, 54, 61, 74, 94, 133, 140, 142, 149–151, 160–161, 170–171, 181, 183–184, 186, 229
jurisprudence 154, 193–194
  of ECJ 5, 7, 9–10, 27–30, 32, 36, 74, 94, 96–101, 104, 111, 128–129, 136, 147, 152, 161, 173, 191, 195–197, 199, 204–205, 212, 229, 240
  of German Constitutional Court 15, 154, 176, 205, 208, 211, 213, 240–241

Kompetenz-Kompetenz 46, 48, 50–51, 54, 62, 65, 100, 137, 184, 208, 216–217, 221–222, 224, 226, 232, 237

law
  European 4–6, 8–11, 27–30, 36–37, 44, 53–54, 64, 67, 71–73, 80, 90–97, 111–112, 117–118, 127, 136, 138–153, 156–161, 165, 169, 172–174, 176, 179, 181–182, 185–186, 188, 190–191, 195, 200, 206, 209, 215, 220, 223, 229, 231, 238, 240, *see also* community law
  international 7, 26–27, 42–43, 47, 50, 60, 89, 90–91, 99, 108, 133–136, 140, 142, 145–146, 149, 154, 156, 183, 194–195, 208–209, 223
  ordinary 9, 18, 31, 76, 84, 88, 90, 99–101, 111, 114, 129, 193, 229
  primary 10, 47, 67, 73, 76, 97, 120–121, 138–140, 141–142, 174, 182, 185, 190, 196, 200, 209, 217, 229
  secondary 9–10, 25, 36–37, 67, 72, 97, 104, 121, 141–143, 173–174, 185, 190–191
  national, domestic 4–6, 10, 16, 24, 26–30, 44, 54, 70–71, 73–74, 76, 90–96, 102, 106, 108–111, 134, 136, 140, 145–146, 148–151, 153–156, 158, 160, 172–173, 175, 179, 181, 185–186, 191, 194–195, 200, 203, 208–209, 211, 217, 219, 221, 230, 240
League of Nations 1
legal basis, foundation (of the EU) 5, 12, 25, 47, 50–51, 53, 57, 60, 64, 89, 120, 137–138, 162–163, 165, 190, 201, 203, 216–217, 221, 226, 234
legislation 6, 8–10, 18, 29, 31–32, 54, 67, 74, 84, 94, 96, 98–99, 103, 108–109, 111, 121, 126, 141–144, 148, 161, 168, 174, 176, 185, 191, 195, 200–203, 229
legislative authority 67, 167, 178, 230
legislative power, legislature 3, 5–6, 8, 25, 30, 35, 63, 66, 72–73, 83, 87, 90, 107, 111, 113, 120, 145–146, 151, 155–157, 170, 172–173, 176, 184, 193, 195–196, 225, 231
legislator 103
legitimacy 14–15, 17, 19, 24, 26–27, 33, 36, 59, 67–69, 76–80, 82, 85–86, 97, 103–104, 106, 108–109, 113, 119–121, 124, 129, 131, 133, 150, 161, 164–165, 189, 191, 201–206, 223, 232, 235, 238
  chain of 66–67, 102, 113, 121
  crises, problem 18, 23, 25, 37, 101, 112, 114, 124, 178, 235
  deficit, gap 11, 15, 23–24, 26, 32, 35, 76, 78, 89, 103, 108–109, 121, 123, 128–129, 167, 178, 234
  democratic 3, 10, 17–18, 25, 57–58, 60, 62, 66–67, 69, 73, 80, 98, 103, 105, 112–113, 119, 121, 189–190, 201, 203, 217–218, 221, 224–225, 238–239
  flow of, stream of 17–18, 24, 26, 33, 79–80, 113, 121, 129, 165, 179–180, 206
  lack of 105–106
legitimacy, legitimation, level of, standard of 69–70, 77, 165, 218–219, 225, 239
legitimation 13, 33, 56, 68, 103, 113–114, 210

chain of 10, 103
democratic 3, 66, 79, 113, 162, 201–202, 210, 215
dualistic 11, 121, 191
external 26, 60, 62, 72, 104
internal 15, 17, 26, 33, 35, 62, 66–67, 72, 79, 104, 124, 180, 191, 202
monistic 103, 121, 191
resources 33, 103, 113, 164, 180
subject of, legitimating subject 51, 59, 220
liberalism, liberalization, liberal 6, 30, 82, 93, 98, 99, 114, 147–148, 168, 198–199, 200, 204, 230
Lisbon judgment 40, 46, 57–58, 62, 70, 75, 80, 112, 127, 184, 205, 215, 221–223, 226, 228, 232, 236

Maastricht judgment 212, 214
market 3, 5–6, 10, 14, 18–19, 22, 29, 34–35, 70–71, 73, 93–94, 98–99, 109–110, 147, 172, 189, 195, 197–198, 200, 230, *see also* common market, single market
Masters of the Treaties 5, 46, 50–51, 62–63, 72, 89, 99–100, 120, 137, 163, 202, 208, 211, 221, 226–227, 232
media 10, 16, 28, 33, 59, 78, 85, 102, 107, 118, 122, 125, 128, 164, 179
member states 3–12, 14–19, 22–26, 28–30, 32–33, 35–37, 40, 42, 44–57, 60–74, 77, 79–80, 89–100, 103, 106, 108–114, 117–122, 124, 127–129, 135–142, 144–149, 152–154, 156–157, 159–165, 168–175, 177–178, 180–181, 185–188, 190–191, 194–200, 202–205, 207–208, 210–211, 216–217, 219–222, 224, 226–227, 229–240
method, methodological 7–8, 27, 91, 108, 127, 172, 192, 194, 202, 204, 223
Monetary Union 19, 34, 170, 234
monopoly
of legitimate use of force 56, 80, 136
of public power 44
on invalidating legislation 147, 160, 195

nation-state 4, 10–11, 13, 24, 31, 34, 44, 48, 58, 64, 73, 114–115, 122–123, 125, 129, 133–135, 137–138, 153, 161–164, 168, 180, 184, 189, 194, 202, 208, 218, 225
negotiation 9, 69, 107, 142–143, 168–171, 174–175, 182, 185
no-confidence vote 68
non-political mode of decision making 10, 12–14, 18, 22, 32, 76, 79, 98, 101, 112, 148, 196, 198–200, 204

opinion, formation of 15–16, 19, 78, 125, 235
opposition 37, 52, 75, 102, 118, 122, 149, 186
order/command to apply European law 91, 151, 187, 209, 211, 220–222, 228
over-constitutionalization 32, 99–101, 104
override clause, Canadian 187

Parliament
European 2, 11–12, 15–17, 23–26, 32–33, 35, 48, 50–51, 57–58, 61–62, 66–68, 72, 75, 77–79, 97–98, 101–109, 111–113, 117–128, 141, 144, 156, 167, 173–174, 178–180, 185, 191, 201–203, 210, 218, 238
German 215, 221, 227–228
parliamentarianism 16, 169
parliamentarization 17, 23, 32, 101–102, 104, 112, 119, 124–125, 127, 129, 180
parliamentary
assembly 3, 66
prerogative 221
system 15, 17, 24, 72, 121, 178
parliaments, national 3, 9, 15, 17, 23, 26, 49, 51, 58, 62, 66–67, 78, 101–103, 105–107, 112, 119, 121, 125–126, 156, 167, 169–170, 172–178, 180, 185, 191, 201, 210, 219, 227
people 10–12, 24, 41–42, 48–50, 57–60, 63, 66–67, 77, 80–84, 86, 97, 102, 108, 118, 120–121, 125, 132, 144, 146, 161–163, 178, 183, 210, 215–216, 218–220, 222, 226, 233, 235–237

people of the Union 60
pluralism 34, 106
plurality of law 228
policy, politics 3, 9, 11, 13–16, 24–25, 30–32, 34–36, 56, 61, 68, 71, 74–75, 86–88, 95–96, 99, 101, 103, 107, 114–115, 118–119, 123–128, 133, 142–143, 147–148, 150, 156, 167, 180, 199, 204, 230, 236
political parties 35, 78, 102, 117, 121, 125, 127–128, 164, 179–180, 218
popular sovereignty 49, 59–60, 81, 132, 203
pouvoir constituant 58, 62, 64, 84, *see also* constituent power
pouvoir constitué 58, 84
powers, *see* competence
precedence, primacy, supremacy 4, 27, 30, 53, 74, 84–85, 91–93, 108, 132, 136, 145–150, 152–153, 160, 165, 173, 186, 188, 191, 209, 213, 220, 222–223
precedence of application 149
preliminary ruling 98
  procedure 149, 195
primary law, *see* law, primary
privatization 6, 29, 96, 110, 199
prohibition of discrimination, ban on discrimination 5, 110
proportionality 94, 157, 175, 197, 200, 219
protectionism 29
public
  authority, public power 13, 31, 34, 41–48, 52, 55–56, 58–59, 62, 66, 82–84, 86–87, 133, 135, 138, 159, 163, 168, 189–190, 221, 223–225
  general 16, 22, 28, 35, 37, 41, 97, 126, 193, 212, 216
  international law 43
  opinion 17, 75, 80, 100
  service 6, 29, 73, 95–96, 110, 198–199, 204
  service institutions 6–7, 29, 110
  sphere, European 16, 33, 59, 102, 120, 196, 199, 218

ratification, ratification law 50–51, 62, 97, 138–141, 151, 168, 170, 182, 187, 209, 211, 213–214, 217, 219, 226–227, 238–239
referendum 12, 50–51, 60, 138–139, 168, 170, 201, 226
regulation 5, 14, 25, 29, 31, 73, 83, 95, 110–111, 133, 157, 159–160, 165, 169, 175, 183, 185, 196–197, 199–200, 230
representatives 24, 48–49, 66, 71, 86, 97, 103, 109, 125, 132, 144, 183, 191, 210
rule of law 56, 140, 153, 160, 170, 228

secondary law, *see* law, secondary
Security Council 43, 135
self-determination, autodetermination, right of 41–43, 47, 53, 56, 63, 90, 120, 133–134, 137, 163, 183, 220, 224, 226
separation of powers 42, 156
Single European Act (SEA) 10, 25, 67, 97, 103, 108–109, 121, 141, 191, 199
single market 29, 93, 98–99
  see also common market
social policy 30, 99, 199, 230
social state 111, 148, 168
society 7, 16, 24–25, 35, 42, 59, 102, 106–107, 112, 114, 123, 125–128, 133, 155, 164, 179
Solange 150–151, 157, 189, 212–213, 221, 240
solidarity 56, 164–165, 204
solidary community, union of solidarity 34
sovereign powers, rights 42, 134–140, 160–160, 169–171, 182–185, 190, 211, 218, 221, 223–224, 227, 239
sovereignty, sovereign 2, 4, 27, 39–49, 51–56, 58–60, 63–65, 69, 81, 91, 109, 132, 134, 146, 152, 171, 183, 194, 203, 205, 208, 214–216, 218–221, 223–227
state 1–7, 11, 13, 18–19, 21–22, 26–27, 34–35, 39–43, 45–49, 51–52, 55–56, 59, 63–64, 67, 69, 71, 73, 75–78, 82, 90, 92, 94, 107–110, 112, 114–115, 118, 124, 128–129, 133–140, 142, 144–146, 153–155, 158–164, 167–171, 174, 178, 183–184, 187, 189–190, 202, 208–209, 215–216, 218–219, 221–222, 224–226, 229–230, 232, 234–237, *see also* member state, nation-state

authority 59, 120, 226
sovereignty 42, 54, 60, 134, 214–215, 223
subsidies, aids 6, 29, 96, 110, 197–198
statehood 64, 69, 124, 141, 152–153, 162, 164, 214–215, 219–222, 235–237, 239–240
subsidiarity, principle of 14, 35, 37, 140, 170, 175, 177, 183, 219
supremacy, *see* precedence, primacy

TEU, *see* Treaty on European Union
TFEU, *see* Treaty on the Functioning of the European Union
trade, commerce 5, 96, 135, 197
transfer of powers, of competences, of sovereign rights 6–7, 18, 28, 33, 36–37, 42, 46–47, 50, 52–54, 62–63, 69, 76–77, 93, 97, 100, 124, 128, 135–137, 139–140, 142, 145, 148, 151, 155, 159–160, 169–174, 182–185, 189, 208, 210–212, 215–216, 218–219, 221, 223–224, 227–228, 232, 235, 238–239
transformation 26, 28, 73, 83–84, 89, 112, 163, 168, 171, 191, 194, 209, 221–222
treaty 4–5, 7, 9, 10, 12, 15, 18, 23, 25–29, 31–32, 35, 37, 40, 42, 49, 51, 53–54, 58, 60–61, 67, 73–76, 78, 89–95, 97, 99–101, 104, 108–111, 114, 129, 135–144, 149, 152, 161, 163, 168–170, 172–173, 182, 185, 187–188, 194–196, 200–201, 203, 208–211, 213–214, 216, 219, 222, 229–230, 233–234, 238–239
amendment, *see* amendment
constitutional 5, 11, 18, 23, 28, 78, 89, 137–139, 162, 200–201, 234
international 3–5, 9, 14, 47, 50, 60, 89, 100, 109, 137, 169–170, 190, 194, 220, 234
interpretation 5–6, 13, 28–30, 32, 54, 65, 91, 97, 99, 110, 149, 151, 172, 187, 195, 198, 200, 211, 213, 216–217, 227, 238–239
of Amsterdam 141, 186
of Lisbon 12, 15, 36, 47, 49, 51, 57–58, 60, 64–65, 67, 75–77, 89, 95, 117, 119, 125, 141, 176–177, 179, 190–191, 199, 207, 214, 218–222, 224–225, 227, 232, 237–239
of Maastricht 11–12, 23, 34, 67, 109, 122, 141, 176–177, 212, 222, 234
of Nice 67
of Rome 89, 145, 186
Treaty on European Union (TEU) 49–50, 57, 60–62, 65, 117–119, 121–122, 128, 175, 177, 188–189, 206, 217, 219, 227
Treaty on the Functioning of the European Union (TFEU) 18, 37, 50, 61, 70–71, 118, 126, 191, 197, 205
treaty violation 54–55, 69, 206

ultra vires action 54, 92, 186, 188, 213, 228, *see also* excess of powers, competence
UN charter 40
unification, European 1–2, 183, *see also* integration, European
union/EU citizens, *see* citizens
union/EU law 5, 27, 37, 44, 53, 72, 95, 118, 138, 142–144, 146, 152–153, 172–173, 181, 185–188, 194, 196, 200, 205, 220, 214, 221–222, 229–231, *see also* community law
United Nations (UN) 13, 40, 42–44, 135, 223
United Nations Security Council (UNSC) 43, 135

World Trade Organization (WTO) 13, 43, 135